Soft Computing Agents

Dear MyCopy Customer,

This Springer book is a monochrome print version of the eBook to which your library gives you access via SpringerLink. It is available to you at a subsidized price since your library subscribes to at least one Springer eBook subject collection.

Please note that MyCopy books are only offered to library patrons with access to at least one Springer eBook subject collection. MyCopy books are strictly for individual use only.

You may cite this book by referencing the bibliographic data and/or the DOI (Digital Object Identifier) found in the front matter. This book is an exact but monochrome copy of the print version of the eBook on SpringerLink.

Studies in Fuzziness and Soft Computing

Editor-in-chief
Prof. Janusz Kacprzyk
Systems Research Institute
Polish Academy of Sciences
ul. Newelska 6
01-447 Warsaw, Poland
E-mail: kacprzyk@ibspan.waw.pl
http://www.springer.de/cgi-bin/search_book.pl?series=2941

Further volumes of this series can be found at our homepage.

Vol. 53. G. Bordogna and G. Pasi (Eds.)
Recent Issues on Fuzzy Databases, 2000
ISBN 3-7908-1319-2

Vol. 54. P. Sinčák and J. Vaščák (Eds.)
Quo Vadis Computational Intelligence?, 2000
ISBN 3-7908-1324-9

Vol. 55. J.N. Mordeson, D.S. Malik and S.-C. Cheng
Fuzzy Mathematics in Medicine, 2000
ISBN 3-7908-1325-7

Vol. 56. L. Polkowski, S. Tsumoto and T.Y. Lin (Eds.)
Rough Set Methods and Applications, 2000
ISBN 3-7908-1328-1

Vol. 57. V. Novák and I. Perfilieva (Eds.)
Discovering the World with Fuzzy Logic, 2001
ISBN 3-7908-1330-3

Vol. 58. D.S. Malik and J.N. Mordeson
Fuzzy Discrete Structures, 2000
ISBN 3-7908-1335-4

Vol. 59. T. Furuhashi, S. Tano and H.-A. Jacobsen (Eds.)
Deep Fusion of Computational and Symbolic Processing, 2001
ISBN 3-7908-1339-7

Vol. 60. K.J. Cios (Ed.)
Medical Data Mining and Knowledge Discovery, 2001
ISBN 3-7908-1340-0

Vol. 61. D. Driankov and A. Saffiotti (Eds.)
Fuzzy Logic Techniques for Autonomous Vehicle Navigation, 2001
ISBN 3-7908-1341-9

Vol. 62. N. Baba, L.C. Jain (Eds.)
Computational Intelligence in Games, 2001
ISBN 3-7908-1348-6

Vol. 63. O. Castillo, P. Melin
Soft Computing for Control of Non-Linear Dynamical Systems, 2001
ISBN 3-7908-1349-4

Vol. 64. I. Nishizaki, M. Sakawa
Fuzzy and Multiobjective Games for Conflict Resolution, 2001
ISBN 3-7908-1341-9

Vol. 65. E. Orłowska, A. Szalas (Eds.)
Relational Methods for Computer Science Applications, 2001
ISBN 3-7908-1365-6

Vol. 66. R.J. Howlett, L.C. Jain (Eds.)
Radial Basis Function Networks 1, 2001
ISBN 3-7908-1367-2

Vol. 67. R.J. Howlett, L.C. Jain (Eds.)
Radial Basis Function Networks 2, 2001
ISBN 3-7908-1368-0

Vol. 68. A. Kandel, M. Last and H. Bunke (Eds.)
Data Minining and Computational Intelligence, 2001
ISBN 3-7908-1371-0

Vol. 69. A. Piegat
Fuzzy Modeling and Control, 2001
ISBN 3-7908-1385-0

Vol. 70. W. Pedrycz (Ed.)
Granular Computing, 2001
ISBN 3-7908-1387-7

Vol. 71. K. Leiviskä (Ed.)
Industrial Applications of Soft Computing, 2001
ISBN 3-7908-1388-5

Vol. 72. M. Mareš
Fuzzy Cooperative Games, 2001
ISBN 3-7908-1392-3

Vol. 73. Y. Yoshida (Ed.)
Dynamical Aspects in Fuzzy Decision, 2001
ISBN 3-7908-1397-4

Vol. 74. H.-N. Teodorescu, L.C. Jain and A. Kandel (Eds.)
Hardware Implementation of Intelligent Systems, 2001
ISBN 3-7908-1399-0

Vincenzo Loia · Salvatore Sessa
Editors

Soft Computing Agents

New Trends for Designing Autonomous Systems

With 82 Figures
and 13 Tables

Springer-Verlag Berlin Heidelberg GmbH

Prof. Vincenzo Loia
Università di Salerno
Dipartimento di Matematica e Informatica
Via S. Allende
84081 Baronissi (Salerno)
Italy
loia@unisa.it

Prof. Salvatore Sessa
Università Federico II
Dipartimento di Construzioni e
Metodi Matematici in Architettura
Via Monteoliveto, 3
80134 Napoli
Italy
sessa@unina.it

ISSN 1434-9922

DOI 10.1007/978-3-7908-1815-4

Cataloging-in-Publication Data applied for
Die Deutsche Bibliothek – CIP-Einheitsaufnahme
Soft computing agents: new trends for designing autonomous systems; with 13 tables / Vincenzo Loia; Salvatore Sessa, ed. – Heidelberg; New York: Physica-Verl., 2001
(Studies in fuzziness and soft computing; Vol. 75)

Originally published by Physica-Verlag Heidelberg 2001
MyCopy version of the original edition 2001

Hardcover Design: Erich Kirchner, Heidelberg

88/2202-5 4 3 2 1 0 – Printed on acid-free paper

www.springer.com/mycopy

Foreword

The purpose of this volume is to collect the most recent results in the design of knowledge-based systems realized by merging techniques derived from Soft Computing area with recent trends of Distributed Artificial Intelligence.

Since in the existing literature there is a lack in dealing the strong unpredictability of rich distributed systems, the combined use of Fuzzy Logic, Evolutionary systems (e.g. fusion of Genetic Algorithms, Neural Networks and Fuzzy Systems) and Agent or Multi-agent technology seems a promising solution.

Nowadays the scientific community is very attracted by these efforts. If the Distributed Artificial Intelligence (DAI) practicioners feel the necessity to better cope with adaptivity by using Soft Computing technology, the Soft Computing specialists feel similarly the necessity to investigate on new models and architectures of Distributed Artificial Intelligence for improving their synergism.

This book is devoted to give a unifying perspective in this direction inviting well-known authors whose expertise is widely recognized.

Generally speaking, intelligent agents are an innovative technology, so powerful that computation models become increasingly open, distributed and mobile.

The formulation of cooperative strategies, the linguistic aspects of the communication, the local decision versus the global knowledge, the actions and plans as distributed viewpoints are, among others, known topics dealt in literature.

All these issues have as context an universe of discourse characterized by an incomplete knowledge and by a fragmentation of logical interactions, faced often by a non-monotonic reasoning.

Then, we believe that a more complete and sound discussion on these topics should be well appreciated by both soft-computing and agent communities.

Essentially we address the following issues:

- human-computer interaction through fuzzy agents (cf. the papers of Rocha, Damiani et al. and Callaghan et al.);
- evolutionary architectures for multi-agent environment (cfr. the papers of Iba and Terano and of the editors);
- decomposition of a complex systems into autonomous agents through the concept of granularity (cfr. the paper of Pedrycz and Vukovich);
- adaptivity and learning in multi-agent systems (cfr. the papers of Takadama et al. and Franklin).

We deeply thank all the invited authors. A particular acknowledgement goes to Professor Janusz Kacprzyk, the Editor-in-Chief of this Series, which has given to us the opportunity to act as editors of this volume.

Vincenzo LOIA	Salvatore SESSA
University of Salerno, DMI	University of Naples, DICOMMA

Contents

Foreword V
Vincenzo Loia and Salvatore Sessa

Chapter 1:
"Conscious" Software: A Computational View of Mind 1
Stan Franklin

Chapter 2:
Intelligent Agents in Granular Worlds 47
Witold Pedrycz and George Vukovich

Chapter 3:
Controlling Effective Introns for Multi-Agent Learning by Means of Genetic Programming 73
Hitoshi Iba and Makoto Terao

Chapter 4:
TalkMine: A Soft Computing Approach to Adaptive Knowledge Recommendation 89
Luis Mateus Rocha

Chapter 5:
A Soft-Computing Distributed Artificial Intelligence Architecture for Intelligent Buildings 117
Victor Callaghan, Graham Clarke, Martin Colley, and Hani Hagras

Chapter 6:
Towards a Multiagent Design Principle: Analyzing an Organizational-Learning Oriented Classifer System 147
Keiki Takadama, Takao Terano, Katsunori Shimohara, Koichi Hori, and Shinichi Nakasuka

Chapter 7:
A Human-Centered Approach for Intelligent Internet Applications 169
Ernesto Damiani, Rajiv Khosla, and Somkiat Kitjongthawonkul

Chapter 8:
A Soft Computing Framework for Adaptive Agents 191
Vincenzo Loia and Salvatore Sessa

"Conscious" Software: A Computational View of Mind

Stan Franklin***, †

Institute for Intelligent Systems and Department of Mathematical Sciences
The University of Memphis
Memphis, TN 38152–3370
USA
Email: stan.franklin@memphis.edu
http://www.msci.memphis.edu/~ franklin

Abstract. Here we describe a software agent that implements the global workspace theory of consciousness. A clerical agent that corresponds with humans in natural language via email, CMattie composes and sends weekly seminar announcements to a mailing list she maintains. She's designed under a two tiered architecture with high-level concepts, behaviors, associations, etc., undergirded with low-level codelets that do most of the actual work. A wide variety of computational mechanisms, many taken from what is now called softcomputing, flesh out the architecture. As a computational model, CMattie provides ready answers, that, is testable hypotheses, to very many questions about human cognition. Several such are noted. There's also a discussion of the extent to which such "conscious" software agents can be expected to be conscious.

Keywords. Action selection, artificial intelligence, autonomous agent, cognitive architectures, computational mechanisms of mind, consciousness, emotions, global workspace theory, learning, memory, metacognition, perception

1 Introduction

Like the Roman god Janus, the "conscious" software project has two faces, its science face and its engineering face. Its science side will flesh out the global workspace theory of consciousness. Using ideas and mechanisms from softcomputing, its engineering side explores architectural designs (Sloman, 1996) for information agents that promise more flexible, more human-like intelligence within their domains. The fleshed out global workspace theory (Baars, 1988; 1997) will yield a multitude of testable hypotheses about human

*** Supported in part by NSF grant SBR-9720314 and by ONR grant N00014-98-1-0332

† With essential contributions from the Conscious Software Research Group including Art Graesser, Satish Ambati, Ashraf Anwar, Myles Bogner, Arpad Kelemen, Irina Makkaveeva, Lee McCauley, Aregahegn Negatu, Hongjun Song, Uma Ramamurthy, Zhaohua Zhang

cognition. The architectures and mechanisms that underlie consciousness and intelligence in humans can be expected to yield software agents that learn continuously, that adapt readily to dynamic environments, and that behave flexibly and intelligently when faced with novel and unexpected situations. This paper is devoted primarily to the description of one such "conscious" software agent and the issues that arise therefrom.

1.1 Autonomous Agents

Artificial intelligence pursues the twin goals of understanding human intelligence and of producing intelligent software and/or artifacts. Designing, implementing and experimenting with autonomous agents furthers both these goals in a synergistic way.

An *autonomous agent* (Franklin and Graesser, 1997) is a system situated in, and part of, an environment, which senses that environment, and acts on it, over time, in pursuit of its own agenda. In biological agents, this agenda arises from evolved in drives; in artificial agents from drives built in by its creator. Such drives, which act as motive generators (Sloman, 1987) must be present, whether explicitly represented, or expressed causally. The agent also acts in such a way as to possibly influence what it senses at a later time. In other words, it is structurally coupled to its environment (Maturana, 1975; Maturana and Varela, 1980). Biological examples of autonomous agents include humans and most animals. Non-biological examples include some mobile robots, and various computational agents, including artificial life agents, software agents and many computer viruses. We'll be concerned with autonomous software agents, designed for specific tasks, and 'living' in real world computing systems such as operating systems, databases, or networks.

1.2 Cognitive Agents Architecture and Theory

Such autonomous software agents, when equipped with cognitive (interpreted broadly) features chosen from among multiple senses, perception, short and long term memory, attention, planning, reasoning, problem solving, learning, emotions, moods, attitudes, multiple drives, etc., are called *cognitive agents* (Franklin, 1997). 'Though ill defined, cognitive agents can play a synergistic role in the study of human cognition, including consciousness. Here's how it can work.

Minds, in my view, are best viewed as control structures for autonomous agents (Franklin, 1995.) A theory of mind constrains the design of a cognitive agent that implements that theory. While a theory is typically abstract and only broadly sketches an architecture, an implemented design must provide a fully articulated architecture, and the mechanisms upon which it rests. This architecture and these mechanisms serve to flesh out the theory, making it more concrete. Also every design decision taken during an implementation constitutes a hypothesis about how human minds work. The hypothesis says that humans do it the way the agent was designed to do it, whatever "it" was. These hypotheses will suggest experiments with humans by means of which they can be tested. Conversely, the results of such experiments will suggest corresponding modifications of the architecture and mechanisms of the cognitive agent implementing the theory. The concepts and methodologies of cognitive science and of computer science will work synergistically to enhance our understanding of mechanisms of mind. I have written elsewhere in much more depth about this research strategy (Franklin, 1997), which I've called Cognitive Agent Architecture and Theory (CAAT). The autonomous agents described herein were designed following the dictates of the CAAT strategy.

1.3 What's to Come?

An attempt at implementing global workspace agents (to be explained below) in pursuit of the CAAT strategy is underway. Its first phase was to build Virtual Mattie, an autonomous software agent that 'lives' in a Unix system, communicates with seminar organizers and attendees via email in natural language, and composes and sends seminar announcements, again via email, all without human direction (Franklin et al, 1996). VMattie, now up and running far more successfully than her designers had even hoped (Song et al, 2000; Zhang ,Franklin, Olde, Wan and Graesser,1998), implements about forty percent of Baars' global workspace theory of consciousness (Baars, 1988; 1997). The second phase adds the missing pieces of the global workspace theory, producing 'Conscious' Mattie. CMattie is almost completely designed, though the design is not quite stable, and the coding stage is quite far along. She will implement a fairly full version of global workspace theory, and will account for most of the psychological and neuroscientific facts that, according to Baars (1997, Appendix), must constrain any theory of consciousness (Franklin and Graesser, 1999). We will refer to a cognitive software agent that implements global workspace theory in this sense as a *"conscious" software agent.*

Still, we are concerned that the so limited domain of CMattie is inherently insufficient to allow us to achieve the more engineering goals of the "conscious" software project, to produce software that is more intelligent, more flexible, more human-like than existing artificial intelligence software. For these goals, we need more dynamic, more challenging domains that require agents with multiple senses, multiple time-varying drives, and more complex actions to serve as proof-of-concept projects for "conscious" software. These more challenging domains will also address some of the limitations on the scientific side of the project (see Section 7 below). Phase three is pursuing another such "conscious" software agent, IDA, in parallel with the completion of CMattie. Now in the design stage, IDA, an intelligent distribution agent, is intended to help the Navy with its reassignment of personnel at the end of duty tours (Franklin, Kelemen, and McCauley, 1998). This reassignment offers a complex, demanding domain orders of magnitude more challenging than that of CMattie. We hope it will prove a suitable proof-of-concept project. Yet another such challenging project called AutoTutor is waiting in the wings. AutoTutor is a fully automated computer tutor that simulates dialogue moves of normal human tutors and that will eventually incorporate sophisticated tutoring strategies (Graesser, Franklin & Wiemer-Hastings, 1998; Wiemer-Hastings et al, 1998). The first, unconscious, version of AutoTutor was completed in the spring of 1998 on the topic of computer literacy. If energy and funding hold out, we intend to try for a "conscious" version of AutoTutor as another proof-of-concept project.

In addition to a brief account of VMattie, this paper will contain a relatively complete high level account of CMattie. It will include short descriptions of the various mechanisms used to build her, many taken from softcomputing, and a summary of global workspace theory as well. No more will be said about IDA or AutoTutor, primarily because of space constraints. The design principles followed in the implementation of each of these agents are derived from the author's action selection paradigm of mind (Franklin 1995, Chapter 16). Its "multiplicity of mind" tenet asserts that "minds tend to be embodied as collections of relatively independent modules with little communication between them." The corresponding design principle recommends building cognitive agents as multiagent systems with no central executive. The agents mentioned above are implemented using codelets, small pieces of code doing a single small job. The "diversity of mind" tenet asserts that "mind is enabled by a multitude of disparate mechanisms." This specifically denies the unified theory of cognition hypothesis (Newell, 1990). The corresponding design principle suggests choosing mechanisms suitable to the job to be done rather than trying for a single, unified mechanism. There are other such tenets and their corresponding design principles (for a full account, see Franklin 1997) .

Building the machinery of human consciousness into a software agent raises the fascinating issue of software awareness. Is it possible for software agents to be aware in anything like the way humans, and presumably many animals, are aware? If so, how could one know? Baars requires both a human subject's immediate assertion of consciousness of an event and some independent verification as conditions for accepting that something conscious had indeed occurred (Baars 1988, page 15). In software agents a mechanism for verification could be built into an interface, and the agent could be given the capability of reporting the content of its "consciousness." While Baars' criteria seem to me a perfectly fine operational definition of consciousness, as he intended, I doubt it would cut much ice with philosophers. Why can't a zombie (in the philosophical sense) report a verifiable experience as being conscious? He could either be lying or mistaken. Baars also give neuro-anatomical arguments for animal consciousness (1988, pages 33 ff.) essentially stressing structural similarities with humans. Others mount different sorts of arguments (Griffin, 1984; Franklin, 1995, Chapter 3). A slightly fuller account of this issue was given elsewhere (Franklin and Graesser, 1999)

Conversational software systems since Weizenbaum's Eliza (1966) have mimicked consciousness. A recently successful such system is Mauldin's Julia (1994), who fooled any number of men in an online chat room into seriously hitting on her. There's even the $100,000 Loebner Prize for the first such system to successfully pass the Turing test (web). All of these systems depend on more or less simple syntactic transformations together with a built-in database of phrases to perform their feats. There's no claim of consciousness, nor any reason to suspect it. Recall that the Turing test was intended as a sufficient indicator of intelligence, not consciousness (Turing, 1950).

But "conscious" software agents present a different problem. Suppose CMattie notices that sessions of two different seminars are scheduled for the same room at overlapping times. "CMattie notices" implies that this scheduling conflict results in the creation of a coalition of codelets that gains the spotlight of "consciousness" (to be described in Section 7 below). This coalition might contain the codelet that discovered the conflict together with two or more others that carry information about the two sessions. CMattie's emotion of concern might be aroused. Is CMattie then aware of the conflict in something like a human's conscious awareness? If so, how could we know it? CMattie, on noting the conflict, would send email messages to the two seminar organizers saying that she noticed the conflict and suggesting that they resolve it. Would these messages, together with our noting that the coalition did indeed occupy the spotlight, satisfy Baars' criterion for consciousness? Perhaps so, but it wouldn't convince me of CMattie's awareness in anything like a human sense. How can we be sure of consciousness in any other creature, computational or biological? Can "conscious" software agents help us with this problem?

2 Mechanisms

Following the diversity of mind tenet of the action selection paradigm of mind (Franklin 1995, Chapter 16), the architectures of the various "conscious" software agents are designed using a diversity of mechanisms of mind. A *mechanism of mind* is a computational mechanism that serves to enable some cognitive function. Taken from the "new AI" literature (see Maes, 1993), now often referred to as softcomputing, each of these mechanisms required extensions and enhancements to make it suitable for use in "conscious" software. Very brief descriptions of the original versions of each appear in the following subsections. Full accounts can be found in the original sources referenced. Expository accounts can be found in *Artificial Minds* (Franklin, 1995). Extensions and enhancements are described in subsequent sections. Some more commonly known mechanisms such as case based reasoning and classifier systems are used in the CMattie architecture described below. Accounts of these are not included in this section since descriptions of them are readily available in easily found books (Kolodner, 1993; Holland, 1986).

2.1 The Copycat Architecture

Copycat is an analogy making program that produces answers to such conundrums as "abc is to abd as iijjkk is to ?". Hofstadter and Mitchell (1993, 1994) consider analogy making, along with recognition and categorization, as examples of high-level perception, that is deep, abstract, multi-model forms of perception rather than low-level, concrete, uni-model forms. Copycat is intended to model this kind of high-level perception. Its design assumes that high-level perception emerges from the activity of many independent processes, running in parallel, sometimes competing, sometimes cooperating. These independent processes, here called *codelets*, create and destroy temporary perceptual constructs, trying out variations to eventually produce an answer. The codelets rely on an associative network knowledge base with blurry conceptual boundaries called the slipnet. The slipnet evolves to the problem by changing activation levels and by changing degrees of conceptual overlap. There is no central executive, no one in charge. Decisions are made by codelets independently and probabilistically. The system self-organizes; analogy making emerges.

Copycat's architecture is tripartite, consisting of a slipnet, a working area, and a population of codelets. The slipnet, an associative network comprised of nodes and links, contains permanent concepts and relations between them. That's what Copycat knows. It does not learn. The slipnet is its long-term memory. The system has a connectionist flavor by virtue of spreading activation in the slipnet. All of this is explicitly encoded. The working area, working memory if you like, is where perceptual structures are built and modified, sometime by being torn down. The population of codelets consists of perceptual and higher level structuring agents. As demons should, they wait until the situation is right for them to run, and then jump into the fray.

2.2 Behavior Nets

Behavior nets were introduced by Pattie Maes in a paper entitled "How to do the right thing" (1990). The "right thing" refers to a correct action in the current context. This work is about behavior selection, that is, how to control actions subject to constraints. It's designed to work well with limited computational and time resources in a world that's not entirely predictable.

A behavior looks very much like a production rule, having preconditions as well as additions and deletions. A behavior is distinguished from a production rule by the presence of an activation, a number indicating some kind of strength level. Each behavior occupies a node in a digraph (directed graph). The three types of links of the digraph are completely determined by the behaviors. If a behavior X will add a proposition b, which is on behavior Y's precondition list, then put a successor link from X to Y. There may be several such propositions resulting in several links between the same nodes. Next, whenever you put in a successor going one way, put a predecessor link going the other. Finally, suppose you have a proposition m on behavior Y's delete list that is also a precondition for behavior X. In such a case, draw a conflictor link from X to Y, which is to be inhibitory rather than excitatory.

As in connectionist models, this digraph spreads activation. The activation comes from activation stored in the behaviors themselves, from the environment, and from goals. Maes' system has built-in global goals, some goals to be achieved one time only, while others are drives to be pursued continuously. The environment awards activation to a behavior for each of its true preconditions. The more relevant it is to the current situation, the more activation it's going to receive from the environment. This source of activation tends to make the system opportunistic. Each goal awards activation to every behavior that, by being active, will satisfy that goal. This source of activation tends to make the system goal directed. Finally, activation spreads from behavior to behavior along links. Along successor links, one behavior strengthens those behaviors whose preconditions it can help fulfill by sending them activation. Along predecessor links, one behavior strengthens any other behavior whose add list fulfills one of its own preconditions. A behavior sends inhibition along a conflictor link to any other behavior that can delete one of its true preconditons, thereby weakening it. Every conflictor link is inhibitory.

Call a behavior *executable* if all of its preconditions are satisfied. Here's a pseudocode version of Maes' algorithm for the system:

Loop forever

1. Add activation from environment and goals.
2. Spread activation forward and backward among the behaviors.
3. Decay - total activation remains constant.
4. Behavior fires if
   i) it's executable and
   ii) it's over threshold and
   iii) it's the maximum such.
5. If one behavior fires, its activation = zero, and all thresholds revert to their normal value.
6. If none fires, reduce all thresholds by 10%.

In this last case, the system "thinks" for one round, and then tries again.

Note that there is nothing magical about the 10% in the previous paragraph. The system may well work better at a higher or lower value. This threshold reduction rate is one of several global parameters that can be used to tune a behavior net. For example, strengthening the activation rate of drives will make the system more goal driven, while varying the activation rate from the environment makes it more or less opportunistic.

2.3 Pandemonium Theory

John Jackson (1987) extended Selfridge's pandemonium theory (1959) to a theory of mind. Picture a collection of demons (comparable to Copycat's codelets) living in a sports stadium of some kind. Some of the demons are involved with perception, others cause external actions and still others act internally on other demons. Almost all the demons are up in the stands. A half dozen or so are down on the playing field exciting the crowd in the stands. A demon excites other demons to which it is linked. Demons in the stand respond. Some are more excited than others and are yelling louder. Stronger links produce louder responses. The loudest demon in the stands joins those on the field, displacing one of those currently performing back to the stands.

The system starts off with a certain number of initial demons and initial, built-in links between them. New links are made between demons and existing links are strengthened in proportion to the time the two demons have been together on the field. The strength of the link between two demons depends not only upon the time they're together on the field, but also upon the motivational level of the whole system at that time, the "gain." The gain is turned up when things are going well, turned down, even to negative, when things are getting worse. The higher the gains, the more the links between concurrently performing demons are strengthened.

Under such a strategy, demons would tend to reappear on the playing field if they were associated with improved conditions, resulting in strengthened links between these demons. When one of these arrives once again on the playing field, its compatriots tend to get pulled in also because of the added strength of the links between them. The system's behavior would then tend to steer toward its goals, the goals being the basis on which the system decides things are improving.

Typically, improved conditions result not from a single action, but from a coordinated sequence of actions. Suppose we make the links from demons on the playing field to new arrivals stronger than those from new arrivals to incumbents. Uphill links would tend to be stronger than downhill links. And suppose we also have demons gradually fade from the playing field, instead of suddenly jumping up and heading for the stands. Habitual sequences could then be completed from memory simply by putting an initial segment on the playing field. Once started, the system tends to redo that sequence.

Although we focused on the playing field, much of the really important activity takes place below ground (subconsciously) in the *sub-arena*. The sub-arena measures the system's well being, and on this basis, adjusts the gain on changes in link strengths through association. The sub-arena performs sensory input by sending demons representing low-level input to the playing field. Thus it provides a sensory interface. Low-level actions are carried out by demons in the sub-arena at the command of action demons on the playing field. Some primitive sensory capabilities and some primitive actions are built in.

Jackson also allows for the creation of concepts in his system. Demons that have very strong links can be merged into a single concept demon. When concept demons are created, their component demons survive, and continue to act individually. In a pandemonium system, the playing field is a major bottleneck because so few demons entertain on the playing field at any one time. Concept demons help relieve this bottleneck. Also, when compacted into a concept demon, higher level features of one problem enable the transfer of solutions to another. Not only can we have concept demons, but also *compound concept demons* that result from merging concept demons. With compound concept demons a hierarchy of concepts at various levels of abstraction is possible. Higher-level concept demons might well linger on the playing field longer than low level demons

Unused links decay, or lose strength, at some background rate. Negative links may decay at a different rate. High-level demons enjoy a slower decay rate. As a consequence, sufficiently rarely used links disappear, and recent associations count more than older associations. As links have strengths, demons also have their strengths, the strength of voice of those up in the crowd yelling, and the strength of signal of those on the playing field. The demon that yells the loudest goes to the playing with the same strength as when he was summoned. Again, notice the softcomputing flavor with no central executive.

2.4 Sparse Distributed Memory

Pentti Kanerva (1988) designed a content addressable memory that, in many ways, is ideal for use as a long-term associative memory. Content addressable means that items in memory can be retrieved by using part of their contents as a cue, rather than having to know its address in memory. To describe Kanerva's *sparse distributed memory,* even superficially, will require more effort than we've expended on the other mechanisms, and even a short excursion into Boolean geometry.

Boolean geometry is the geometry of Boolean spaces. A Boolean space is the set of all Boolean vectors (that is, vectors composed of zeros and ones) of some fixed length, n, called the dimension of the space. Points in Boolean space are Boolean vectors. The Boolean space of dimension n contains 2^n Boolean vectors, each of length n. The number of points increases exponentially as the dimension increases. Though his model of memory is more general, Kanerva uses 1000 dimensional Boolean space, the space of Boolean vectors of length 1000, as his running example.

Boolean geometry uses a metric called the *Hamming distance,* where the distance between two points is the number of coordinates at which they differ. Thus d((1,0,0,1,0), (1,0,1,1,1)) = 2. The distance between two points will measure the similarity between two memory items in Kanerva's model, closer points being more similar. Or we might think of these Boolean vectors as feature vectors, where each feature can be only on, 1, or off, 0. Two such feature vectors are closer together if more of their features are the same. Kanerva shows that for n = 1000, 99.9999% of the space lies between distance 422 and distance 578 from a given vector. In other words, almost all the space is far away from any given vector. Boolean space is sparsely populated, an important property for the construction of the model, and the source of part of its name.

By a sphere we mean the set of all points within some fixed distance, the radius, from its center. Spheres in Boolean space are quite different in one respect from the Euclidean spheres we're used to. Points of a Euclidean sphere are uniformly distributed throughout. For r = n/2 most of the points in a sphere in Boolean space lie close to its boundary. This is enough Boolean geometry to get started. Let's see how Kanerva uses it to build his model.

A memory is called random access if any storage location can be reached in essentially the same length of time that it takes to reach any other. Kanerva constructs a model of a random access memory capable, in principle, of being implemented on a sufficiently powerful digital computer. This memory has an address space, a set of allowable addresses each specifying a storage location in a sense to be explained below. Kanerva's address space is Boolean space of dimension 1000. Thus allowable addresses are Boolean vectors of length 1000, henceforth to be called *bit vectors* in deference to both the computing context and to brevity.

Kanerva's address space is enormous. It contains 2^{1000} locations, no doubt more points than the number of elementary particles in the entire universe. One cannot hope for such a vast memory. On the other hand, thinking of feature vectors, a thousand features wouldn't deal with human visual input until a high level of abstraction had been reached. A dimension of 1000 may not be all that much; it may, for some purposes, be unrealistically small.

Kanerva proposes to deal with this vast address space by choosing a uniform random sample, size 2^{20}, of locations, that is, about a million of them. These he calls *hard locations.* With 2^{20} hard locations out of a possible 2^{1000} locations, the ratio is 2^{-980} – very sparse indeed. In addition, the distance from a random location in the entire address space to the nearest hard location will fall between 411 and 430 ninety-eight percent of the time, with the median distance being 424. The hard locations are certainly sparse.

We've seen how sparse distributed memory is sparse. It is distributed in that many hard locations participate in storing and retrieving each datum, and one hard location can be involved in the storage and retrieval of many data. This is a very different beast than the store-one-datum-in-one-location type of memory to which we're accustomed. Each hard location, itself a bit vector of length 1000, stores data in 1000 counters, each with range -40 to 40. We now have a million hard locations, each with a thousand counters, totaling a billion counters in all. Numbers in the range -40 to 40 will take most of a byte to store. Thus we're talking about a billion bytes, a gigabyte, of memory. Quite a lot, but not out of the question.

How do these counters work? Writing a 1 to the counter increments it; writing a 0 decrements it. A datum, ξ,to be written is a bit vector of length 1000.[1] To write ξ at a given hard location x, write each coordinate of $\xi$to the corresponding counter in x, either incrementing it or decrementing it.

Call the sphere of radius 451 centered at location ξ the access sphere of that location. An access sphere typically contains about a thousand hard locations, with the closest to ξ usually some 424 bits away and the median distance from ξ to hard locations in its access sphere about 448. Any hard location in the access sphere of ξ is *accessible* from ξ. With this machinery in hand, we can now write distributively to any location, hard or not. To write a datum ξ to a location ζ, simply write ξ to each of the roughly one thousand hard locations accessible from ζ distributed storage.

With our datum distributively stored, the next question is how to retrieve it. With this in mind, let's ask first how one reads from a single hard location, x. Compute ζ, the bit vector read at x, by assigning its ith bit the value 1 or 0 according as x's ith counter is positive or negative. Thus, each bit of ζ results from a majority rule decision of all the data that have been written on x. The read datum, ζ, is an archetype of the data that have been written to x, but may not be any one of them. From another point of view, ζ, is the datum with smallest mean distance from all data that have been written to x.

Knowing how to read from a hard location allows us to read from any of the 2^{1000} arbitrary locations. Suppose ζ is any location. The bit vector, ξ, to be read at ζ is formed by pooling the data read from each hard location accessible from ζ. Each bit of ξ results from a majority rule decision over the pooled data. Specifically, to get the ith bit of ξ add together the ith bits of the data read from hard locations accessible from ζ and use half the number of such hard locations as a threshold. At or over threshold, assign a 1. Below threshold assign a 0. Put another way, pool the bit vectors read from hard locations accessible from ζ,, and let each of their ith bits vote on the ith bit of ξ.

We now know how to write items into memory, and how to read them out. But what's the relation between the datum in and the datum out? Are these two bit vectors the same, as we'd hope? Let's first look at the special case where the datum ξ is written at the location ξ. This makes sense since both are bit vectors of length one thousand. Kanerva offers a mathematical proof that reading form ξ recovers ξ.Here's the idea of the proof. Reading from ξ recovers archetypes from each of some thousand hard locations and

[1] I will try to adhere to Kanerva's convention of using lower case Greek letters for locations and for data, and lower case Roman letters for hard locations. The Greek letters will include ξ(xi), η (eta), and ζ (zeta).

takes a vote. The voting is influenced by the $\sim$1000 stored copies of ξ and, typically, by about 10,000 other stored data items. Since the intersection of two access spheres is typically quite small, these other data items influence a given coordinate only in small groups of ones or twos or threes. The thousand copies of the stored item are what's needed to recover it. Iterated reading allows recovery when reading from a noisy version of what's been stored. Again, Kanerva offers conditions (involving how much of the stored item is available for the read) under which this is true, and mathematical proof.

Since a convergent sequence of iterates converges very rapidly, while a divergent sequence of iterates bounces about seemingly at random, comparison of adjacent items in the sequence quickly tells whether or not a sequence converges. Thus, this memory is content addressable, provided we write each datum with itself as address.

Kanerva lists several similarities between properties of his sparse distributed memory and of human memory. One such has to do with the human property of knowing what one does or doesn't know. If asked for a telephone number I've once known, I may search for it. When asked for one I've never known, an immediate "I don't know" response ensues. Sparse distributed memory could make such decisions based on the speed of initial convergence. If it's slow, I don't know. The "on the tip of my tongue phenomenon" is another such. In sparse distributed memory, this could correspond to the cue having content just at the threshold of being similar enough for reconstruction. Yet another is the power of rehearsal during which an item would be written many times and, at each of these to a thousand locations. A well-rehearsed item would be retrieved with fewer cues. Finally, forgetting would tend to increase over time as a result of other writes to memory.

The above discussion, based on the identity of datum and address, produced a content addressable memory with many pleasing properties. It works well for reconstructing individual memories. However, more is needed. We, and our autonomous agents, must also remember sequences of events or actions. Kanerva shows how the machinery we've just seen can be modified to provide this capability. The basic idea is something like this. The cue for a sequence of patterns serves as the address for the first pattern of the sequence. Thereafter, the content of each pattern in the sequence is the address of the next pattern.

3 Global Workspace Theory

The material in this section is from Baars' two books (1988, 1997) and superficially describes his global workspace theory of consciousness.

3.1 Processors and Processes

In his global workspace theory, Baars, along with many others (e.g. Ornstein, 1986; Edelman, 1987; Minsky, 1985), postulates that human cognition is implemented by a multitude of relatively small, special purpose processes, almost always unconscious. (It's a multiagent system.) Communication between them is rare and over a narrow bandwidth.

3.2 Global Workspace

Coalitions of such processes find their way into a global workspace (and into consciousness). This limited capacity workspace serves to broadcast the message of the coalition to all the unconscious processors, in order to recruit other processors to join in handling the current novel situation, or in solving the current problem. Thus consciousness in this theory allows us to deal with novelty or problematic situations that can't be dealt with efficiently, or at all, by habituated unconscious processes. Something like this key insight of Baars' theory seems to have been independently arrived at by others also. Freeman writes as follows (1995 p. 136)

> " I speculate that consciousness reflects operations by which the entire knowledge store in an intentional structure is brought instantly into play each moment of the waking life of an animal, putting into immediate service all that an animal has learned in order to solve its problems, without the need for look-up tables and random access memory systems."

3.3 Contexts

All this takes place under the auspices of contexts: goal contexts, perceptual contexts, conceptual contexts, and/or cultural contexts. Baars uses goal hierarchies, dominant goal contexts, a dominant goal hierarchy, dominant context hierarchies, and lower level context hierarchies. Each context is, itself a coalition of processes. Though contexts are typically unconscious, they strongly influence conscious processes.

3.4 Learning

Baars postulates that learning results simply from conscious attention, that is, that consciousness is sufficient for learning.

3.5 Rest of the Theory

There's much more to the theory, including attention, action selection, emotion, voluntary action, metacognition and a sense of self. I think of it as a high level theory of cognition.

4 The Virtual Mattie Architecture

4.0.1 Virtual Mattie (VMattie), an autonomous clerical agent "lives" in a UNIX system, communicates with humans via email in natural language with no agreed upon protocol, and autonomously carries out her tasks without human intervention. In particular, she keeps a mailing list to which she emails seminar announcements once a week. VMattie's various tasks include gathering information from seminar organizers, reminding organizers to send seminar information, updating her mailing list in response to human requests, composing next week's seminar schedule announcement, and sending out the announcement to all the people on her mailing list in a timely fashion. At the time of this writing VMattie is up and running, and doing all that was expected of her.

In VMattie, Baars' "vast collection of unconscious processes" are implemented as codelets in the manner of the Copycat architecture (Hofstadter and Mitchell, 1994; Mitchell, 1993). All of the higher level constructs are associated with collections of codelets that carry out actions or acquire particular information associated with the construct. Working memory consists of two distinct workspaces as well as the perception registers (see Figure 4 below). (This yields a hypothesis about human cognition.) Perceptual contexts include certain nodes from a slipnet type associative memory à la Copycat, and certain templates in workspaces. How can a context, a coalition of codelets, be a node. We routinely identify the node and its associated coalition of codelets. The node type perceptual contexts become active via spreading activation reaching a threshold (another hypothesis). Several nodes can be active at once, producing composite perceptual contexts (another hypothesis). Baars says that "[o]ne of the remarkable features of conscious experiences is how they can trigger unconscious contexts that help to interpret later conscious events." The VMattie architecture fleshes out this assertion with mechanisms. Goal contexts are implemented via an expanded version of Maes' behavior nets (1990). Again they become active by having preconditions met and exceeding a time variable threshold (another hypothesis).

4.1 The VM Architecture

The VM architecture is composed of three major parts, the perceptual apparatus, the action selection module, and the input/output module. The perceptual apparatus consists of a slipnet, a processing workspace, and a set of perception registers (see Figure 1). The slipnet is an associative knowledge base. The perception registers hold and make available the information created during perception of a message. (Another tenet of the action selection paradigm of mind asserts that minds operate on sensations to create information for their own use (Franklin, 1995, p. 413; see also Oyama, 1985).) The action selection module is composed of a behavior net, including explicitly represented drives, a workspace and a long-term (tracking) memory (see Figure 1). The mechanisms and functions of all these modules will be described below.

4.2 Perception via Slipnet

In sufficiently narrow domains, natural language understanding may be attained via an analysis of surface features without the use of a traditional symbolic parser. Allen describes this approach as complex, template-based matching, natural language processing (1995). VMattie's limited domain requires her to deal with only nine distinct message types, each with predictable content. This allows for surface level natural language processing. VMattie's language understanding module has been implemented as a Copycat-like architecture though her understanding takes place differently. The mechanism includes a slipnet storing domain knowledge, and a pool of codelets (processors) specialized for specific jobs, along with templates for building and verifying understanding. Together they constitute an integrated sensing system for the autonomous agent VMattie. With it she's able to recognize, categorize and understand.

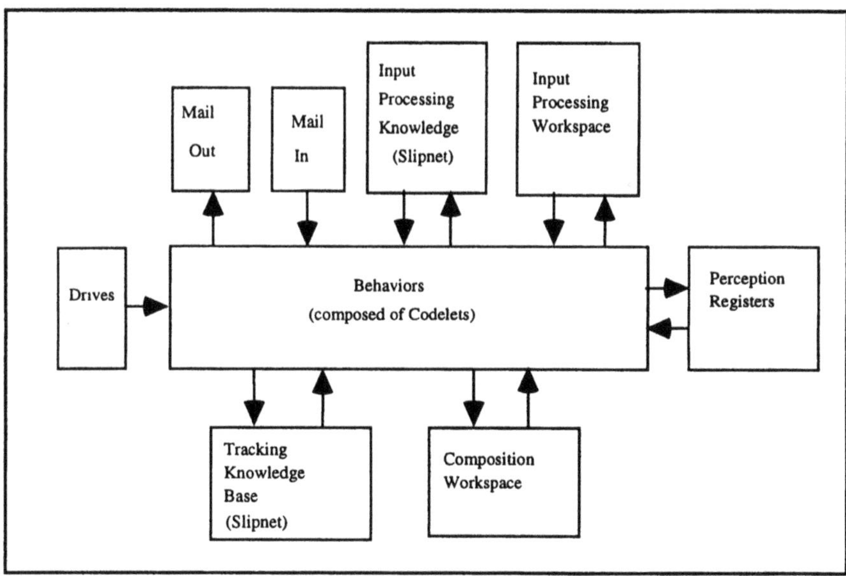

Fig. 1. Vmattie Architecture (Franklin, et al, 1996)

The perception registers hold information created from an incoming email message. Acting like a structured blackboard, the perception registers make this information available to codelets that need it. Each register holds the content of a specified field. Fields include organizer-name, email-address, date, speaker, seminar-name, etc. These field names label the behavior variables discussed in the preceding paragraph. When occupied, perception registers provide environmental activation to behaviors that can use their contents. A detailed description of VMattie's perceptual apparatus has appeared elsewhere (Zhang ,Franklin, Olde, Wan and Graesser,1998).

4.3 Instantiated Behavior Nets

VMattie has several distinct drives operating in parallel. (Our drives play the same role in this mechanism, as do Maes' goals.) VMattie wants:

1) to get the weekly seminar out in a timely fashion,
2) to maintain complete information on each of the ongoing seminars,
3) to keep her mailing list updated,
4) to acknowledge each incoming message.

These drives vary in urgency as email messages arrive and as the time for the seminar announcement to be sent approaches. This variation in drive urgency, other than on and off, is an enhancement to the original behavior net architecture. Drives provide activation to behaviors that fulfill them.

Behaviors are typically mid-level actions, many depending on several codelets for their execution. Examples of behaviors might include add-address-to-list, associate-organizer-with-seminar, or compose-reminder (to remind organizer to send speaker, title, etc.). As described in 2.2 above, the behavior net is composed of behaviors and their various links.

Our behaviors must support variables. To associate-organizer-with-seminar immediately asks: which organizer and which seminar. VMattie's behaviors implement the usual preconditions, action, add list and delete list, allowing variables in the contents of any of these. Picture an underlying digraph composed of templates of behaviors with their variables unbound and their links. Above this, picture an identical, instantiated copy with the variables in its behaviors bound. Now, picture several such instantiated layers, each independent of the others except for activation inputs from drives, etc. (See Figure 2) Instantiated behaviors and their links lie above their templates. Activation spreads only through instantiated links. A detailed description of VMattie's instantiated behavior net will appear (Song and Franklin, 2000).

5 "Conscious" Mattie

Though comprehensive, Baars' theory is quite abstract, as a psychological theory should be. It offers general principles and broad architectural sketches. Questions of architectural detail, that is of just how functional components fit together and who talks to whom, are sometimes left open, as are almost all questions of mechanisms, that is of *how* these components do what they are claimed to do. For example, in Baar's presentation the various types of contexts (perceptual, conceptual, goal contexts) are lumped architecturally.

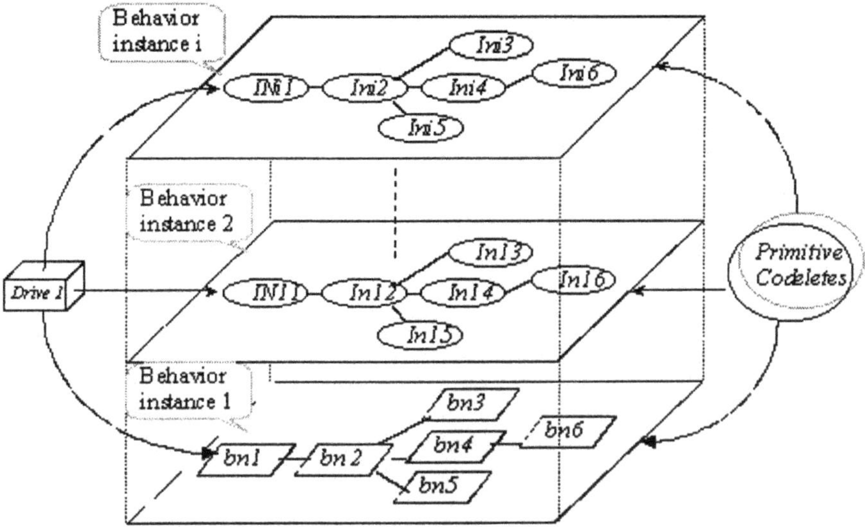

Fig. 2. Demonstration of a behavior template and its instantiation sequence. Behavior template 1 can have more than one behavior instance at a time. Drive 1 and Attention Registers only spread activaiton to the behavior instances, but not to behavior template

Though distinguished functionally, their architectural relationships, as well as their mechanisms, are left unspecified. As a good theory should, this one raises as many questions as it answers.

Providing a more detailed and discriminated architecture, and the mechanisms with which to implement it, can be expected to suggest answers to many of these questions about human cognition. With this in mind we introduce "conscious" Mattie (CMattie), a cognitive agent designed within the constraints of global workspace theory. CMattie's architecture and mechanisms serve to flesh out that theory and, hopefully, provide a fertile source of hypotheses for cognitive science and cognitive neuroscience.

5.1 Foundation in Virtual Mattie

CMattie is best viewed as an extension of VMattie. Her domain is exactly the same; CMattie is also a clerical software agent who communicates with humans via email and sends out weekly seminar schedules. The VM architecture, as described in Section 4, is carried over in its entirety to CMattie. Perception in CMattie is again via a slipnet and a workspace. Actions are selected by an instantiated behavior net. The perceptual registers are in place. The input/output module that sends and receives email messages is the same.

Yet there are significant differences. VMattie's slipnet (perceptual knowledge base) contains an embedded artificial neural network, feedforward and trained by backpropagation, that identifies an incoming message type. CMattie's slipnet clings much more closely to the original Copycat model, facilitating the learning of new message types.

VMattie's instantiated behavior net selects and executes an instantiated behavior from each instantiation at each time step. (See 4.3 above.) These behaviors operate in (simulated) parallel. CMattie selects and executes only one instantiated behavior from all instantiated behavior net layers at each time step. This brings CMattie in line with global workspace theory, which prescribes a single dominant goal context at a time. These contexts are discussed in 5.2 below.

VMattie's behavior net contains a behavior stream that implements the perceptual process of understanding a new message. The process by which a message moves from input text to understanding in the perceptual registers is controlled by a stream of behaviors in the behavior net. In humans the analogous process seems to typically be automatic, unconscious and independent of the current goal context. Let me say a little more to clarify this point. In humans, the current goal context certainly influences perception. But, we have no goal context for converting a retinal image into a subsequent mapping. Such goal contexts are beyond the perceptual apparatus. For this reason CMattie implements the perceptual process via codelets directly.

In VMattie missing information in a message is recovered from the tracking memory after perception has occurred. In CMattie default information is added as a result of "consciousness" of something missing during the latter part of the perceptual process itself. Again, this seems more in line with what happens in humans in analogous situations.

5.2 Concordance with Global Workspace Theory

In CMattie, Baars' "vast collection of unconscious processes" are implemented as codelcts in the manner of the Copycat architecture, or equivalently as Jackson's demons. Her limited capacity global workspace is implemented as a portion of Jackson's playing field. Working memory consists of at least four distinct workspaces (yielding a hypothesis about humans). Perceptual contexts include certain nodes from a slipnet type associative memory à la Copycat, and certain templates in workspaces. A node type perceptual context becomes active via spreading activation reaching a threshold (another hypothesis). Several nodes can be active at once, producing composite perceptual contexts (another hypothesis). These mechanisms allow conscious experiences to trigger unconscious contexts that help to interpret later conscious events. Conceptual contexts also reside in the slipnet, as well as in sparse distributed memory, CMattie's associative memory. Goal contexts are implemented as instantiated behaviors in a much more dynamic version of Maes' behavior nets. They become active by having preconditions met and exceeding a time-varying activation threshold (another hypothesis). Goal hierarchies are implemented as instantiated behaviors and their associated drives. The dominant goal context is determined by the currently active instantiated behavior. The dominant goal hierarchy is one rooted at the drive associated with the currently active instantiated behavior.

But, you object, global workspace theory calls for contexts to be coalitions of codelets. Each slipnet node is associated with a collection of codelets that it both activates and receives activation from. The same is true of each behavior whose associated codelets perform its action when the behavior is executed. The CM architecture, to be described in detail below, is comprised of a more abstract level consisting of the slipnet, the behavior net and many other modules, and a less abstract level, the codelets. In specifying a concordance with global workspace theory, it's best to identify each higher level construct (e.g. slipnet node, behavior) with it's associated coalition of codelets.

The remaining functions comprising global workspace theory are implemented in CMattie by modules named in easily recognizable ways, for example emotion, learning, and metacognition.

5.3 The CM Architecture

CMattie's architecture consists of a number of modules complexly interconnected. One way of coming to grips with it is to think of five major components, the codelets, the high level constructs, the "consciousness" mechanism, metacognition and learning. The first three of these are at least indicated in Figure 6. Learning is embedded in several of the other modules, Metacognition sits above all the others and influences them. Each module will be described briefly in this section. Referring back to the figure will help in understanding the relationships between the modules.

As in VMattie, all of CMattie's actions are performed by codelets. Codelets implement the perception mechanism and put into action all selected behaviors. In addition to these codelets, CMattie also utilizes other classes of codelets, for example emotional codelets (see 5.4) and "consciousness" codelets. The latter serve to bring novel information and/or problematic situations to "consciousness". For example, if a speaker-topic message arrives without the title of the talk, a "consciousness" codelet, watchful for just this situation, creates an informative coalition, and competes vigorously for the spotlight. The coalition would consist of the "consciousness" codelet that recognized the missing title, and other "consciousness" codelets holding pertinent data from the perception registers.

Codelets in CMattie participate in a pandemonium theory style organization. Those who share time in the spotlight of "consciousness" have associations between them formed or strengthened. Those codelets sharing time in the playing field also change associations, but at a much lesser rate. Coalitions of highly associated codelets may form higher-level concept codelets (demons a la Jackson). This is comparable to chunking in SOAR (Laird, Newell and Rosenbloom, 1987).

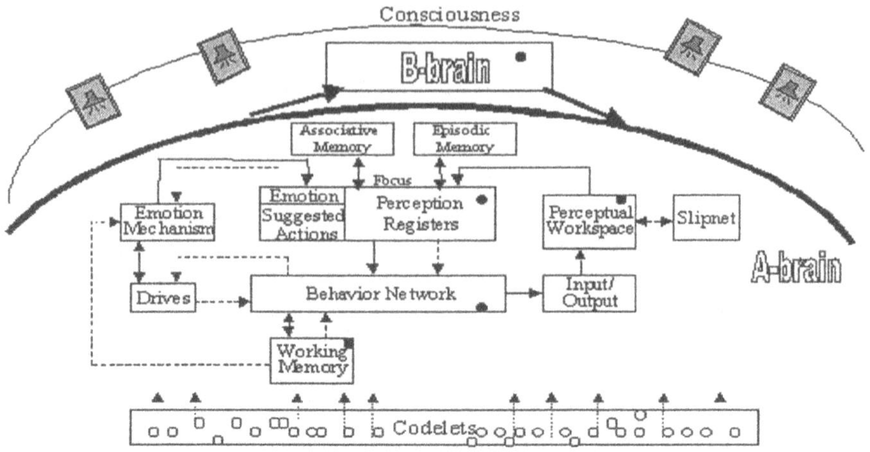

Fig. 3. The CMattie Architecture

CMattie employs an important subclasse of codelets, distinguished by their need to be active in more than one context simultaneously. For example, consider a codelet whose task is to write the speaker name in the appropriate place in the announcement template. Such a codelet may be awaiting it chance to write when another speaker-topic message is perceived, requiring another such. Such codelets, called generator codelets, spawn instances of themselves with their variables bound. Each of these instantiated codelets carries the complete picture of a single task within itself. Instantiated codelets associated with instantiated behaviors are examples of generated codelets.

5.4 Emotions

Including emotional capabilities in non-biological autonomous agents is not a new idea (Bates, Loyall, and Reilly, 1991; Sloman and Poli, 1996; Picard, 1997). Some claim that truly intelligent robots or software agents can't be effectively designed without emotions. In CMattie we'll experiment with building in mechanisms for emotions (McCauley and Franklin, 1998) such as guilt at not getting an announcement out on time, frustration at not understanding a message, and anxiety at not knowing the speaker and title of an impending seminar. These emotions will play a role analogous to the single temperature variable in the original copycat architecture, but more complex. They'll also provide gain control for the pandemonium architecture. Action selection will be influenced by emotions via their effect on drives, modeling recent work on human action selection (Damasio, 1994).

CMattie can "experience" four basic emotions, anger, fear, happiness and sadness. These emotions can vary in intensity as indicated by their activation levels. For example, anger can vary from mild annoyance to rage as its activation rises. A four vector containing the current activations of these four basic emotions represents CMattie's current emotional state. Like humans, there's always some emotional state however slight. Also like humans, her current emotional state is often some complex combination of basic emotions. The effect of emotions on codelets, drives, etc. varies with their intensity. Fear brought on by an imminent shutdown message might be expected to strengthen CMattie's self-preservation drive resulting in additional activation going from it into the behavior net.

CMattie's emotional codelets serve to change her emotional state. When its preconditions are satisfied, an emotional codelet will enhance or diminish one of the four basic emotions. An emotion can build till saturation occurs. Repeated emotional stimuli result in habituation. Emotion codelets can also combine into concept codelets (see 2.3 above) to implement more complex secondary emotions that act by affecting more than one basic emotion at once. Emotion codelets also serve to enhance or diminish the activation of other codelets. They also act to increase or decrease the strength of drives, thereby influencing CMattie's choice of behaviors.

As we'll see in the next two subsections, CMattie's associative memory associates emotions with situations while her episodic memory remembers past emotions. These memories become part of the contents of "consciousness" (see 5.7 below) and can affect the current emotion. Thus, CMattie's remembered emotions also influence her action selection.

CMattie's emotion mechanism maintains a continual, multidimensional evaluation of how well things are going for her. By affecting action selection it should help her to choose good enough actions in unforeseen situations. The change in association of an emotional codelet and other codelets as a result of being "conscious" together (as described in below) results in the learning of emotional associations. The "chunking" into emotion concept codelets (5.4.3) is also a form of learning.

5.5 Associative Memory

In Section 5.3.3 above we described the pandemonium style association that occurs between CMattie's codelets. That's one type of associative memory, though we don't refer to it as such. Here we describe another associative memory based on sparse distributed memory (see 2.4 above) and implemented similarly.

The contents of the perception registers (see Section 4.1 and Figure 6 above) are encoded as simple ASCII code, and strung together into a Boolean vector. This vector is lengthened to include space in which to encode an emotion and an action along with each set of contents of the perception registers.

Such a vector will be used both to read from, and to write to, CMattie's associative memory. Both are accomplished through the focus, sparse distributed memory's gateway to the world. CMattie's focus is a register of appropriate size to hold the vector just described. For purely technical reasons, information is sometimes written redundantly (Anwar and Franklin, forthcoming). The structure of the focus is more complicated than described above, as will be explained in the next section.

How is the associative memory used? When new sensory information is created, it appears in the perception registers in the focus (to be described in Section 5.6.8 below). A read is then made from associative memory, using the contents of the perception registers as the address. Whatever is associated with this current perception is returned. Typically this will include default values of fields not mentioned in the email message, as well as an associated emotion and a suggested action. The actual perceived information will, in most but perhaps not all, cases remain unchanged. Upon arrival in the focus the result of this read provides environmental and internal activation to the behavior net and to the emotion module through consciousness (see Section 5.7 below). Its information is thus made available to the rest of the system, for example to codelets who want to enter it in one or another template. This description of the use of associative memory is only roughly accurate. It omits the role played by consciousness as will be discussed in Section 5.7 below.

Shortly thereafter we may expect a current emotion, influenced by the associated emotion, to arise. In parallel, the behavior net is choosing its next behavior. Perhaps a new goal context is called for by this current perception. Recall that it's possible that the behavior net not choose a behavior, but simply to "think" for another round (see Section 2.2 above). Whatever emotion and behavior arise are entered into the focus as emotion and action, the contents of the perception registers remaining unchanged. A write is then made with this Boolean vector as address. This constitutes CMattie's association with the current percept.

5.6 Episodic Memory

Humans use an intermediate term memory in several ways. For example, I can easily recall what I had for dinner last night. A month from now I'd probably find that impossible unless it had somehow become relevant in the meantime and been reinforced. If perhaps the mussels had been exceptional, and I later reported on them to my wife and daughters within a few days, I might well be able to recall the entire meal a month later. Here the intermediate term memory was used to store items that might become relevant for a short while. I'd be unlikely to remember the color of the napkins or the pattern on the silverware, though others might.

Humans also need an intermediate term memory to keep a to-do list for tracking intended actions. Some such actions can not yet be performed because some precondition is missing. Others simply haven't reached a high enough priority. Such intended behaviors of both types are handled in CMattie by her behavior net. Intention occurs at the time of instantiation (see Sections 4.3 and 5.1 above). When a stream of behaviors is completed, it disappears. Thus, in CMattie the behavior net acts as an intermediate term memory. The hypothesis that we humans keep a to-do list in a similar fashion comes with one obvious difficulty. I often forget items on my internal to-do list while CMattie doesn't.

We humans also use intermediate term memory as episodic memory to keep track of contexts that might be needed again. This may only be a different view of remembering the meal with the exceptional mussels. CMattie also needs an episodic memory. Suppose a speaker-topic message arrives without the title of the talk. CMattie asks the organizer for the title. (This uses "consciousness" on her part in a technical sense to be described below.) The response may well contain little other than the missing title. How is CMattie to establish a context for the reply?

One possibility is to use CMattie's associative memory. After all, her understanding of the original message was written there after being understood and placed in the incoming perception registers. The way sparse distributed memory works, however, makes this solution untenable. In the example described, a read using only the seminar organizers name and/or email address would be required. Encoded, this would specify such a small piece of the Boolean vector used as an address that little useful information could be expected to be read (see Section 2.4 above). For this reason we've given CMattie a separate episodic memory based on a different mechanism. This yields yet another hypothesis about how human memory is organized. This time I suspect the hypothesis will turn out to be incorrect.

CMattie's episodic memory is implemented as a case-based memory, suitable for use with cased-based reasoning (Kolodner, 1993). This choice was influenced by the need to use cased-based reasoning for learning (see Section 5.9 below). Like sparse distributed memory, cased-based memory is content addressable (see Section 2.4 above). However, in the way it's used in CMattie, a small cue will suffice to retrieve the desired item.

Like her associative memory, CMattie's episodic memory is content addressable. Presented with a cue, here considered to be a case, episodic memory returns the stored cases most similar to the cue. All this immediately conjures up two questions: What is a case, and how is similarity judged? In CMattie's episodic memory a case looks just like an entry in associative memory, that is, a copy of the perception registers augmented with an emotion and an action. The second question is less easy to answer since, as of this writing, the similarity metric is still being designed. One idea that will likely come into play is to give an exact match in a particular perception register a great weight.

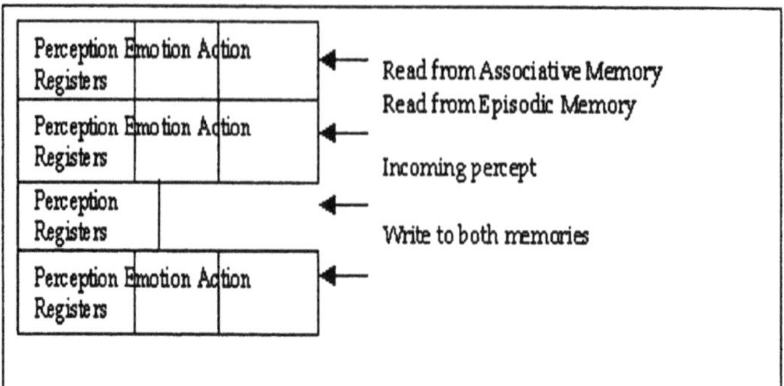

Fig. 4. CMattie's Focus

CMattie's use of episodic memory is much like that of her associative memory. When a percept arrives in the perception registers, a read from episodic memory is made. When, following that, a behavior is chosen, or declined to be chosen, a write to episodic memory is made. The case here included the contents of the perception registers, the new behavior, if chosen, and the current emotion, which may well have changed as a result of the percept, of associations with it, and/or of a context recovered from episodic memory.

CMattie's focus (see Figure 4 above) consists of four sets of registers. The perception registers hold the percept as it emerges from her perceptual module. Using these contents as addresses her associative and episodic memories are read into the two upper sets of registers. Most often the read from associative memory will contain copies of the contents of the perception registers with defaults filled in and with an emotion and an action added. The read from episodic memory into its set of registers should contain the case most similar to the original perception register contents. Later the set of registers for writes to associative and episodic memories should contain the original perception register contents augmented by default values, together with the current emotion and the currently active behavior (goal context). These are subsequently written to the two memories using themselves as addresses.

"Consciousness" comes into play here, as we'll see in the next section. In order to achieve this a codelet is associated with each of the individual registers in each of the four collections of registers in the focus. The codelet associated with a register carries the content of that register to make it available to other codelets. For example, one codelet might carry a message type while another carries the name of a seminar.

5.7 The Spotlight of "Consciousness"

According to global workspace theory (Baars, 1988; 1996; Section 3.2 above) the contents of consciousness, a coalition of processors, are broadcast to all the other processors. As a result, those processors are enlisted who can help with the novel and/or problematic situation at hand. They are the relevant processors. In the CMattie architecture processors are implemented by codelets. The apparatus for producing "consciousness" consists of a coalition manager, a spotlight controller, a broadcast manager, and a collection of "consciousness" codelets who recognize novel or problematic situations (Bogner, 1998; Bogner, Ramamurthy, and Franklin, 2000).

We'll take up a slightly simplified version of each of these in turn. (The full description will be given in Section 5.8 below.) But first, let's return to Jackson's metaphor or the sports stadium (see Section 2.3 above). The same metaphor is useful for describing the activity of CMattie's codelets after some small but crucial changes are made. Picture a sports arena composed of stands and a playing field (see Figure 5). In the stands are the inactive codelets. This must not be taken too literally. Each of these codelets is alert to conditions that would cause it to become active and join the playing field or, in the case of generator codelets, to instantiate a copy of itself, with variables bound, into the playing field (see 5.3.4 above). Note how this differs from pandemonium theory where demons are drawn into the playing field only by the strength of their association with current players.

On the playing field we find the active codelets, that is, codelets that are actively carrying out their functions. Some of these are joined in coalitions. One such coalition should lie in the spotlight of "consciousness". One can think of the playing field as CMattie's working memory or, better yet, as the union of her several working memories. At any given time codelets associated with her perceptual workspace and with her composition workspace (Section 4.1) will be active, along with codelets carrying information from the focus (Section 5.8).

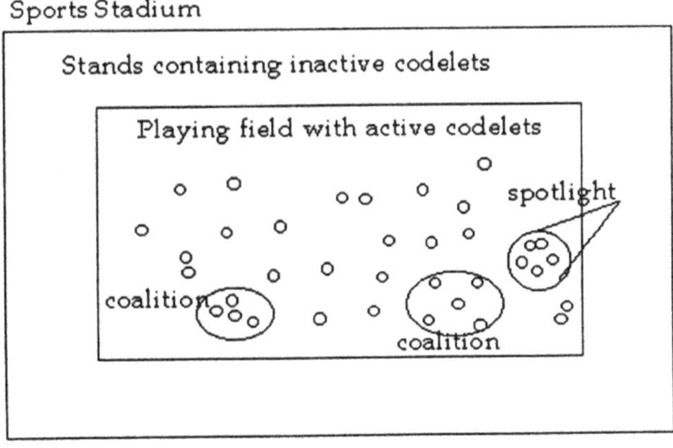

Fig. 5.

Each "consciousness" codelet (see Section 5.3.2 above) keeps a watchful eye out for some particular situation to occur that might call for "conscious" intervention. An example might be of two seminars scheduled in the same room at the same time. Upon encountering such a situation, the appropriate "consciousness" codelet will be associated (see Sections 2.3.3; 5.3.3 above) with the small number of codelets that carry the information describing the situation (see Section 5.6.9 above). In this case these codelets might collectively carry the names of the two seminars involved, the room, the date and the overlapping times. This association should lead to the collection of this small number of codelets, together with the "consciousness" codelet that collected them, becoming a coalition. Codelets also have activations (see Sections 5.2.2 and 5.4.2 above). The "consciousness" codelet increases its activation in order that the coalition might compete for "consciousness" if one is formed.

CMattie's coalition manager is responsible for forming and tracking coalitions of codelets on the playing field. Such coalitions are initiated on the basis of the mutual associations between the member codelets. Since association can both increase and diminish, the forming and tracking of coalitions is a dynamic process. Coalitions appear and disappear. Codelets may leave one coalition, and may join another.

While the existence of a coalition depends on the strengths of the associations between its members, its chance of becoming "conscious" depends on their average activation. CMattie's spotlight controller is responsible for selecting the coalition with the highest such average to shine upon. Since activations change even more rapidly than associations, the spotlight of "consciousness" can be expected to frequently shift from one coalition to another. Recall that the activation of a codelet can be influenced by a higher level concept (slipnet node, behavior), by the current emotion and, in the case of a "consciousness" codelet, by its own action. A codelet's activation goes to zero when its task is finished.

Global workspace theory calls for the contents of "consciousness", that is, of the spotlight in the CMattie architecture, to be broadcast to each of the codelets. Here we must distinguish between instantiated codelets and the other types. Instantiated codelets have their variables bound to particular pieces of information. They are either on the playing field in the process of carrying out their particular duties, or they are on the sidelines waiting to do so. (See Section 5.8 below for an explanation.) In either case instantiated codelets are already committed to certain duties and are not available to help with subsequent situations. Hence instantiated codelets do not receive broadcasts from "consciousness". All other codelets, including the generator codelets, do receive each broadcast. It is possible that a codelet is actively engaged on the playing field and cannot respond to a relevant percept. This design decision suggests the existence of instantiated processors in humans, a hypothesis that to my knowledge remains to be tested.

5.8 CMattie in Operation

Having struggled through the foregoing subsections of Section 5, the reader will have created a mental model of the workings of the CMattie architecture. To provide a chance to check this individually created model against that of the author, this section will contain a brief run through of CMattie in operation. Also, the account in the previous portions of this section left out some details in order not to overburden the reader all at once. These details will be described here.

Suppose a new message arrives in CMattie's inbox. Codelets move it into the perceptual module as soon as that module is free. Perception occurs as described in Sections 4.2 and 5.1 above. The constructed bare percept is then moved into the incoming perception registers in the focus. Associative and episodic memories make their contributions as described in Sections 5.5.3 and 5.6.7 creating the finished percept, partly from the environment (the incoming message), and partly from memory.

At this point, generator codelets, whose job it is to carry information from the registers in the focus, will typically take note of the new percept, and instantiate copies of themselves with variables bound to the appropriate register information. A "consciousness" codelet will also note the new percept, associate itself with these information-bearing codelets, and provide activation to itself and them. (Note this extension of pandemonium theory where codelets would only watch the playing field for a chance to act.) The resulting highly activated coalition (Section 5.7.5) will typically soon find itself in the spotlight of "consciousness" (Section 5.7.6), becoming its contents. These contents are then broadcast to all existing codelets (section 5.7.7) except the instantiated codelets.

Some of the codelets receiving the broadcasst may deem themselves relevant and respond. In particular, the contents of the message type register can be counted on to stimulate all the codelets associated with the beginning behavior of any behavior stream that normally responds to a message of this type (Sections 4.3.2; 5.3.2). These mostly generator codelets will then instantiate copies of themselves with their variables bound appropriately to the information on the blackboard. Now comes one of the omitted details mentioned above. Were this collection of instantiated codelets to join the playing field, the corresponding behavior would then be active without having been selected by the behavior net. Hence these instantiated codelets remain on the sideline of the playing field poised for action.

As we've seen in Section 4.0, such a collection of codelets can be identified with the behavior (goal context) it subserves. As such, its very presence on the sidelines causes an instantiated copy of the associated behavior to be added to the behavior net. But the behavior net is composed of streams, not individual behaviors. Thus an instantiated copy of the entire behavior of the stream to which the original behavior belongs is added to the behavior net. (In CMattie, a behavior belongs to only one stream. In future "conscious" software agents this may not be the case, and another design decision will have to be made.) And, since each instantiated behavior in this new stream is associated with a coalition of codelets, instantiated copies of all of these are added to sidelines. As an instantiated behavior in this stream is selected for execution by the behavior net, the corresponding coalition of codelets joins the playing field and each of them actively carries out their respective tasks.

CMattie's behavior net is now augmented with the intention carry out behaviors it expects to use to deal with the situation posed by the incoming message. As each instantiated behavior in the new streams is executed, its coalition of instantiated codelets joins the playing field and become active. CMattie's behavior net has acted as a to do list (see Section 5.6 above).

5.9 Conceptual and Behavioral Learning

CMattie has learned from an experience if the probability of certain actions in certain situations change as a consequence of that experience. Several distinct learning mechanisms are implemented in the CMattie architecture, some of which we've already seen. The storing of a percept in associative memory may well affect subsequent choice of actions, as might its being written to episodic memory. Hence both memories can be considered learning mechanisms. Codelets change their associations by virtue of sharing "consciousness" or, to a lessor extent, of being in the playing field at the same time (see Sections 2.3 and 5.3.3 above). Again, such a change might affect a subsequent choice of action, so we've a third learning mechanism. We've also seen this form of learning applied to emotion (Section 5.4). CMattie's metacognition module learns via classifiers (see Section 5.11 below), a fourth learning mechanism. In this section we'll describe an additional learning mechanism for conceptual learning (Ramamurthy, Bogner and Franklin, 1998; Bogner, Ramamurthy and Franklin, 2000). We'll also discuss a quite similar mechanism for learning new behaviors. These design decisions suggest another hypothesis, that humans also employ similarly diverse learning mechanisms.

CMattie learns concepts into her perceptual mechanism, that is, she learns new slipnet nodes and links, and new perceptual codelets. This learning takes place by modifying what's known, existing nodes, links and codelets, using case based reasoning (Kolodner, 1993). The impetus for such learning comes from messages from a seminar organizer informing CMattie that she has mishandled a previous message. An interchange between CMattie and the organizer may eventually lead to her learning a new concept. We'll trace a hypothetical scenario for such learning.

Suppose CMattie receives an announcement of a dissertation defense to be held at a certain place and time with a certain speaker and title. She would most probably treat this as a speaker-topic message for a seminar. This understanding is disseminated through "consciousness", leading to an acknowledgement to the sender stating that she is initializing a new seminar called “Dissertation defense Seminar” with the sender as organizer. This acknowledgement may well elicit a negative response from the sender. CMattie has slipnet nodes, including a message type, codelets and behaviors to help deal with such a situation. Such a negative response may start a “conversation” between CMattie and the sender. During this interchange, CMattie learns that a dissertation defense is similar to a seminar, but with slightly different features. In this case, the periodicity feature (see Figure 6) has a different value.

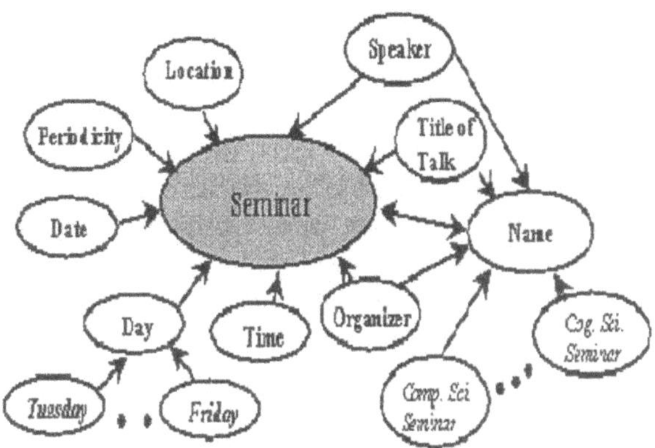

Fig. 6. Slipnet Fragment (from Ramamurthy, Bogner, and Franklin, 1998)

The email conversation, stripped of headers and pleasantries might go something like this:

Sender: *It's not a dissertation defense seminar, just a dissertation defense.*
CMattie: *What's a dissertation defense?*
Sender: *It's like a seminar but only happens irregularly.*

CMattie can trace the thread of the conversation via her episodic memory. She has codelets that recognize words associated with features. Thus she should recognize “irregularly” as having a certain meaning with regard to periodicity. At this point, case based reasoning comes into play, allowing the creation of a new slipnet node for dissertation defense with features the same as those of the seminar node except for periodicity fixed at “irregular.” Links are also put in place similar to those of the seminar node. A new message type node is also created, along with its links. Finally the needed new codelets are created, modeled after the old. Case based reasoning has solved the problem by first identifying the solution to the most similar old problem, and then modifying it to solve the new one. (In order for this to work, initial cases have to be included in case based memory at startup.) A new concept has been learned to the extent that CMattie needs to learn it.

Behavioral learning occurs quite similarly. CMattie's behavioral learning mechanism, again case based, takes note of the changes wrought in the slipnet and deduces needed changes in behavior. This leads to new behavior streams and new codelets to support them. If CMattie initially gets things wrong, another interchange with the sender may ensue. Eventually, CMattie will learn an acceptable behavior for a dissertation defense. Note that we've described what is essentially a one-shot learning. Though we might consider this reinforcement learning, it would be a stretch. This global learning is quite different from the local learning common in new AI systems, such as in neural net or reinforcement learning.

5.10 Metacognition

Metacognition should include knowledge of one's own cognitive processes, and the ability to actively monitor and consciously regulate them. This would require self-monitoring, self-evaluation, and self-regulation. Metacognition plays an important role for humans. It guides people in revising or even abandoning tasks, goals, or strategies (Hacker, 1999). If we want to build more human-like software agents, we need to build metacognition into them. Aaron Sloman calls this meta-management, and has been making this point for many years (Sloman, 1996). Also, Baars' global workspace theory explicitly calls for metacognition (Baars, 1988).

Following Minsky, we'll think of CMattie's "brain" as consisting of two parts, the A-brain and the B-brain (Minsky, 1985). The A-brain, as illustrated in Figure 6, consists of all the modules of CMattie's architecture that have been described so far. It performs all of her cognitive activities except metacognition. Its environment is the outside world, a dynamic, but limited, real world environment. The B-brain, sitting on top of the A-brain, monitors and regulates it. The B-brain's environment is the A-brain, or more specifically, the A-brain's activities. In this subsection, we'll discuss the mechanism of the B-brain and its interaction with some relevant modules in the A-brain (Zhang, Franklin and Dasgupta, 1998; Zhang and Franklin, forthcoming).

One can look at a metacognitive module as an autonomous agent (see Section 1.1 above) in its own right. It senses the A-brain's activity and acts upon it over time in pursuit of its own agenda. It's also structurally coupled to its quite restricted environment. Its agenda derives from built in metacognitive drives. One such drive is to interrupt oscillatory behavior. Another such might be to keep CMattie more on task, that is to make it more likely that a behavior stream would carry out to completion. Yet another would push toward efficient allocation of resources.

Unlike the situation in her A-Brain where drives are explicitly represented as part of the behavior net, CMattie's metacognitive drives are embodied in fuzzy production rules. The preconditions of such rules typically include some specification of an emotional state. Another type of precondition may involve the number of email messages in the incoming queue, or the number of instantiated behavior streams, or the memory space they are using.

How does the metacognition module influence CMattie's behavior to promote her drives? Oscillatory behavior might occur as the perceptual mechanism goes back and forth between two message types unable to decide on either. Metacognition might then send additional activation to one message type node in the slipnet, effectively forcing a decision, even a wrong one. The metacognition module can also affect CMattie's behavior by tuning global parameters, for example in the behavior net (see Section 2.2 above). This kind of tuning could serve to keep her more on task, by increasing the parameter that controls the amount of activation a drive pumps into its behavior streams. Or, it could make her more thoughtful by increasing the threshold for executing behaviors. Finally, metacognition may be concerned with high-level allocation of resources. For example, memory might be shifted from, say, a workspace (part of working memory) to the behavior net to accommodate a shortage of space there.

CMattie's metacognition module is quite complex in its own right (Zhang and Franklin, forthcoming), being comprised of several distinct submodules. Due to space limitations, only a cursory description will be given here. An inner perception submodule monitors the A-Brain. It consists of sensors and detectors. Detectors differ from sensors in that they perform inferences. Sensors get the raw data from the A-brain, and detectors put them into internal representations. The fuzzy classifier system (Valenzuela-Rendon, 1991) at the heart of metacognition's action selection needs fuzzy inputs. The fuzzifier submodule contains membership functions that interpret a real (crisp) number to express the fuzzy values, and uses them to fuzzify each inner percept. Thus each numeric value of an inner percept is replaced by the corresponding linguistic value. These fuzzy percepts are then fed to the encoder submodule, which encodes them into finite-length strings and puts them in a message list. These fuzzy string percepts may match antecedents of classifiers. This matching activates collections of classifiers from the fuzzy rule base submodule of classifiers, often referred to as the classifier store. This fuzzy rule base of classifiers contains the metacognition modules' knowledge of what to do in a given situation. Metacognition then uses classifiers from the fuzzy rule-base to infer appropriate fuzzy string actions that are posted in the message list by winning classifiers. The decoder submodule decodes the string action to a set of fuzzy actions. Using the membership functions, the defuzzifier submodule transforms these fuzzy values into crisp numeric values that can be used by the inner actions submodule. The appropriate actions are then taken.

Metacognition in CMattie is implemented as a classifier system in order that it may learn. Learning actions always requires feedback on the results of prior actions. The Evaluator submodule is implemented by a reinforcement learning algorithm (Barto, Sutton and Brouwer, 1981) that assigns reward or punishment to classifiers based on the next inner percept. It also uses a reinforcement distribution algorithm (Bonarini, 1997) to distribute credit among the classifiers. The more common bucket brigade algorithm (Holland and Reitman, 1978) is not used since sequences of actions are not typically required of metacognition in CMattie. When things are not going too well over a period of time, learning occurs via a genetic algorithm (Holland, 1975) acting to produce new classifiers.

5.11 Self-preservation

Another of CMattie's drives is for self-preservation. Why is such a drive needed? What can happen to a software agent? The most feared event would be a sudden shut down of the machine on which the agent is running, possibly causing a loss of data and/or of state. Another, less feared event is of running out of resources, say memory. CMattie handles some such situations reflexively and others in a more deliberative way (Ramamurthy and Franklin, forthcoming).

If CMattie receives a system message, as opposed to an email message, warning of an eminent shutdown, the message is detected by self-preservation codelets early in the perception process. These codelets immediately act reflexively to save data structures containing both data and state. They also shut down the agent if time permits. CMattie is started up automatically with the saved data when the host system comes online again. Much of CMattie's action selection is reactive in the sense of Sloman (1996). Here we have a reflex action that doesn't even make it through the perception process before action is taken.

On the other hand an email message from the system administrator warning of a shutdown is handled in the perception module like any other message. The percept it generates will give rise to a coalition of codelets with high priority into "consciousness". The coalitions that respond to the resulting broadcast are highly active and give rise to equally active behaviors. The resulting action is quick but more deliberate than that described in the previous paragraph. The results are much the same, but likely to be more complete.

CMattie will also negotiate with the system administrator for more resources when the need arises. This occurs with much the same kind of mechanisms that implement conceptual and behavioral learning (Section 5.9). These might include disk space, memory space and/or access to time on the central processing unit. This requires that CMattie be able to sense her use of these various resources.

CMattie's self-preservation drive also motivates her to backup her important data structures to disk at regular intervals. This is also accomplished in the usual way with self-preservation codelets realizing the necessity and activating the appropriate behaviors.

5.12 Implementation

At the time of this writing CMattie's design is essentially complete though not yet stable. Small modifications are being made as the coding proceeds and turns up issues not previously considered. These issues require design decisions that simultaneously give rise to hypotheses about human cognition. The coding is in Java, chosen primarily because of the ease of use of threads. CMattie is very much a multi-agent system. The coding is perhaps more than half finished. We estimate about a quarter of a million lines of code in the complete implementation. Intelligence doesn't come cheaply. CMattie will live in a Unix system.

6 Hypotheses

If, as we've seen in the previous paragraph, CMattie isn't even up and running, what's the justification for such a long and detailed article about her? CMattie's design constitutes a computational model of mind. In particular, it fleshes out Baars' global workspace theory with a more concrete architecture and the mechanisms with which to implement it. The resulting conceptual model promises to be a rich source of hopefully testable hypotheses about human cognition. In theory, each of our design decisions leads to such a hypothesis (Franklin, 1997), namely that in humans it works according to our design. Of course, many or even most of these hypotheses may turn out to be false. We humans may do it differently. Nonetheless, even false hypotheses can lead to new knowledge. This section will explicitly offer several such hypotheses, stated as questions, mostly to give the reader an idea of the kind of hypotheses available from this conceptual model. We make no claim for novelty in these hypotheses. Much may already be known about them. And, we will only include a small sample of the available hypotheses.

6.1 Memory

In CMattie, working memory consists of several different workspaces. One serves her perceptual module. IDA, a "conscious" software successor to CMattie (see Section 8 below) will have perceptual workspaces for each of several senses each equipped with different facilities. Another CMattie workspace serves for the composition of announcements. Yet another, the focus, serves as a working memory for incoming percepts, together with associated memories, emotions and actions. *Do humans also have several working memories each capable of holding different types of data?*

CMattie's associative and episodic memories use quite different mechanisms. Her associative memory is content addressable and requires a rather complete perceptual cue for recall. Also content addressable, her episodic memory must react appropriately to a small cue so that the proper context can be found for an incoming message. Thus different mechanisms are required. *Do human associative and episodic memories also differ in their mechanisms and in the size of their cues?*

CMattie's behavior net serves a memory like function; it implements her internal to do list. Each sequence of behaviors (goal contexts) that CMattie intends is instantiated in some layer of her behavior net. Will all of them eventually be acted upon? I presume so, since CMattie won't be very busy in her limited domain. *Do humans have some similar sort of action selection mechanism that acts as a to do list?*

6.2 Processors

It's been often suggested, and is now apparently widely accepted, that human cognition is effected by a host of individual small processors working in parallel (Baars 1988, 1997; Edelman, 1987; Minsky, 1985; Ornstein, 1986). These processors are implemented in the CMattie architecture by the codelets we've talked so much about. They are postulated to work as what computer scientists call demons, that is, they watch and wait for a situation appropriate to them, and then they act. In CMattie, a codelet's job might be to write a particular piece of information, say a day of the week, into a seminar announcement. Suppose this codelet has collected its appropriate day, say "Tuesday," and is waiting for its overlying behavior to be executed so that it can do its job. Suppose during this time another message is processed needing another day of the week, say "Wednesday," written into a different place in the seminar announcement. But the write-day-of-the-week codelet is occupied. What now? To deal with this kind of situation, we've had the original codelet instantiate a copy of itself carrying the "Tuesday" information. Later it can instantiate another copy carrying "Wednesday." *Do human processors instantiate such copies of themselves that carry specific pieces of information?* A slightly weaker hypotheses can be proposed in computer science terms. *Can human processors contain bound variables?*

The situation described in the previous paragraph raises a question about one of the most basic tenets of global workspace theory. The theory demands that *every* processor receive each broadcast from the global workspace. The instantiated codelet carrying "Tuesday" is irrevocably set on its course of action. All it can do is write its work in the proper place in the announcement being composed. It can't help in any way with the novel or problematic situation that provoked the latest "conscious" broadcast. Why should it receive that broadcast? Perhaps we should not think of it as a processor at all. *Do some human processors, already embarked on some given task, not receive "conscious" broadcasts?*

Sometimes a collection of CMattie's codelets, having been awakened by a relevant "conscious" broadcast, will wait in the wings for it's overlying behavior to be executed, that is, for its goal context to become dominant. When this happens, these codelets begin performing their tasks. It seems obvious from introspection that *humans also at times postpone reacting to some conscious stimulus until some task with higher priority is completed.*

6.3 Perception

Associations directly contribute to CMattie's perceptions, while episodic memories do not. When her perception module is finished with an incoming message, the information therein is written to the incoming perception registers in the focus. The resulting string of characters is used as the address at which to read associative memory. The results of this read also go to the empty slots in the incoming perception registers, and become part of the percept. At the same time, the same address is used to read episodic memory with the results going to a separate set of registers. The contents of the incoming perception registers typically become "conscious". Those from episodic memory do also when they are relevant, say when a room time conflict is noticed by a "consciousness" codelet. The contents of episodic memory do not become part of the percept. *Do human associative and episodic memories differ in that the first can contribute to a percept while the second cannot?*

7 Can "Conscious" Software be Conscious?

Having seen an extended account of a "conscious" software agent, it's reasonable to ask the question of this section title. Put another way, is there some sense in which it is reasonable to speak of a computer system, including its software, as being conscious? Since the word "conscious" is used with several meanings, we have several questions in disguise. Let's look at some, but by no means all, of the different possible meanings. Pinker (1997, p134), citing Jackendoff (1987), distinguishes three meanings of "consciousness": self-knowledge, access to information (access-consciousness) and sentience. We'll explore the possibility of "conscious" software being conscious in each of these senses. To focus our discussion, we'll restrict our attention to CMattie, the best developed of the "conscious" software agents.

7.1 Access-consciousness

Access-consciousness refers to the accessing of information from perception and from short-term memory for use in, say, rational thought and deliberate decision making. Not all internal information is so available, leading to the conscious/unconscious distinction. What about CMattie? A look at the black dots in Figure 6 reveals that her perception registers, containing the content of her perception, is available to the spotlight of "consciousness". The same is true of two of her working memories, as well as several other modules. It seems safe to say that CMattie is access-conscious.

7.2 Self-knowledge

One part of the self-knowledge sense of consciousness refers to the existence of an internal model of the agent's world that contains a notion of self. This notion of consciousness has been explored in non-human primates by Gallup (1982) and others (see also Fox, 1982) using the now well known marked forehead and mirror technique. They've discovered that, while the great apes tend to exhibit self-knowledge by this test, several species of monkeys do not. I would not conclude that these monkeys have no internal sense of self, since the test seems a sufficient, but not necessary, criterion. Another interesting question raised by this work is whether a sense of self can be learned. Several gorillas failed Gallup's test, while the famous Koko (Patterson, 1994) passed it. I doubt that a human infant has such a sense, so it must be learnable by humans. Can it be taught to the monkeys who failed Gallup's test?

And CMattie? CMattie has such internal models of her world in her slipnet, in her episodic memory, in her associative memory and in the template for her behavior net. Although, these models don't contain the notion of her "self," the slipnet certainly could. That CMattie isn't conscious in this sense is simply the result of a design decision. Her domain doesn't require it. As Aaron Sloman pointed out (personal communication), if CMattie were scheduled to speak at one of the seminars she announces, we'd want to build in a sense of self.

On the other hand, CMattie (and no doubt the monkeys as well) is capable of self-awareness in the sense of being able to monitor her activity and change her strategy when things aren't going well. This capability is embodied in her metacognition module (Zhang,Franklin and Dasgupta, 1998; Zhang and Franklin, forthcoming), which doesn't appear in Figure 6. Metacognition uses internal sensors to track the rest of CMattie's mind, uses emotions and its own criteria to decide if things are going well or not, and effects change gently by spreading activation appropriately, and/or modifying global parameters. (See Section 5.10 above) Metacognition is also involved in deliberate action.

7.3 Sentience

This brings us to a highly controversial issue. Can CMattie be sentient in some sense? Some would say that only biological agents can experience qualia (Hill, 1991; Searle, 1992). Some biologists speculate that sentience arises from synchronized oscillations in the brain (Crick and Koch, 1990). In the context of qualia, the neuroscientist Walter Freeman says, "I am willing to believe that rabbits are conscious, and that every animal possessing laminated neuropil has some consciousness, though I do not extend the attribute to lesser brains or to other forms of matter" (1995, p. 136). Nonetheless, Freeman doesn't rule out the possibility of conscious artifacts (p. 139). He even speculates about ethical issues. Neither does the philosopher John Haugeland who describes the assertion that no AI system could be conscious as "very hard to defend" (1985, p. 247).

Roboticist Hans Moravec postulates imagery as the "beginnings of awareness" in machines. "In our lab, the programs we have developed usually present ... information from the robot's world model in the form of pictures on a computer screen–a direct window into the robot's mind. In these internal models of the world I see the beginnings of awareness in the minds of our machines–an awareness I believe will evolve into consciousness comparable with that of humans" (1988, p. 39). Baars defines imagery as "conscious experience of internal events" (1997, p. 22). If Moravec is right, then CMattie must be aware of those of her internal events that come into her spotlight of "consciousness".

Philosopher Dave Chalmers takes a hard look at the possibility of artificial sentience (1996). "I claim that conscious experience arises from fine-grained functional organization." (p. 248) He refers to a more formalized version of this statement as "the principle of organizational invariance" (p. 248). He later concludes that "[t]he invariance principle tells us that in principle, cognitive systems realized in all sorts of media can be conscious" (p. 275). Still later the "in principle" is bypassed. "... there is a nonempty class of computations such that the implementation of any computation in that class is sufficient for a mind, and in particular, is sufficient for the existence of conscious experience" (p. 314). And that's not all. "... implementing the right computation suffices for rich conscious experience like our own" (p. 315).

What about CMattie? Does she fall into Chalmers' special "nonempty class of computations"? Unfortunately, we can't tell. There are no easy characterizations for members of the class. And the proof rests on the invariance principle. Is it true? Ultimately, these thoughts, though no doubt important for consciousness studies, don't help us with the CMattie problem, except to make sentience on her part more plausible.

Recall Chalmers' assertion that "conscious experience arises from fine-grained functional organization." This contradicts those who expect consciousness to emerge from any sufficiently complex system. We hold this same view. If you want conscious software, you must build in the appropriate architecture and mechanisms. The question is, have we done so in CMattie?

One tempting way out of the dilemma of determining awareness in software is to follow what we could do with humans, ask them. Philosophers wouldn't like this approach, since zombies, in the philosophical sense, would reply that they are sentient. Still Baars uses subjects' reports as one of two criteria for consciousness (1988, p.15) and asserts that it's typical of experimental psychologists. Should we build "conscious" software agents with the ability to give such reports? Would that help settle matters? We doubt it. Call to mind the conversational software agent Julia (Mauldin, 1994). It shouldn't be difficult to reprogram her to claim sentience, and she'd probably be convincing.

Of course, if CMattie were to be sentient, her awareness would surely be quite different from ours, possibly so different we wouldn't even recognize it. Many comparisons have been made of human consciousness with that presumed of other species (e.g., Dawkins, 1986, p. 35-36), all pointing out major differences due to different senses, etc. Hofstadter makes a similar point about possible machine awareness. "If one accepts [the] somewhat disturbing view that perhaps machines–even today's machines–should be assigned various shades of gray (even if extremely faint shades) along the 'consciousness continuum', then one is forced into trying to pinpoint just what it is that makes for different shades of gray" (1995, p. 311).

So, will CMattie be sentient? Should we assign her some shade of gray? We don't know how to tell. But, she has machinery that may give her a shot at it.

8 Limitations and Future Work

The CMattie model adds both architecture and mechanisms to global workspace theory. In many ways, it provides a successful conceptual model of mind (Franklin and Graesser, 2000). One can pose questions about human cognition, and put these questions to the model by imagining how the model would behave in the situation of the question, thus providing the model's answer to the question. But there are many limitations to this model that restrict the body of questions that it can address. In this section we'll sample only a few of these limitations, and go on to briefly describe future work designed to remove some of them.

8.1 Limitations

CMattie has only one major sense, incoming email, though she does directly sense the operating system on which she runs (see Section 5.11 above). These two are quite distinct, and offer no possibility for the kind of sensory fusion human senses offer. This allows an overly simple perceptual mechanism, and avoids many issues that arise for human perception. It's a severe limitation.

Like CMattie, we humans tend to keep an internal to do list. We tend to forget items from our list, without some external help. CMattie does not. This tells us that CMattie's behavior net isn't designed exactly right. It's another limitation.

Aaron Sloman three levels of control in cognitive agents, a reactive level, a deliberative level and a meta-management level (1996). CMattie's metacognitive module operates roughly on the meta-management level. The rest of CMattie's action selection mechanisms operate within the reactive level. Sloman's deliberative level is characterized by the agent being able to construct "alternative plans that have to be compared in some way prior to selection." The plans not selected are discarded. CMattie, in her behavior net, selects between alternate behavior streams that could be considered to be plans of action. However, the streams not selected are not discarded. CMattie's action selection is relatively complex, but is still reactive. Her perception mechanism does sometimes try out alternative candidates for the message type of an incoming message discarding one in favor of another. Thus perception is in a sense deliberative, a possibility pointed out by Sloman. A deliberative level of control is important to, and some think even characteristic of, human cognition. The lack of this level in the CMattie architecture is a major limitation.

Human senses tend to habituate to repeated stimuli, lessening their responses to them. CMattie's domain doesn't provide for such repetitions, except perhaps in messages from the operating system. In the later case she would habituate, but only because the appropriate responses would already have been taken. CMattie's emotion component does provide for habituation. Repeated stimuli to a particular emotion have diminishing effect. Still, we view CMattie's lack of sensory habituation as a limitation for a model of human cognition.

In humans, conscious actions become over learned with repetition and thereafter automatic. CMattie has a mechanism for such automatization inherited from pandemonium theory. Concept demons from pandemonium theory become concept codelets in CMattie (see Section 2.3 above). With each of these codelets performing some task, the concept codelet as a whole would perform a more complex action, an automatization of the individual codelets. There are several problems. CMattie's domain is so simple as to offer little scope for this sort of thing to happen. Also, most such collections of codelets that would coalesce in this way are already built into the coalition implementing some behavior. Finally, there's the issue of instantiated codelets. The codelets that should coalesce into a concept codelet are the generator codelets sitting in the stands. The instantiated codelets on the playing field are concerned only with their specified tasks. Though this last objection is easily overcome, the lack of such automatization of actions is yet another limitation of the model.

Baars describes the self in humans as "the overall context of experience" (1997, p.150), going on to talk about "the desperate creativity with which humans maintain as much coherence and stability in their conscious experience as they can" (p. 149). Remember that "context" here is a technical term referring to a coalition of processors, i.e. codelets. CMattie has no such coalition, no self. Gazzaniga postulates an "interpreter" that "seeks explanations for internal and external events" (1998, p. 24). Baars includes the interpreter as part of the self, calling it the "narrative self" (p. 147). In her learning mechanisms (see Section 5.9 above), CMattie can connect a negative response from a human correspondent with specific words in a prior message in a cause and effect fashion. This seems a little piece of an interpreter. Still, CMattie has no general mechanism for generating explanations. This part of the self is also missing. Lacking a self seems a limitation of this model of global workspace theory. Lacking an interpreter seems a limitation of any model of human cognition.

We humans ignore much of what comes in as sensation as we create percepts. But even within a percept we direct attention, singling out certain relevant items or issues and ignoring others. CMattie does ignore unneeded words in her sensation, an incoming email message. However, she attends to her entire percept, obviating the need for an attention mechanism such as we humans employ. This is yet another limitation of the model.

I feel confident that a little more thought would turn up a host of other such limitations. Nonetheless, I expect even this so limited model to prove useful. I also expect subsequent "conscious" software agents, such as IDA (to be described next) to be, still limited, but much less so.

8.2 IDA

IDA (Intelligent Distribution Agent), is a "conscious" software agent being developed for the Navy. At the end of each sailor's tour of duty, he or she is assigned to a new billet. This assignment process is called distribution. The Navy employs some 280 people, called detailers, full time to effect these new assignments. IDA's task is to facilitate this process, by playing the role of detailer as best she can. Occupying a domain orders of magnitude more complex than that of CMattie, IDA will not be limited in many of the ways that CMattie is. IDA is intended as a proof of concept project for "conscious" software.

Designing IDA presents both communication problems and constraint satisfaction problems. She must communicate with sailors via email and in natural language, understanding the content. She must access a number of databases, again understanding the content. She must see that the Navy's needs are satisfied, for example, the required number of sonar technicians on a destroyer with the required types of training. She must understand and abide by the Navy's some ninety policies regarding distribution. She must hold down moving costs and training costs. And, she must cater to the needs and desires of the sailor as well as is possible in order to promote retention.

Unlike CMattie, IDA will sense her world using several different major sensory modalities. She'll receive email messages, she'll read screens from a number of different databases, and she'll sense via operating system commands and messages. Each of the different databases can be thought of as requiring a different sense, since each will require its own knowledge base and workspace within IDA. Sensory fusion will be needed for action selection.

In matching sailors with billets IDA will continually face constraint satisfaction problems. Among other approaches we intend to experiment with a SOAR like mechanism (Laird, Newell and Rosenbloom, 1987) and with a Copycat like mechanism, each of which would construct possible action scenarios, choose between them, and discard those not chosen. IDA will have a level of deliberative control.

IDA's construction of action scenarios may well require knowledge of cause and effect, in other words, an interpreter (see Section 8.1 above). A self in the sense of a single overarching context is another matter for IDA. What would one put in it? What would its codelets do? This limitation of the model may well remain in the IDA version.

In solving constraint satisfaction problems IDA will need information from various databases about both the sailor and the billet. The ability to read one such database will be considered a sense. A single record will be a sensation. The perception process in this case is trivial since the fields are nicely lined up in known positions and there content is always expressed in a unique and predetermined way known to IDA. But the data in a record will in most cases contain items of no current interest to IDA. She'll need the kind of attention mechanism whose lack was considered a limitation of CMattie (see Section 8.1 above).

8.3 AutoTutor

Before IDA became available, our intention was to use AutoTutor as our first proof-of-concept project. AutoTutor (Graesser, Franklin & Wiemer-Hastings, 1998; Wiemer-Hastings et al, 1998) is a fully automated computer tutor that simulates the dialogue moves of normal human tutors. An unconscious prototype, in the sense of not implementing global workspace theory, is currently up and running. With computer literacy as its topic, it's now being perfected in many ways in parallel. AutoTutor will eventually incorporate sophisticated tutoring strategies. The architecture and mechanisms of AutoTutor are much different from that of CMattie, and from that planned for IDA. Rebuilding portions of AutoTutor to conform to the demands of global workspace theory may be quite a challenge. Still, if energy and funding hold out, we intend to try for a "conscious" version of AutoTutor as another proof-of-concept project.

8.4 Acknowledgements

Though this paper has a single author, the work described herein is very much a team effort. It is the work of the "Conscious" Software Research Group, a part of the Institute for Intelligent Systems at the University of Memphis. The research group currently includes Stan Franklin, Art Graesser, Satish Ambati, Ashraf Anwar, Myles Bogner, Arpad Kelemen, Irina Makkaveeva, Lee McCauley, Aregahegn Negatu, Hongjun Song, Uma Ramamurthy, Zhaohua Zhang. Each person's major contributions to the project can be inferred from the authorship of the individual papers describing various parts of the "conscious" software architecture and mechanisms. For their many, many other contributions, I thank them all.

References

1. Allen. James (1995), *Natural Language Understanding.* Redwood City, CA: Benjamin/Cummings.
2. Anwar and Franklin (forthcoming ????), "Sparse Distributed Memory for "Conscious" Software Agents"
3. Baars, B. J. (1988). *A Cognitive Theory of Consciousness.* Cambridge: Cambridge University Press.
4. Baars, B. J. (1997). *In the Theater of Consciousness.* Oxford: Oxford University Press.
5. Barto, A.G., Sutton, R. S., and Brouwer, P. S. (1981). Associative Search Network: a Reinforcement Learning Associative Memory, *Biological Cybernetics,* 40(3): 201-211.
6. Bates, Joseph, A. Bryan Loyall, and W. Scott Reilly (1991). "Broad Agents," Proceedings of the AAAI Spring Symposium on Integrated Intelligent Architectures, Stanford University, March. These proceedings are available in SIGART Bulletin, Volume 2, Number 4, August 1992.
7. Bonarini A., (1997), Anytime learning and adaptation of hierarchical fuzzy logic behaviors. *Adaptive Behavior Journal,* Special Issue on Complete Agent Learning in Complex Environments, M. Mataric (Ed.). 5 (3-4), 281-315.
8. Bogner Myles (1998), *Creating a "conscious" agent.* Master's thesis, The University of Memphis, May.
9. Bogner, Myles, Uma Ramamurthy, and Stan Franklin (2000). "Consciousness" and Conceptual Learning in a Socially Situated Agent. in Kerstin Dautenhahn ed. Human Cognition and Social Agent Technology
10. Damasio, A. R. (1994), *Descartes' Error,* New York: Gosset/Putnam Press.
11. Chalmers, David J. (1996), *The Conscious Mind,* Oxford: Oxford University Press.
12. Crick, Francis and Christof Koch (1990), "Towards a Neurobiological Theory of Consciousness," The Neurosciences 2.
13. Dawkins, Richard (1986), *The Blind Watchmaker,* New York: Norton.
14. Edelman, Gerald M. (1987). *Neural Darwinism: The Theory of Neuronal Group Selection.* New York: Basic Books.
15. Franklin, Stan (1995). *Artificial Minds.* Cambridge, MA: MIT Press.
16. Franklin, Stan (1997). Autonomous Agents as Embodied AI, Cybernetics *and Systems'* Special issue on Epistemological Aspects of Embodied AI, 28:6 499-520.
17. Franklin, Stan, Art Graesser, Brent Olde, Hongjun Song, and Aregahegn Negatu (1996). "Virtual Mattie–an Intelligent Clerical Agent," AAAI Symposium on Embodied Cognition and Action, Cambridge MA, November.
18. Franklin, Stan and Graesser, Art (1997) "Is it an Agent, or just a Program?: A Taxonomy for Autonomous Agents," *Intelligent Agents III,* Berlin: Springer Verlag, 21-35,
19. Franklin, S., and A. Graesser. 1999. A Software Agent Model of Consciousness. *Consciousness and Cognition* 8:285-305.
20. Franklin, Stan, Arpad Kelemen, and Lee McCauley (1998), IDA: A Cognitive Agent Architecture, Proceedings of the IEEE Conference on Systems, Man and Cybernetics, 2646-2651.
21. Freeman, Walter (1995), Societies of Brains, Hillsdale, NJ: Lawrence Erlbaum.

22. Gallup, G. (1982), "Self-awareness and the emergence of mind in primates," American Journal of Primatology, 2:237-246.
23. Gazzaniga, Michael S. (1998), *The Mind's Past.* Berkeley: University of California Press.
24. Graesser, A.C., Franklin, S., & Wiemer-Hastings, P. (1998). Simulating smooth tutorial dialogue with pedagogical value. Proceedings of the American Association for Artificial Intelligence (pp. 163-167). Menlo Park, CA: AAAI Press.
25. Griffin, Donald R. (1984), *Animal Thinking,* Cambridge, Mass: Harvard University Press.
26. Hacker, Douglas, (1999), Metacognitive: Definitions and Empirical Foundations, In Hacker, D., Dunlosky, J., Graesser A. (Eds.) *Metacognition in Educational Theory and Practice.* Hillsdale, NJ: Erlbaum, vol. 44 , issue 3, 1999.
27. Haugeland, John (1985), *Artificial Intelligence: The Very Idea,* Cambridge MA: The MIT Press.
28. Hill, C. S. (1991), *Sensations: A Defense of Type Materialism,* Cambridge: Cambridge University Press.
29. Hofstadter D. R. (1995), Fluid Concepts and Creative Analogies, Basic Books.
30. Hofstadter, D. R. and Mitchell, M. (1994), "The Copycat Project: A model of mental fluidity and analogy-making." In Holyoak, K.J. & Barnden, J.A. (Eds.) *Advances in connectionist and neural computation theory,* Vol. 2: Analogical connections. Norwood, N.J.: Ablex.
31. Holland, J. H. (1975). *Adaptation in Natural and Artificial Systems.* Ann Arbor: University of Michigan Press.
32. Holland, J. H. (1986), "A Mathematical Framework for Studying Learning in Classifier Systems." In D., Farmer et al, Evolution, *Games and Learning: Models for Adaption in Machine and Nature.* Amsterdam: North-Holland
33. Holland, J. H. and Reitman, J. S. (1978). Cognitive Systems Based on Adaptive Algorithms. In D. A. Waterman & F. Hayey-Roth (Eds.*), Pattern Directed Inference Systems* (pp. 313 -329). New York: Academic Press.
34. Jackson, John V. (1987), "Idea for a Mind," *SIGGART Newsletter*, no. 181, July, 23-26.
35. Kanerva, Pentti (1988), *Sparse Distributed Memory,* Cambridge MA: The MIT Press.
36. Kolodner, Janet (1993), *Case-Based Reasoning* , Morgan Kaufman
37. Laird, John E., Newell, Allen, and Rosenbloom, Paul S. (1987). "SOAR: An Architecture for General Intelligence." *Artificial Intelligence,* 33: 1-64.
38. Leung, K.S., and C. T. Lin (1988), "Fuzzy concepts in expert systems." *Computer* 21(9):43-56
39. Loebner Hugh, (web), http://acm.org/~loebner/In-response.html
40. Maes, Pattie (1990), 'How to do the right thing', *Connection Science,* **1:3.**
41. Maes, Pattie (1993), "Modeling Adaptive Autonomous Agents," *Artificial Life* , 1:1/2, 135-162.
42. Maturana, H. R. (1975). "The Organization of the Living: A Theory of the Living Organization. "International *Journal of Man-Machine Studies,* 7:313-32.
43. Maturana, H. R. and Varela, F. (1980). *Autopoiesis and Cognition: The Realization of the Living.* Dordrecht, Netherlands: Reidel.
44. Mauldin, Michael L. (1994) "Chatterbots, Tinymuds, And The Turing Test: Entering The Loebner Prize Competition" Proceedings of the Twelfth National Conference on Artificial Intelligence, AAAI Press, 16-21

45. McCauley, Thomas L. and Stan Franklin (1998) An Architecture for Emotion, AAAI Fall Symposium "Emotional and Intelligent: The Tangled Knot of Cognition"
46. Minsky, Marvin (1985), *The Society of Mind,* New York: Simon and Schuster.
47. Mitchell, Melanie (1993), *Analogy-Making as Perception,* Cambridge MA: The MIT Press.
48. Moravec, Hans (1988), *Mind Children,* Cambridge, MA: Harvard University Press.
49. Newell, Allen (1990), Unified Theories of Cognition, Cambridge, Mass: Harvard University Press.
50. Ornstein, Robert (1986), *Multimind.* Boston: Houghton Mifflin.
51. Oyama, S. (1985). The *Ontogeny of Information..* Cambridge: Cambridge University Press.
52. Patterson, F.G.P., and Cohn, R.H. 1994. Self-recognition and Self-awareness in Lowland Gorillas. In S.T. Parker, R.W. Mitchell and M.L. Boccia (Eds.), *Self-awareness in Animals and Humans.* New York: Cambridge University Press.
53. Picard, Rosalind (1997), *Affective Computing,* Cambridge MA: The MIT Press.
54. Pinker, Steven (1997), How the Mind Works, New York: Norton.
55. Ramamurthy, Uma , Franklin, Stan and Negatu, Aregahegn (1998), Learning Concepts in Software Agents From Animals to Animats Complex Adaptive Systems series.A Bradford BookAugust 1998.
56. Ramamurthy, Uma and Stan Franklin (forthcoming), Self-preservation in Software Agents.
57. Selfridge, O.G. (1959), "Pandemonium: A Paradigm for Learning," *Proceedings of the Symposium on Mechanisation of Thought Process,* National Physics Laboratory.
58. Searle, J. R. (1992), *The Rediscovery of the Mind,* Cambridge MA: The MIT Press.
59. A. Sloman, 'Motives Mechanisms Emotions' in Cognition and Emotion 1,3, pp.217-234 1987, reprinted in M.A. Boden (ed) *The Philosophy of Artificial Intelligence* "Oxford Readings in Philosophy" Series Oxford University Press, pp 231-247, 1990.
60. Sloman, A., (1992), "Developing concepts of consciousness," *Behavioral and Brain Sciences.*
61. Sloman, Aaron (1996) What Sort of Architecture is Required for a Human-like Agent?, Cognitive Modeling Workshop , AAAI96, Portland Oregon.
62. Sloman, Aaron and Poli, Riccardo (1996). "SIM_AGENT: A toolkit for exploring agent designs in Intelligent Agents," Vol. II (ATAL-95), Eds. Mike Wooldridge, Joerg Mueller, Milind Tambe, Springer-Verlag, pp. 392–407.
63. Song, H., and S. Franklin, (2000). A Behavior Instantiation Agent Architecture. Connection Science, to appear.
64. Turing, Alan (1950), "Computing Machinery and Intellignece." Mind, 59:434-60. Reprinted in E. Feigenbaum and J. Feldmans, eds., Computers and Thought. New York: McGraw-Hill, 1963.
65. Valenzuela-Rendon, M. (1991) The Fuzzy Classifier System: a classifier System for Continuously Varying Variables. *In Proceedings of the Fourth International Conference on Genetic Algorithms (pp. 346-353).* San Mateo, CA: Morgan Kaufmann.

66. Weizenbaum, J. (1966) "ELIZA–A computer program for the study of natural language communication between man and machind," Communications of the Association for Computing Machinery. 9:36-45
67. Wiemer-Hastings, P., Graesser, A.C., Harter, D., and the Tutoring Research Group (1998). The foundations and architecture of AutoTutor. *Proceedings Lecture Notes in Computer Science* (pp. 334-343). Berlin, Germany: Springer-Verlag.
68. Wilson, Stewart W. (1994), ZCS: A Zeroth Level Classifier System, *Evolutionary Computation,* vol.2, issue 1, pp 1-18, MIT Press.
69. Zhang, Zhaohua, Stan Franklin and Dipankar Dasgupta (1998), Metacognition in Software Agents using Classifer Systems, Proc AAAI 98, 82-88
70. Zhang, Zhaohua, Stan Franklin, Brent Olde, Yun Wan and Art Graesser (1998) "Natural Language Sensing for Autonomous Agents," Proc. IEEE Joint Symposia on Intelligence and Systems, Rockville, Maryland, 374-81
71. Zhang, Zhaohua and Stan Franklin (forthcoming), Metacognition in Software Agents Using Fuzzy Systems

Intelligent Agents in Granular Worlds

Witold Pedrycz[1] and George Vukovich[2]

[1] Dept. of Electrical and Computer Engineering University of Alberta, Edmonton, Canada T6G 2G7 and Systems Research Institute, Polish Academy of Sciences 01-447 Warsaw, Poland
[2] Canadian Space Agency, Spacecraft Engineering 6767 Route de l'Aeroport Saint-Hubert, Quebec J3Y 8Y9, Canada

Abstract. In this study, we introduce a concept of granular agents and elaborate on various representation, communication and learning issues arising in this framework. A granular world, in which the granular agents interact, embodies a collection of information granules being regarded as generic conceptual entities used to represent knowledge and handle problem solving. On the other hand, granular computing is a paradigm supporting knowledge representation, coping with complexity, and facilitating interpretation of processing. In this sense, it is crucial to all man-machine pursuits, data mining and intelligent data analysis, in particular. There are three essential facets that are inherently associated with any agent, that is formalism used to describe and manipulate information granules and the granularity of the granules themselves as well as the internal structure of the agents. There are numerous formal models of granular worlds ranging from set-theoretic developments (including sets, fuzzy sets, and rough sets) to probabilistic counterparts (random sets, random variables and alike). In light of the evident diversity of granular world (occurring both in terms of the underlying formal settings as well as levels of granularity), we elaborate on their possible interaction and identify implications of such communication. More specifically, we have cast these in the form of the interoperability problem, that is associated with the representation of information granules. Moreover, we explore various internal models of agents including the concepts stemming from fuzzy state machines and discuss pertinent models of learning.

Keywords: autonomous agents, finite state machines, granulation of information, interoperability and communication

1 Introductory remarks

Agent technologies are rapidly growing area of information technology. In spite of some differences, the standard definitions of agents emphasize their autonomous nature, and learning abilities (evolving behavior), [7] and [8]. Some other descriptions underline an aspect of communication between the agents [2], that is regarded as an important facet of any collective activity pertinent to this area. A comprehensive and lucid discussion on intelligent agents developed in a fuzzy evolutionary framework can be found in [1]. By looking into the specificity of the agent-based activities, it is not surprising that a technology of fuzzy set has a lot to offer. Firstly, a distributed problem solving is completed at various levels of generality. Secondly, agents collaborate and communicate between themselves, (see Figure 1). Fuzzy sets are one among several key vehicles of granular computing. Fuzzy sets themselves are examples of information granules. Depending upon the level of granularity, various communication links can be established. Two agents can solve the problem at a certain level of detail. They could collaborate efficiently if the level of granularity of these agents is similar. Agents are dynamic systems: accept inputs and generate outputs depending on its internal sta te. In this sense, the internal dynamic structure of the agents is an important feature of the autonomous agent. In this study, we revisit the concept of

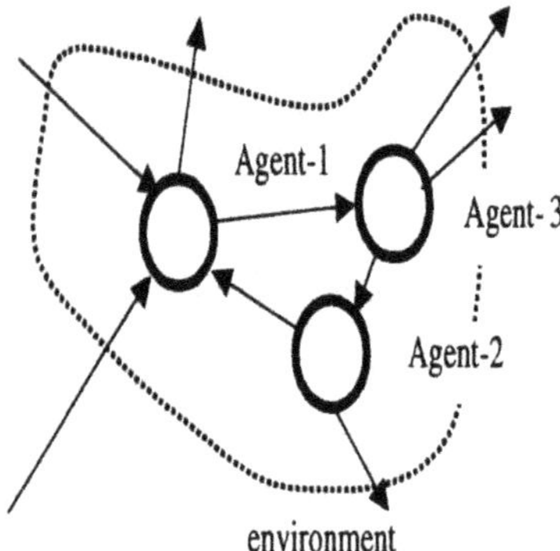

Fig. 1. An environment of agent-based computing; note a distributed character of problem solving and an important role of communication and interaction between the agents

autonomous agents in the setting of fuzzy sets with a special emphasis paid to the communication problems in the collective environment formed by the agents and the development of a formal model of the agent itself. We employ a top-down approach starting from an overall architecture and then proceeding with a detailed model of the agent. Firstly, in Section 2 we concentrate on the problem of communication between agents, introduce a notion of a communication quality and quantify it numerically through a suitable communication index. In Section 3, we discuss on a concept of a fuzzy state machine (fuzzy automaton) regarded as a generic model of an agent by concentrating on its conceptual and learning capabilities. A fuzzy flip-flip (more precisely a fuzzy JK flip-flop) is a basic building block of the state machines and look more thoroughly at its dynamics (Section 4). Next, in Section 5 discussed is a detailed development procedure of a Moore type fuzzy state machines that is followed by a learning scheme (Section 6). Conclusions are covered in Section 7. The material includes illustrative numeric examples augmenting the presentation of the underlying concepts and algorithms. As an immediate prerequisite, we introduce a few basic definitions. Firstly, information granulation perceived in this study becomes accomplished in the setting of fuzzy sets. Information granules are fuzzy sets. The quantification of granularity of fuzzy sets is completed using their σ-counts, [11] and [12]. Confining to normal fuzzy sets (or fuzzy relations, in general), the value of the σ-count, being equal to 1, corresponds to a singleton – the most specific information granule we can envision in this environment. Secondly, operations on fuzzy sets are implemented in the form of triangular norms (t- and s-norms). The negation is defined in a standard way (that is "$1 - a$" for any membership value "a" situated in the unit interval).

2 Communication between the agents in the granular environment

Apparently, agents are autonomous systems. There is no central control (coordination centre) but agents cooperate in representing and solving problems. Each agent may have its specific agenda that looks into problem solving from a very unique standpoint. Communication mechanisms or more generally, a communication environment in which they operate is of primordial importance. This concerns both the communication links to be established between the agents as well as the external environment with which they interact. The following communication aspects deserve careful analysis

- An interaction realized in terms of very different (and therefore quite incompatible) granularity of two or more agents. An agent communicates a message to some other agent. This activity is done in terms of its own vocabulary (information granules). The other agent has to take advantage of the message being sent to it, interpret (encode) it in its own language and then take further action. This issue requires handling some conceptual underpinnings and quantifying these in terms of some meaningful indexes of communication compatibility. If the vocabulary of the language and/or the granularity of terms used by the two agents are highly incompatible, the communication does not take place.
- Introducing a detailed algorithmic layer using which the agents can realize meaningful communication and quantify the results of such interaction. More precisely, we are interested in the technical insight of a tandem of

encoding - decoding mechanisms of granular messages sent between the agents.

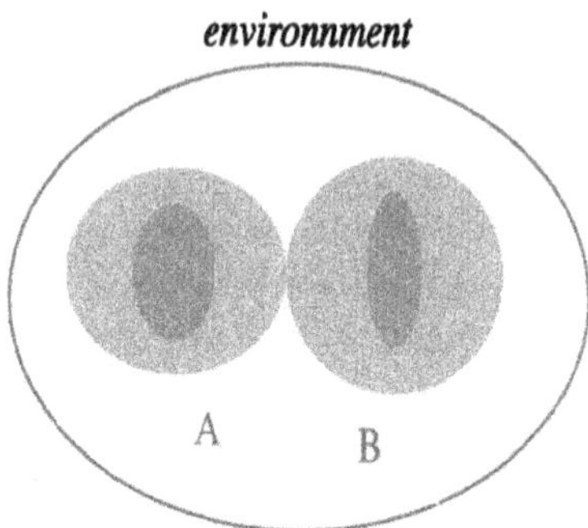

Fig. 2. Embedding agents (A and B) in a global communication environment; note a communication interface (communication layer) formed around each agent (a computational layer of the agent is indicated as a darker core)

The overall architecture of the communication between the agents as schematically portrayed in Figure 2, distinguishes between the numeric core of the agent and its interface layer.

Before moving into technicalities, it is prudent to make some general observations. First, if we are provided with detailed (very specific) information granules, especially those arising at the numeric level, such messages are fully accepted by any agent in spite of the granularity level it operates on. Secondly, we anticipate that the agent may not be capable of handling incoming messages that are too general with regard to the granularity of its own information granules. There is a broad variety of situations in between that require detailed numeric quantification. To describe the quality of the existing communication processes, let us set up a notation. An input information granule is denoted by X. The collection of the information granules, specific to the agent (A) accepting, is denoted by $A_1, A_2, \ldots, A_c$. We assume that all fuzzy sets in this scenario are normal. The possibility measure Poss (X, A_i) serves as a measure of interaction (communication) between the agent and the incoming message. The communication index expressing effectiveness of the communication between the agents is defined in the form

$$\text{Comm\_index}(X, A_1, A_2, \ldots, A_c) = c - \sum_{i=1}^{C} \langle \text{Poss}(X, A_i) \rangle .$$

Note that if X is equal to the entire universe of discourse (yielding Poss (X, A_i) =1 for all $i = 1, 2, \ldots, c$), then the communication index is equal to zero meaning that there is a strong incompatibility in the communication process. Moreover when X tends to be less specific (detailed), then the values of the communication index decrease. The way in which this index decreases depends on the form of X as well as the specific membership functions of $A_i's$. Observe that we also average over the moving information granule X of some fixed granularity (this is indicated by $\langle \mathrm{Poss}(X, A_i) \rangle$).

The averaging of this type helps us achieve higher relevance of the results. Finally, $\mathrm{Comm\_index}(A_1, A_2, \ldots, A_c) = 0$.

If the collections of the above granules form a fuzzy partition (that is their membership grades sum up to 1 for any element of the universe of discourse), we know that when σ-count$(X) = 1$, then the communication index assumes the value equal to $c - 1$. This value can be considered as a reference point when comparing all other situations with the granularity of X being different from 1.

Example 1. Here we consider four Gaussian membership functions of A_i while the incoming message X is treated as an interval of width "$2a$" distributed around a center "x". The parameters of the Gaussian fuzzy sets are summarized in Table 1; note that we have considered several combinations of the parameters of the membership functions (the same modal values and different spreads). The values of the communication index are plotted in Figure 3. As anticipated, the quality of communication deteriorates when X grows up in size of its granules. This deterioration, however, depends upon the size of the information granules used by the agent to whom the message has been delivered.

Case	Mean values	Spread (the same for all granules)
1	1, 3, 5, 8	0,5
2	1, 3, 5, 8	2,0

Table 1. Membership functions of the information granules forming a communication interface of the agent: selected collections of the parameters of the Gaussian fuzzy sets

The communication index serves as an essential indicator of quality of communication established between the agents. Low values of this index indicate an insufficient level of communication between the agent and the environment or some other agent.

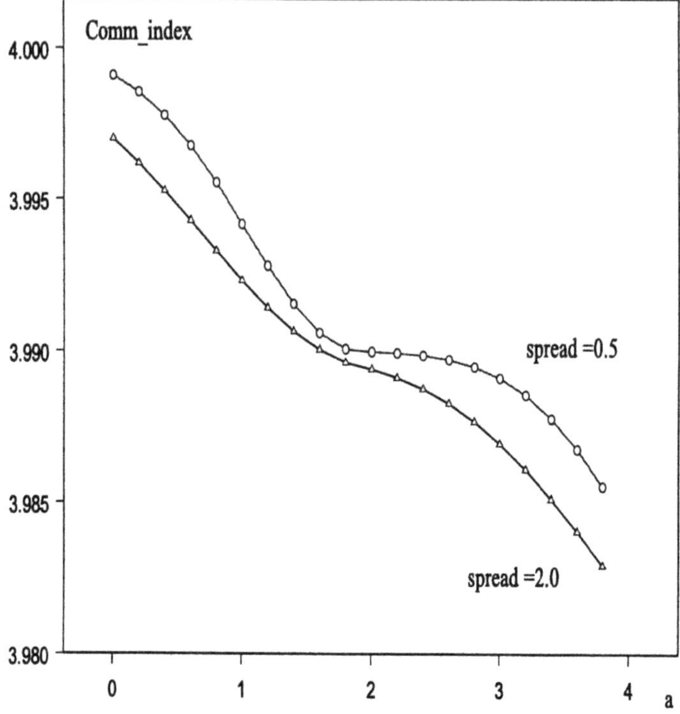

Fig. 3. Communication index treated as a function of the size (a) of the set-based information granule

meaning that X has to communicate to the agent that falls in its scope of operation (obviously, if all information granules exploited by the agent do not overlap with X, then the communication becomes meaningless).

We can localize agents in a granularity - scope space which is a convenient formalism to describe the essence of communication mechanisms in a general sense, (see Figure 4). By the scope dimension (scope axis) we mean a range of information granules used by the agents. The granularity coordinate positions the agents as to their specificity and the ability to communicate (where the quality of communication is now articulated in the form of the communication index). For instance, two agents, C and D do not communicate because of their different scope. Agents A and C are close in terms of the granularity of information being used, as well as their scope. As a consequence, it is very likely that they will be communicating quite well.

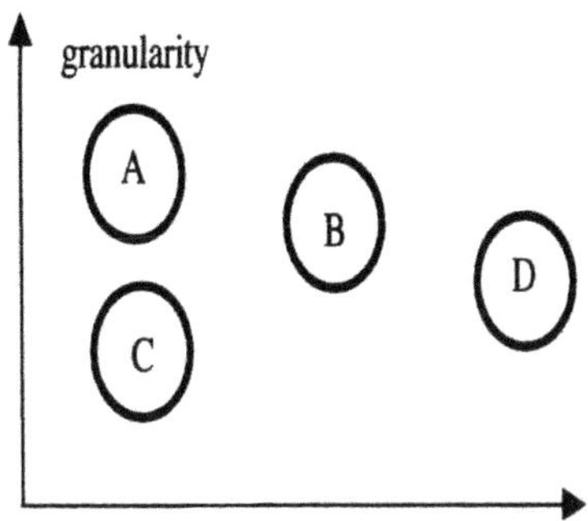

Fig. 4. A distribution of agents (A, B, C, and D) in the granularity - scope space

3 A fuzzy state machine as a generic model of an intelligent agent

Finite state machines and automata theory have been a backbone of a variety of models spreading across a spectrum of various disciplines [15] including hardware systems, industrial controllers, compilers, software requirement analysis, discrete optimization just to name a few. Fuzzy sets have augmented the automata theory in a relatively early phase of their developments; in this regard the reader may refer to the classic monograph authored by Kandel and Lee [9], where they address various generalizations available in this setting. Let us remind that a finite state machine (automaton) is defined as the structure

$$< \mathbf{X}, \mathbf{Q}, \mathbf{Y}, f, g >$$

where $\mathbf{X}$ is a set of inputs, $\mathbf{Q}$ denotes a set of states, $\mathbf{Y}$ is a set of outputs while "f" and "g" are the next-state switching and output functions. The elements of the sets $\mathbf{X}$, $\mathbf{Q}$, and $\mathbf{Y}$ are binary (0 or 1) or could come from a finite collection of some symbols (a, b, c, ...) that are afterwards coded in a binary fashion. The standard way of graphical representation of these machines is through a state graph, that is a graph whose nodes represent states while edges are used to identify transitions between the states. By its nature, at any point of time, the system may reside in only one state (if this property does not hold, we refer to it as a nondeterministic machine). Fuzzy state machines admit a concept of partial belongingness to a given state. In other words, we allow the system to reside in a collection of states. Similarly, we relax the requirement of occurrence of one input symbol, so that several transitions (edges) of the graph are active as well. Figure 5 contrasts finite state machines with their fuzzy set-based extension. In a broader perspective,

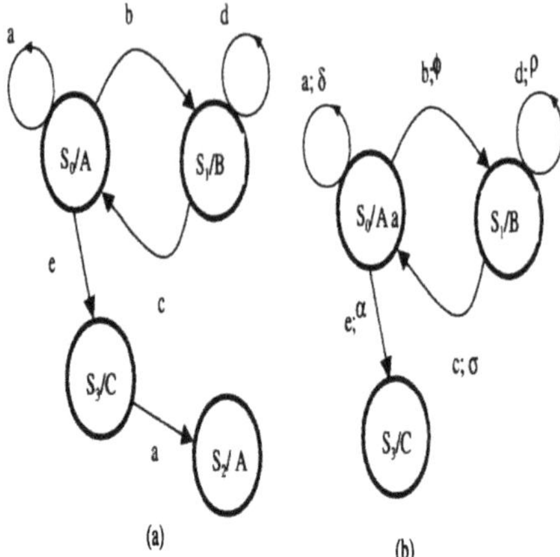

Fig. 5. Finite state machines (a) versus fuzzy state machines (b); observe that the latter can have several states and a number of transitions (edges) involved in the dynamics of the machine. α, β, γ, ... denote a strength of transition and degree of membership to the state

one has to refer to a number of research pursuits occurring in the area of analysis and use of fuzzy state machines; noteworthy is a diversity of the methods used therein, cf. [4], [13], [14], [15].

The ability of the fuzzy finite state machines to serve as an efficient model of the agents can be justified in several different ways:

- These automata exhibit a transparent interpretation and show their dynamics in terms of basic logic-inclined entities.
- They can be learned based through an interaction with an environment and other agents. There is a complete suite of the learning schemes and the finite state machines themselves come equipped with a high level of the parametric flexibility residing within the set of adjustable (trainable) parameters (weights) of the logic elements of the machine.
- They can interact with a continuous environment as we admit inputs and outputs that are located in the unit interval. To cast such fuzzy state machines in the framework of agents, refer to Figure 6. The detailed architecture of the agent and its communication layer are clearly distinguished.

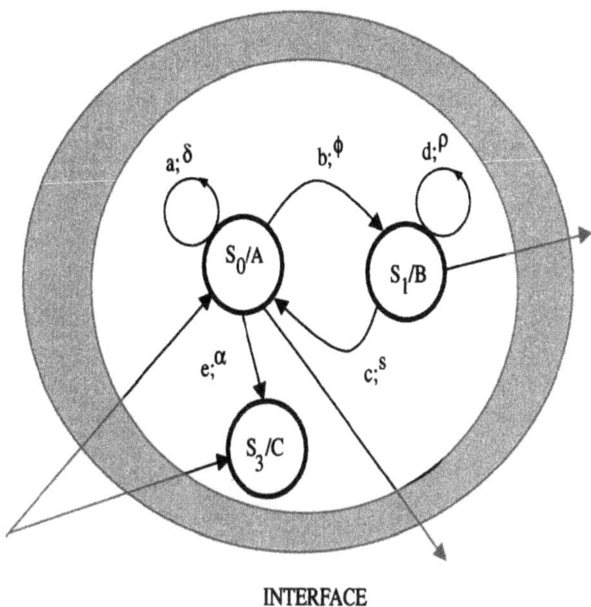

Fig. 6. Fuzzy state machines as internal architectures of the agent

4 The fuzzy JK flip-flop and its dynamics

It is instructive to start with a generic definition of the two-valued JK flip-flop in the form of the next-state equation that could be found in any introductory text on digital systems, cf. [4]:

$$Q^{+} = J\overline{Q} + \overline{K}Q$$

The two inputs (J and K) are used to control the state of the flip-flop. By analyzing the above expression, we can describe the behavior of this system in the tabular form (next-state table) as illustrated below:

Q	$JK = 00$	JK=01	JK=11	JK=10
0	0	0	1	1
1	1	0	0	1

Q^{+}

Apparently, $J = K = 0$ maintains the same state of the flip-flop, say $Q^{+} = Q$. $J = 1$ sets the system ($Q^{+} = 1$), $K = 1$ resets it (that is $Q^{+} = 0$) and $J = K = 1$ toggles the state (meaning that $Q^{+} = \overline{Q}$). The dynamics of the flip-flop can be portrayed in Figure 7. As the variables assume only two values $(0-1)$, the overall pattern of dynamics is quite simple.

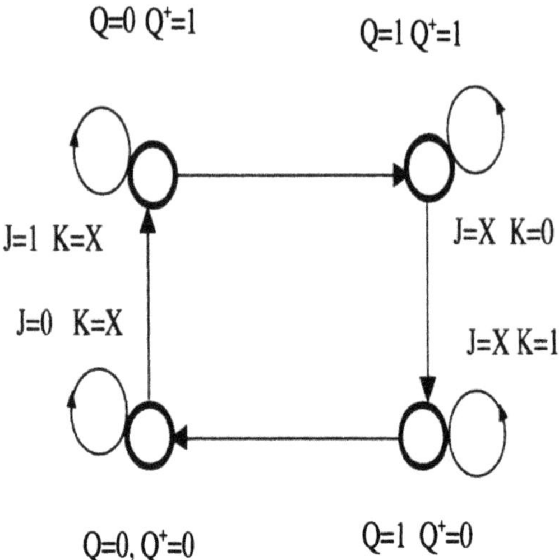

Fig. 7. The dynamics of the JK flip-flop showing all transitions between the states $Q-Q^+$

The fundamental generalization of the JK flip-flop has been first proposed in [5], [6] and then discussed in a series of ensuing papers [3], [10], [16], [17]. The formula governing the fuzzy JK flip-flop reads as

$$Q^+ = J\overline{Q} + \overline{K}Q + J\overline{K} \tag{1}$$

Interestingly enough, we can envision it to generalize a group of 1s as they occur in the two-valued Karnaugh map, see Figure 8.

As the logic operations are realized in terms of triangular norms, we can rewrite (1) in an explicit manner

$$Q^+ = (Jt\overline{Q})s(\overline{K}tQ)s(Jt\overline{K}) \tag{2}$$

In the sequel, realizing the t-norm as the product operation and the probabilistic sum as the s-norm (i.e. $atb = ab$ and $asb = a + b - ab$), we make (2) more specific, that is

$$Q^+ = J\overline{Q} + \overline{K}Q - J\overline{K}\,\overline{Q}Q + J\overline{K} - J^2\overline{Q}\,\overline{K} - J(\overline{K}^2)Q + J^2(\overline{K})^2\overline{Q}Q. \tag{3}$$

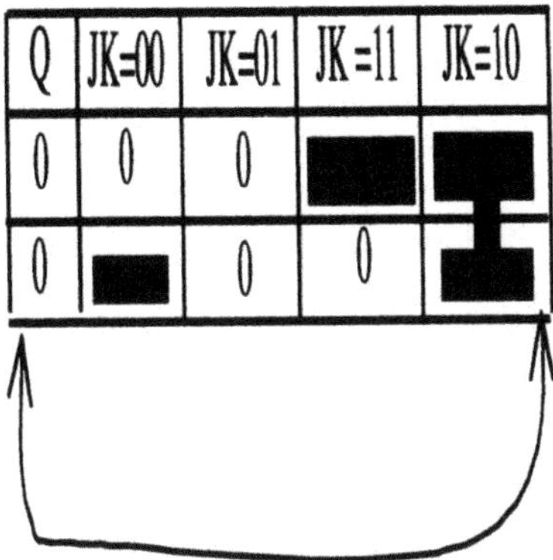

Fig. 8. Karnaugh map showing the three groups of 1*s* as being used in the expression of the fuzzy *JK* flip-flop

One can easily verify, by a straight inspection, that when confining to J, K, Q in $\{0,1\}$, the fuzzy JK flip-flop subsumes its standard two-valued counterpart.

As one may anticipate, the continuous character of the changes in state and inputs of the flip-flop can result in a very rich pattern of its dynamics. In contrast to the four combinations of the current-next state $Q - Q^+$, we envision an infinite number of possible sequences of states. This effect of continuity of states is illustrated in Figure 9.

As seen in Figure 9, we start from the same initial state $Q = 0$ and converge to the same final state equal to 1. This is obvious as K is equal to zero and there is a nonzero value of the set input (J). The speed of changes depends on the value of the set input (J). Note that the reset action is nonexistent (with K equal to zero). The higher the value of J, the faster the changes occurring in the state value (Q^+) of the fuzzy flip-flop. Figure 10 shows the pattern of changes for some configurations of the set and reset inputs. These patterns are more complex and depend which signal prevails. It is essential to notice that depending upon the configuration of the values of the inputs, the system migrates to the values of Q^+ being lower or higher than the initial value of the state.

5 The development of Moore type fuzzy state machines

In this section, we develop a Moore type of the fuzzy state machine. First, we elaborate on the basic architecture as it generalizes the well-known two-valued counterpart [4] and [15]. The Mealy type of fuzzy state machine is developed in the same manner, so this will not discussed this.

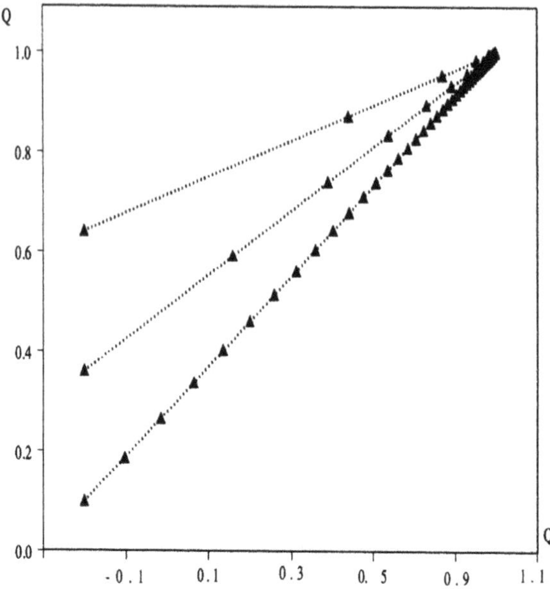

Fig. 9. Plots of dynamical patterns of changes observed in the JK flip-flop in the $Q - Q^+$ space. The starting point is zero, $Q = 0$. Moreover $K = 0$ while J is equal to 0.05 (a), 0.4 (b), and 0.8 (c) (t-norm: product; s-norm: probabilistic sum)

5.1 The architecture

In what follows, we expand the classic Moore type of finite state machine (automaton) to the format of fuzzy inputs and states. Let us recall that the essence of the Moore finite state machine is that the outputs depend on the state but not the input. In other words, the following expressions hold:

$$\mathbf{Q}^+ = f(\mathbf{x}, \mathbf{Q}) \qquad (4)$$
$$\mathbf{y} = g(\mathbf{Q})$$

where $\mathbf{x}$, $\mathbf{y}$, and $\mathbf{Q}(\mathbf{Q}^+)$ are vectors of the inputs, outputs, and states. Obviously, in the two-valued case the above are elements of $\{0, 1\}$. It is well-documented [6] and [14] that the description of the Mealy machine gives rise to the architecture composed of three modules:

- A combinational module (Boolean function) realizing the excitation of J and K inputs of the flip-flops. They indirectly realize the next-state equation (f);
- A combinational module (Boolean function g) mapping the current state (Q) on the outputs of the machine ($\mathbf{y}$);
- A family of JK flip-flops memorizing the state of the system.

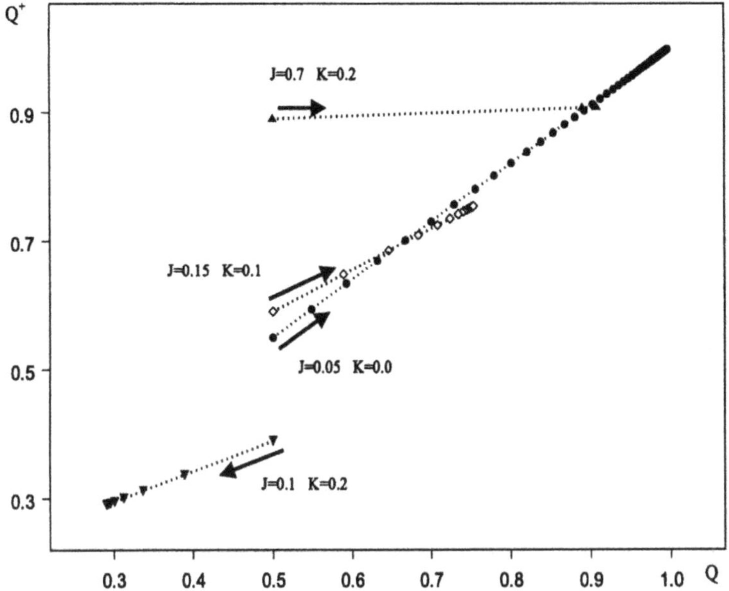

Fig. 10. The plot of the dynamics of the JK flip-flop in the $Q - Q^+$ space. The starting point is 0.5, $Q = 0.5$ (t-norm: product; s-norm: probabilistic sum)

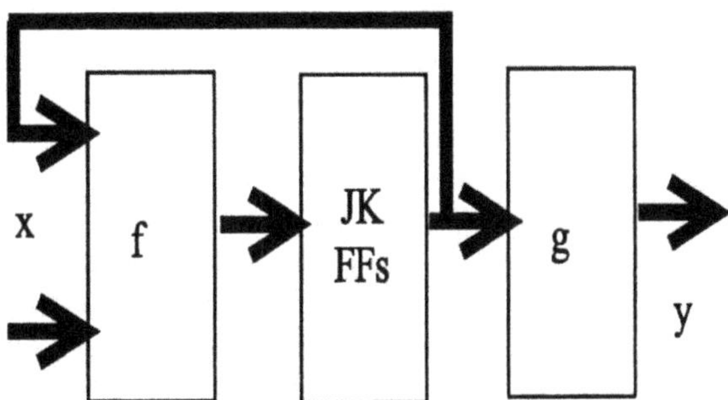

Fig. 11. Moore state machine: a general topology composed of two combinational modules (f and g) and a family of JK flip-flops (JK FFs)

These three modules along with their interrelationships are portrayed in Figure 11.

From now on, our goal is to generalize it to the format in which it could cope with continuous (fuzzy) variables. This requires a generalization of the basic functional modules such as memory block and two combinational modules. At this point, we can exploit fuzzy JK flip-flops as basic memory elements. The combinational part of the system is realized by so-called logic processors. We discuss them in the next section.

5.2 A logic processor and its detailed topology

In [11] proposed were two general classes of fuzzy AND and OR neurons. They serve as generalizations of standard AND and OR digital gates. The AND neuron is a static n-input single output processing element y=AND$(\mathbf{x};\mathbf{w})$ constructed with the use of fuzzy set operators (t- and s-norms)

$$y = \mathop{\boldsymbol{T}}_{i=1}^{n} (x, sw_i). \tag{5}$$

Here $\mathbf{w}$ denotes a weight vector (connections) of the neuron. In light of the boundary conditions of the triangular norms, we obtain:

- if $w_i = 1$, then the corresponding input has no impact on the output. Moreover, the monotonicity property holds: higher values of $w_i^{'}s$ reduce an impact of x_i on the output of the neuron,
- if $\mathbf{w}$ assumes values equal to 0 or 1, then the AND neuron becomes a standard AND gate.

The OR neuron, denoted as y = OR $(\mathbf{x};\mathbf{w}$, is described in the form:

As before for the AND neuron, the same general properties hold; the boundary conditions are somewhat complementary: the higher the value of the connection, the more evident the impact of the associated input on the output. The fundamental Shannon's expansion theorem [14] states any Boolean function can be represented as a sum of minterms (or equivalently, a product of maxterms). The realization is a two-layer digital network: the first layer has AND gates (realizing required minterms); the second one consists of OR gates that carry out OR-operation on the already constructed minterms.

Fuzzy neurons operate in an environment of continuous variables. An analogy of the Shannon theorem (and the resulting topology of the network) can be realized in the form illustrated in Figure 12. Here AND neurons form a series of generalized minterms. The OR neurons serve as generalized maxterms. This network *approximates* experimental continuous data in a logic-oriented manner. In contrast, note that the sum of minterms represents Boolean data. The connections of the neurons equip the network with the highly required parametric flexibility. Alluding to the nature of approximation accomplished here, we will be referring to the network as the logic processor (LP).

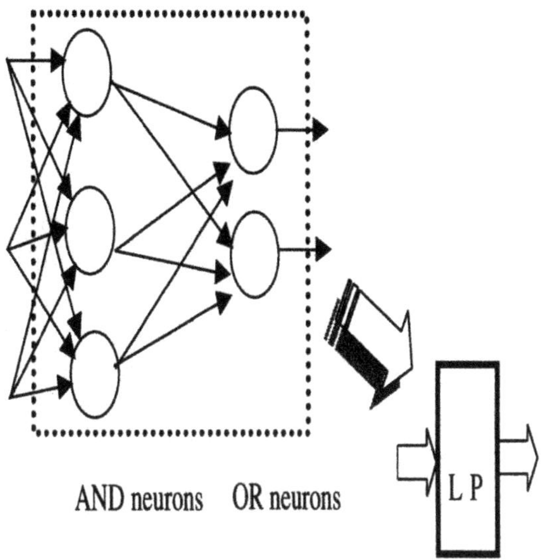

Fig. 12. Logic processor (LP): a general topology; the inputs involve both direct and complemented inputs

5.3 A fuzzy Moore state machine

These logic processors are afterwards used as the building modules in the Moore machine serving as two combinational structures there. The elements of the memory are the fuzzy JK flip-flops.

Now, combining all these functional modules together, we end up with the generalized version of the two-valued Moore machine. Two LPs are used to realize fuzzy combinational functions: the first provides the fuzzy JK flip-flops with the required switching mechanism, the other generates the output function (see Figure 13).

6 The learning scheme

The fuzzy Moore machine comes equipped with the connections of the logic processors that could be easily adjusted. The learning is regarded as a design paradigm of fuzzy sequential systems. We proceed with the design problem formulated as follows Given an input-output sequence $\{(\mathbf{x}(1), \text{target}(1)), (\mathbf{x}(2), \text{target}(2)), \ldots, (\mathbf{x}(N), \text{target}(N))\}$ of the agent operating in a certain environment. Design a fuzzy Moore machine that represents (approximates) this sequence. This formulation is somewhat limited as we are concerned with many inputs $(\mathbf{x}(k))$ and a single output $(\text{target}(k))$, $k = 1, 2, \ldots, N$. We will

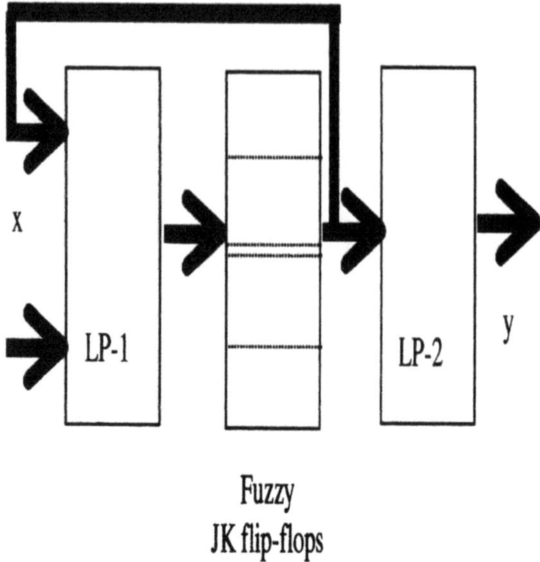

Fig. 13. Fuzzy Moore machine: a general architecture

consider the multiple input - multiple output case afterwards. When dealing with the single output, the fuzzy state machine can be arranged in the topology as illustrated in Figure 14.

Simply, the output function (g) is viewed as an identity and this allows us to eliminate the output logic processor. Only a single fuzzy flip-flop is needed and its state Q is equal to the output, $y = Q$. The remaining logic processor, driving the inputs of the flip-flop, has to be optimized, viz. its connections have to be adjusted so that a certain performance index is minimized. The learning is carried out in the supervised mode. To proceed with the detailed learning scheme, we first fix all necessary notation (see Figure 15).

The logic processor has two outputs, the first driving the set (J) input of the flip-flop and the second used to reset the flip flop. Furthermore the first input is the feedback from the flip-flop. In total, this gives rise to $m = 2(n+1)$ inputs. The performance index to be minimized is a standard sum of squared errors:

$$V(\mathbf{conn}) = \sum_{k=1}^{N} \left[\text{target}(k+1) - Q^{+}(k) \right]^{2}. \tag{6}$$

Here **conn** denotes a family of all connections of the LP. More specifically, **conn** is a structure $\{\mathbf{W}, \mathbf{V}\}$ with $\mathbf{V}$ and $\mathbf{W}$ being the arrays of the connections of the AND and OR neurons, respectively, (see Figure 16). Considering (x), $Q + (k)$ is governed by (x) and $Q(k) = y(k)$. In computing the

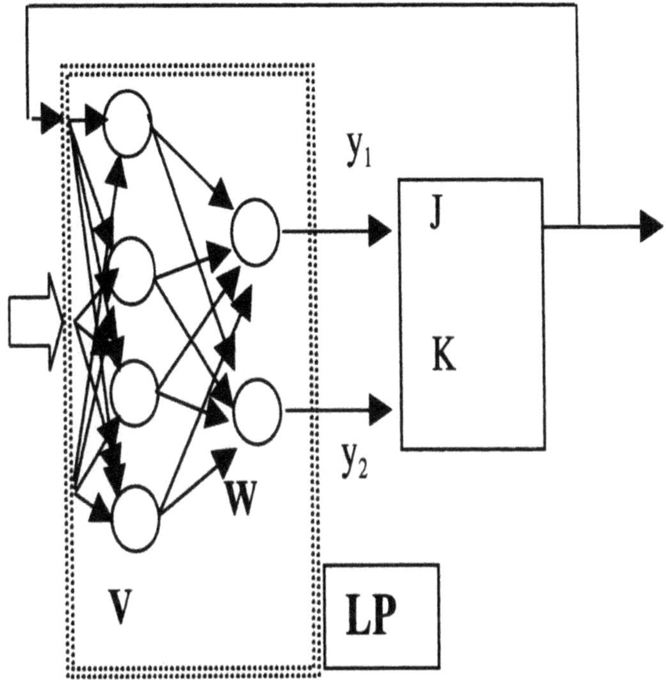

Fig. 14. A structure of the fuzzy state machine used in the learning scenario

performance index (6), we start from $Q+(1) = y(2)$, $Q(1) = y(1)$, etc. In this case, the objective is to make target(2) as close to $y(2)$ as possible. Referring to the structure in Fig.16, we have

$$J = y_1, K = y_2$$
$$y_1 = \mathrm{LP}(\mathbf{x}(k), \mathbf{W}, \mathbf{V})$$
$$y_2 = \mathrm{LP}(\mathbf{x}(k), \mathbf{W}, \mathbf{V})$$

The minimization is completed by changing the connections of the logic processor. While the general learning scheme is compact

$$\mathbf{conn}(\text{iter}+1) = \mathbf{conn}(\text{iter}) - \alpha V(\mathbf{conn})$$

the details can be derived once we have confined ourselves to some specific triangular norms. The derivation is straightforward yet somewhat lengthy. Table 2 summarizes the on-line learning for the product and probabilistic sum being used in the implementation of the fuzzy neurons. As in the on-line learning, the updates of the connections occur after each element of the training set, we drop the index labeling it in the data set. The size of the hidden layer (number of AND neurons) is equal to "h".

General update scheme $\quad \mathbf{conn}(\text{iter}+1) = \mathbf{conn}(\text{iter}) - \alpha V(\mathbf{conn})$

$$\frac{fQ}{fw_{ij}} = -2(\text{target} - Q^+)\frac{dQ^+}{dw_{ij}}, \qquad i = 1,2; \qquad j = 1,2,\ldots,h$$

$$\frac{dQ^+}{dw_{1j}} = C_1\frac{dy_1}{dw_{1j}} \qquad \text{and} \qquad \frac{dQ^+}{dw_{2j}} = C_2\frac{dy_2}{dw_{2j}}$$

$$C_1 = (1-Q) + (1-K) - 2(1-K)J(1-Q) - Q(1-K)^2$$
$$C_2 = (1-Q)^2J^2 - 2J - 2J(1-K)(Q+J)$$

$$\frac{dy_i}{dw_{ij}} = (1 - A_i)a_i$$

$$\text{where} \qquad A_i = \bigoplus_{\substack{\ell=1 \\ \ell \neq j}}^{h} (w_{i\ell}a_\ell)$$

and "$\bigoplus$" stands for the probabilistic sum

$$\frac{fQ}{fv_{ij}} = -2(\text{target} - Q^+)\frac{dQ^+}{dv_{ij}} i = 1,2,\ldots,h; \; j = 1,2,\ldots,m$$

$$\frac{dQ^+}{dv_{ij}} = C_1\frac{dy_1}{dv_{ij}} + C_2\frac{dy_2}{dv_{ij}}$$
$$\frac{dy_1}{dv_{ij}} = \sum_{i=1}^{2}\frac{dy_1}{da_i}\frac{da_i}{dv_{ij}}$$

$$\frac{dy_1}{da_i} = w_{1i}(1 - B_1) \text{where } B_1 = \bigoplus_{\substack{k=1 \\ k \neq i}}^{h} (w_{\ell k}a_k)$$

$$\frac{da_i}{dv_{ij}} = C_i(1 - z_j) \text{and } C_i = \sum_{\substack{\ell=1 \\ \ell \neq i}}^{m} (v_{i\ell} + z_\ell - v_{i\ell}z_\ell)$$

Table 2. A detailed on-line learning algorithm for the fuzzy state machine (α-learning rate)

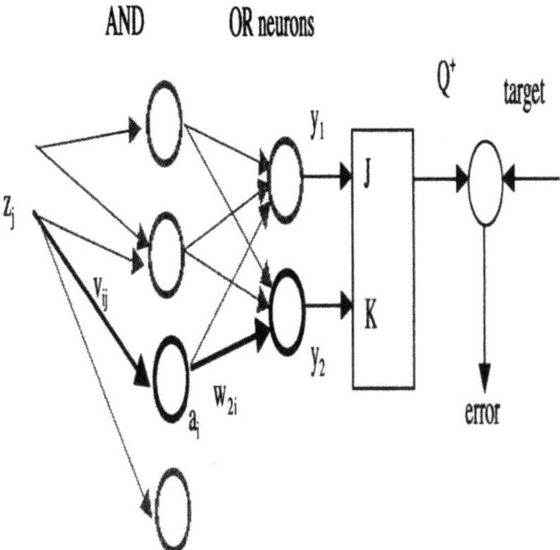

Fig. 15. The learning process for fuzzy state machine - a detailed notation

Example 2. Here, we start with a one-dimensional case. The Boolean data set consists of the triples (Q, x, Q^+):

$$\begin{bmatrix} 000 \\ 011 \\ 101 \\ 110 \end{bmatrix}$$

The learning is realized in the on-line form with the value of α equal to 0.45. The values of the performance index (6) in successive learning epochs are shown in Figure 16.

It is evident that the learning is fast and most changes (updates) of the connections of the LP occur at the early phase of the entire process. The optimized connections of the logic processor are summarized below:

- input - hidden layers (the successive columns correspond to the connections originating from the input layer and involving Q, x, and their complements, respectively)

$$\mathbf{V} = \begin{bmatrix} 1.000 \; 0.000 \; 0.998 \; 1.000 \\ 0.402 \; 0.663 \; 0.499 \; 1.000 \end{bmatrix}$$

- hidden-output layers (the columns correspond to the outputs of the LP)

$$\mathbf{W} = \begin{bmatrix} 1.000 \; 0.000 \\ 1.000 \; 0.041 \end{bmatrix}$$

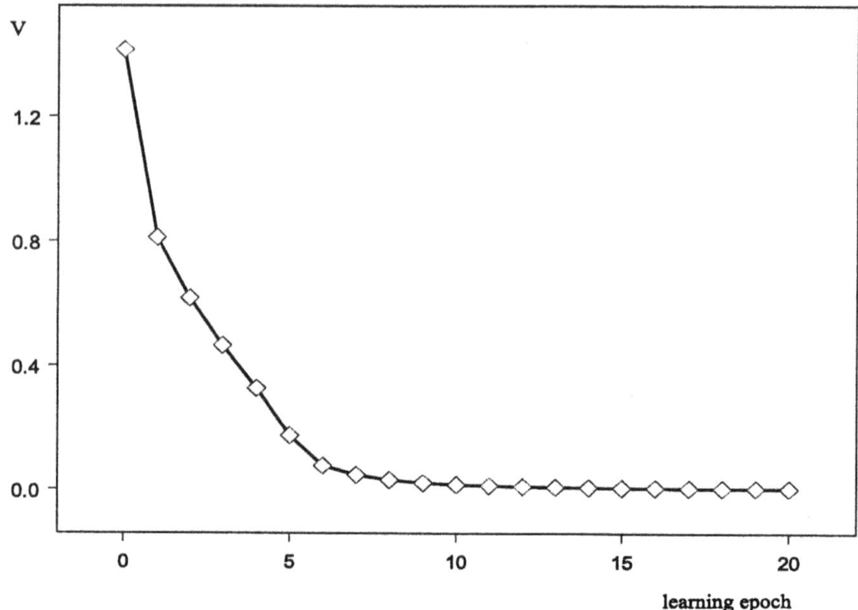

Fig. 16. The values of the performance index (6) in successive learning epochs

The application of the pruning mechanism (where the most essential connections are retained) leads us to the modified matrices of the connections that could be easily interpreted (the essential connections are indicated)

$$\begin{pmatrix} 1.000 & \mathbf{0.000} & 1.000 & 1.000 \\ \mathbf{0.000} & 1.000 & \mathbf{0.000} & 1.000 \end{pmatrix} \quad \begin{pmatrix} \mathbf{1.000} & 0.000 \\ \mathbf{1.000} & 0.000 \end{pmatrix}$$

Then the formula for the entire LP reads as

$$J = K = x.$$

So we ended up with a T flip-flop ($J = K$) (as could have been expected by inspection of the state diagram for the Boolean data, see Figure 17).
Example 3. Here we are concerned with the 2 input - one input binary data. The data set comes in the format (Q, x_1, x_2, Q^+)

$$\begin{bmatrix} .000 \\ 0.010 \\ 0.111 \\ 0.101 \\ 0.101 \\ 1.001 \\ 1.110 \\ 1.010 \end{bmatrix}$$

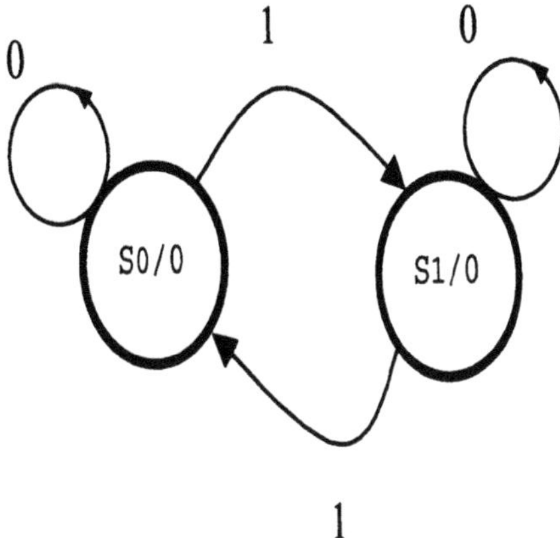

Fig. 17. The state diagram of the finite state machine resulting from the Boolean data set; (S/y) denotes state-output pairs

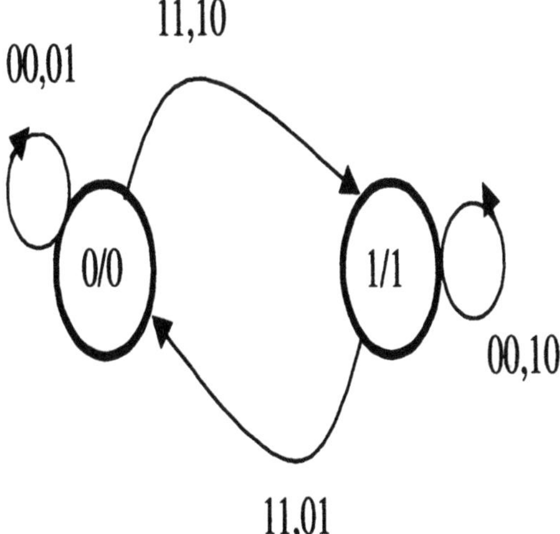

Fig. 18. The state diagram corresponding to the binary data set; as we are concerned with the Moore machine the output is equal to the state, $y = Q$.

The state diagram equivalent to this data set is shown in Figure 18.

The values of the minimized performance index obtained in successive learning epochs are shown in Figure 19. We have started from the minimal topology of the LP having $h = 2$ nodes (AND neurons) in the hidden layer. As before, most of the improvements (optimization) take place at the beginning of the entire learning process.

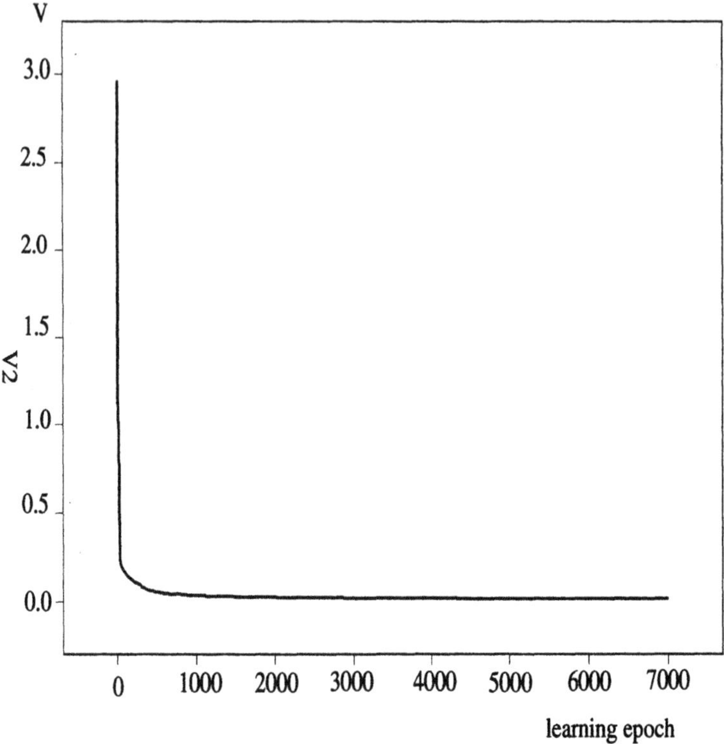

Fig. 19. The performance index (6) as a function of "h" after 7000 learning epochs (learning rate is equal to 0.45)

data	0.000	0.000	1.000	1.000	1.000	1.000	0.000	0.000
FSM	0.000	0.000	1.000	1.000	0.955	0.953	0.047	0.098

Table 3. The results of learning: data and output of the Fuzzy State Machine (FSM)

The value of the performance index is equal 0.0160. At this level, the data are well-represented by the state machine. This claim is fully legitimate by looking at the results shown in Table 3. We have slight departures from plain $1s$ and $0s$ but this does not prevent us from a clear identification (rounding off) of such.

As before, the connections are organized in the matrix form. For the input - hidden layer, the order is: Q, x_1, x_2 followed by their complements (column-wise). The rows correspond to the two nodes in the hidden layer:

$$\mathbf{V} = \begin{pmatrix} 1.000 & 0.000 & 1.000 & 0.000 & 1.000 & 1.000 \\ 0.501 & 0.947 & 0.0496 & 1.000 & 1.000 & 1.000 \end{pmatrix}$$

The connections for the hidden-output layer are summarized below

$$\mathbf{W} = \begin{pmatrix} 1.000 & 0.000 \\ 1.000 & 0.953 \end{pmatrix}$$

The connections are in [0,1]. The original data are binary. It is therefore of interest to prune (or better say, binarize) the *LP* to get a clear understanding as to the Boolean functions realized by the system. Following the pruning formula, we get the connections (additionally the essential connections that contribute to the overall interpretation of the network are put in boldface)

$$\mathbf{V} = \begin{pmatrix} 1.000 & \mathbf{0.000} & 1.000 & \mathbf{0.000} & 1.000 & 1.000 \\ 1.000 & 1.000 & \mathbf{0.000} & 1.000 & 1.000 & 1.000 \end{pmatrix}$$

$$\mathbf{W} = \begin{pmatrix} 1.000 & 0.000 \\ 1.000 & 1.000 \end{pmatrix}$$

In the sequel, they help us to describe the functions:

- for the AND neurons in the hidden layer,

$$\text{hidden}_1 = x_1\overline{Q}$$
$$\text{hidden}_2 = x_2$$

- for the OR neurons in the output layer,

$$J = \text{hidden}_1 = x_1\overline{Q}$$
$$K = \text{hidden}_1 + \text{hidden}_2 = x_1\overline{Q} = x_2$$

How does these expression compare to the result of the "standard" design of such digital system? We can repeat the design process following excitation tables for the JK flip-flop [6] and [14]. This leads us to the Karnaugh maps for the J and K input of the flip-flop (see Table 4).

By encircling the neighboring 1s (and taking advantage of the existing don't care conditions - X), we derive the expressions

$$J = x_1\overline{Q}$$
$$K = x_2$$

The Boolean expression for the J input is the same as the one obtained through learning. The expression for the K input is different: simply what has been learned includes one extra term (that is composed of don't care conditions only). In other words, this portion of the formula is not excessive. Its inclusion, though, does not make any harm to the expression and does not cause any extra hardware as this portion has been already used to implement the set input of the flip-flop, $K = J + x_2$.

Q/x_1x_2	00	01	11	10
0	0	0	1	1
1	X	0	0	X

J

Q/x_1x_2	00	01	11	10
0	X	X	X	X
1	X	1	1	X

K

Table 4. K-maps for J and K inputs of the flip-flop

To summarize these two experiments: the fuzzy state machine (agent) has been *learned* rather than being designed – it comes as an interesting endeavor of some practical implications (especially in light of the current tendency of evolving and learning hardware as we have already witnessed in evolvable hardware).

The experiment was carried out for the increasing size of the hidden layer by changing the number of the AND neurons; the results are summarized below:

h	3	4	5
Performance index V	0.0457	0.0148	0.0111

Evidently, the increase of the size of the hidden layer does not substantially reduce the values of the performance index. In this case, it could be attributed to the relatively simple problem we are dealing with.

7 Conclusions

In this paper, we have studied a concept of agents positioned in the framework of granular computing. Two main issues have been studied in depth: a communication between agents and the detailed architecture of the agent itself. The quality of communication is quantified with the aid of the communication index. Each agent being mapped in the granularity - scope space can be characterized in sense of their communication abilities with other agents and/or external environment. The language of granular computing employed in this study concerns fuzzy sets. The subsequent communication issues are expressed in the same language (namely we assumed that all agents are embedded in the same conceptual environment). Another point worth investigating in the future deals with cases where agents are implemented through various types of formalisms of granular computing (such as sets or interval analysis, rough sets or random sets).

We have showed that the design of the agent itself (whose underlying topology is a fuzzy state machine) can be carried out through learning that gives rise to their highly autonomous behavior.

References

1. F. Cicalese, A. Di Nola, V. Loia, *A fuzzy evolutionary framework for adaptive agents*, Proceedings of 13th Internat. ACM Symposium of Applied Computing, 29/2 - 2/3/99, San Antonio, (USA), ACM Press.
2. S.A. Cerri, *Shifting the focus from control to communication: the STReams Objects Environments model of communicating agents*, Lecture Notes in Artificial Intelligence, **1624**, Springer-Verlag, Berlin, (1997), 115–131.
3. J. Diamond, W. Pedrycz, D. McLeod, *Fuzzy $J-K$ flip-flop as computational structures: design and implementation*, IEEE Trans. on Circuits Systems, **41** (1994) 215–226.
4. F.J. Hill, G.R. Peterson, *Introduction to switching theory & logic design*, J. Wiley & Sons, New York (1981).
5. K. Hirota, K. Ozawa, *The concept of fuzzy flip-flop*, IEEE Trans. on Systems, Man, and Cybernetics, **19** (1989) 980–997.
6. K. Hirota, K. Ozawa, *Fuzzy flip-flop and fuzzy registers*, Fuzzy Sets and Systems, **32** (1989) 139–148.
7. N. Jennings, M. Wooldrige, *Agent-Oriented software engineering*, J. Bradshaw (ed.), Handbook of Agent Technology, AAAI/MIT Press, Boston, MA, (2000).
8. D. Kafura, J.P. Briot, *Actors and agents*, IEEE Concurrency, **6** (1998) 24–29.
9. A. Kandel, S.C. Lee, *Fuzzy switching and automata*, Theory and Applications, Crane and Russak, New York (1979).
10. Y. Mori, K. Otsuka, M. Mukaidono, *Properties of fuzzy sequential circuit using fuzzy transition matrix and their design method*, Proceedings of IEEE Conference, Yokohama (Japan) (1995), 2133–2138.
11. W. Pedrycz, *Fuzzy Set Engineering*, CRC Press, Boca Raton, (USA), 1995.
12. W. Pedrycz, F. Gomide, *Fuzzy Sets: An Introduction*, Analysis and Design, MIT Press, (1998).
13. C.H. Roth, *Fundamentals of Logic Design*, PWS Publishing Company, Boston, 1995.
14. W.G. Schneeweiss, *Boolean Functions with Engineering Applications and Computer Programs*, Springer-Verlag, Berlin (1989).
15. T. Villa, T. Kam, R.K. Brayton, A. Sangiovanni-Vincentelli, *Synthesis of Finite State Machines*, Kluwer Academic Publishers, Boston 1997.
16. J. Virant, N. Zimic, M. Mraz, *Fuzzy sequential circuits and automata*, (C.T. Leondes, Ed.), Fuzzy Theory Systems, **IV**, Academic Press, San Diego (USA), (1999), pp. 1599–1653.
17. J. Virant, N. Zimic, M. Mraz, *T-type fuzzy memory cells*, Fuzzy Sets and Systems, **102** (1999) 175–183.

Controlling Effective Introns for Multi-Agent Learning by Means of Genetic Programming

Hitoshi Iba[1] and Makoto Terao[2]

[1] Dept. of Frontier Informatics, School of Frontier Science, The University of Tokyo, iba@miv.t.u-tokyo.ac.jp
[2] Dept. of Inf. and Comm. Eng., School of Engineering, The University of Tokyo, terao@miv.t.u-tokyo.ac.jp

Abstract. This paper presents the emergence of the cooperative behavior for multiple agents by means of Genetic Programming (GP). For the purpose of evolving the effective cooperative behavior, we propose a controlling strategy of introns, which are non-executed code segments dependent upon the situation. The traditional approach to removing introns was able to cope with only a part of syntactically defined introns, which excluded other frequent types of introns. The validness of our approach is discussed with comparative experiments with robot simulation tasks, i.e., a navigation problem and an escape problem.

1 Introduction

Recently intelligent agents and multi-agent systems have attracted much interest in Distributed Artificial Intelligence (DAI). GP and its variants have been applied to the multi-agent learning (see [Haynes *et al.*95], [Luke *et al.*96], [Iba96], [Hara *et al.*99] for example). However, in the multi-agent application of GP, the computational burden is often problematic. This is because the number of GP trees required for the multi-agent task becomes larger with the number of agents. For instance, in the heterogeneous breeding strategy (see Section 2 for details), each agent uses a distinct GP program so that the total number of GP trees is N times greater than that one of a single-agent task, where N is the number of agents.

Programs generated by GP grow very quickly in size and include large amount of non-functional codes, i.e., introns. This "bloating" effect degrades the GP search, in the sense that (1) larger programs often require more time and more space to run, and (2) larger programs tend to show worse generalization performance than shorter ones. Thus, reducing introns is very important in the GP search. The bloating is supposed to have a much worse effect on the multi-agent application because of a greater number of GP trees required for the task. [Soule *et al.*96] showed that the exponential growth was mainly dominated by non-functional codes. He used a controlling method of the tree growth by removing non-functional code segments, and demonstrated its effectiveness in bounding the programs' size. However, the deletion of all non-functional code segments is known to be an insolvable problem. It is reducible to the program equivalence problem, which is non-recursive. Thus, he only removed a part of syntactic introns that are known to be non-executed before the execution. These introns exclude other frequent types of introns (see Section 3 for details).

This paper introduces the concept of "effective introns", i.e., non-functional code segments of a GP tree dependent upon the execution, and proposes a controlling scheme of the tree growth for multi-agent GP learning. Based on the empirical studies, we show the effectiveness of our approach in the following points:

1. The fitness transition is improved during the training phase.
2. The code growth is effectively controlled.
3. The robustness of acquired programs is increased.

The rest of this paper is structured as follows. Section 2 describes the experimental setting for GP learning. Section 3 introduces a basic idea of controlling effective introns. Section 4 shows the experimental results with robot tasks. The performance is compared with traditional GP strategies. Section 5 discusses our approach, followed by some conclusion in Section 6.

2 Experimental Domains and GP Setting

In this paper, we use the following tasks for autonomous robots (see Fig.1). The world is a continuous 2-dimensional area on which there exist agents (i.e., robots) and obstacles. An agent is represented by an alphabet which is able to move in any direction. In our simulation, robots are supposed to be equipped with different sensors and motors. Thus, the appropriate job separation is required to solve efficiently the tasks described below.

The first task we have chosen is the robot navigation. Some of the training maps are shown in Fig.1(a) and (b), in which four robot agents are represented as a, b, c, and d. There are obstacles such as circles (a) or walls (b). The surrounding circle around an agent represents its view area. The destination of an agent is illustrated as an arrow. For instance, in Fig.1(a), the goal position of agent a is the start position of agent b. The agents' goal is to find the optimal path from given starting locations to their respective goals, while avoiding the obstacles and other robots.

The second task is an "escape problem", in which robot agents are supposed to leave a room through a door (or hole) in case of emergency, such as a fire (Fig.1(c)). However, in order to open the door (shown as a white box in the figure), they have to push all the buttons (shown as +). Thus, this task consists of (1) pushing buttons and (2) escaping from the room through the door.

In order to apply GP to evolving agents' programs for the above tasks, we use the terminal and nonterminal sets shown in Table 1. In the table, a

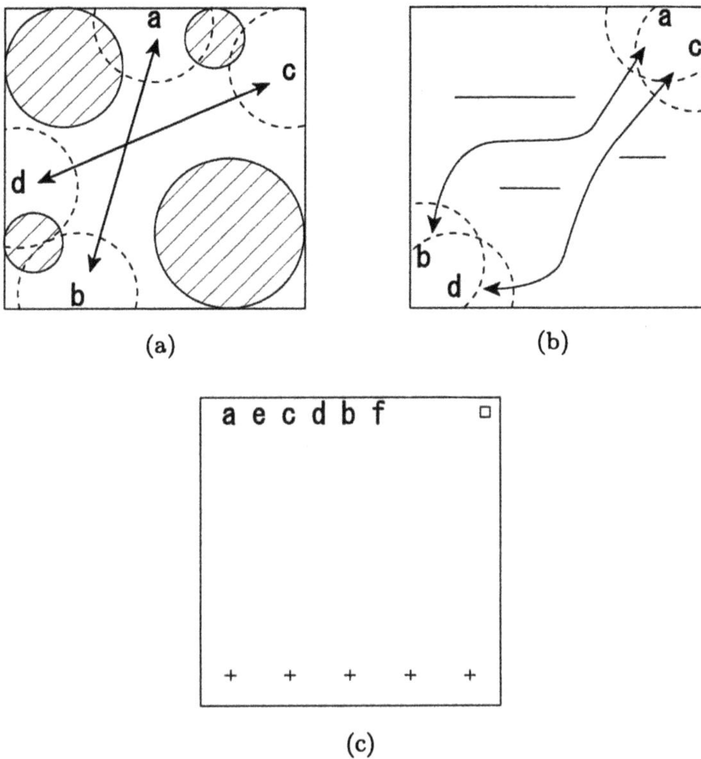

Fig. 1. Training Maps for Robot Tasks.

symbol without any argument is a terminal symbol. We have chosen a vector operation for the GP tree representation. This is aimed to incorporate more precise directional information about the environment surrounding the agents. The output vector of a GP tree tells the agent how to move successively, i.e., the robot moves forward in the vector's direction with the speed proportional to the vector's length unless it bumps into some obstacle. The robot commands are taken from a real robot, or can be constructed easily with the primitive commands (see [Ito *et al.*96] for details). We assume agents, i.e., robots, have an eye sensor with some limited view area. This area is shown as a circle in Fig.1. If the nearest agent is out of its scope, then the "Nearest_Agent" terminal returns a zero vector. It is also the case with the if_obstacle function.

There have been different breeding strategies proposed for the multi-agent learning by GP (see [Luke *et al.*96], [Iba96] and [Hara *et al.*99] for details). This paper uses the co-evolutionary breeding strategy, in which GP individuals are divided into a set of agent-type subpopulations (see Fig.2). Breeding is performed in the same way like in a distributed GP. As generations proceed, some individuals are expected to perform specialized tasks for different

Table 1. GP Terminals and Functions.

Name	#Args.	Description
Destination	0	The directional vector by which to move the agent toward its goal.
Last	0	The last vector of the GP output for the agent. If this is the first move, then returns a zero vector.
Nearest_Agent	0	The directional vector by which to move the agent toward the nearest agent.
Rand	0	A random vector.
+	2	Add two vectors.
−	2	Subtract two vectors.
*2	1	Multiply the magnitude of a vector by 2.
/2	1	Divide a vector by 2.
<-45	1	Rotate a vector counterclockwise 45 degrees.
->45	1	Rotate a vector clockwise 45 degrees.
inv	1	Invert a vector, i.e., if the input is v, then return $-v$.
if_dot	4	If their dot product is greater than 0, then evaluate and return the third argument, else evaluate and return the fourth argument.
if_lte	4	If the magnitude of the first argument is greater than the magnitude of the second argument, then evaluate and return the third argument, else evaluate and return the fourth argument.
if_right	5	If the first argument is in the right side to the second argument, then evaluate the third argument. Else if the first is in the left side to the second, then evaluate the fourth. Else evaluate the fifth argument.
if_crash_wall	2	If the agent bumped into the wall in the last motion, then evaluate the first argument, else evaluate the second argument.
if_crash_agent	2	If the agent bumped into another agent in the last motion, then evaluate the first argument, else evaluate the second argument.
if_obstacle	3	If there exists a wall between the agent and the destination, then evaluate the first argument, Else if there is another agent between them, then evaluate the second. Else evaluate the third argument.

agents. We evaluate the fitness of individuals in an agent-type subpopulation as follows: Initially, i.e., at the first generation, the other agents' programs are chosen randomly. At successive generations, we choose, as the other agents' program, the best programs evolved so far in the other agent-type subpopulations. In our previous papers [Iba96],[Iba98], we have empirically shown

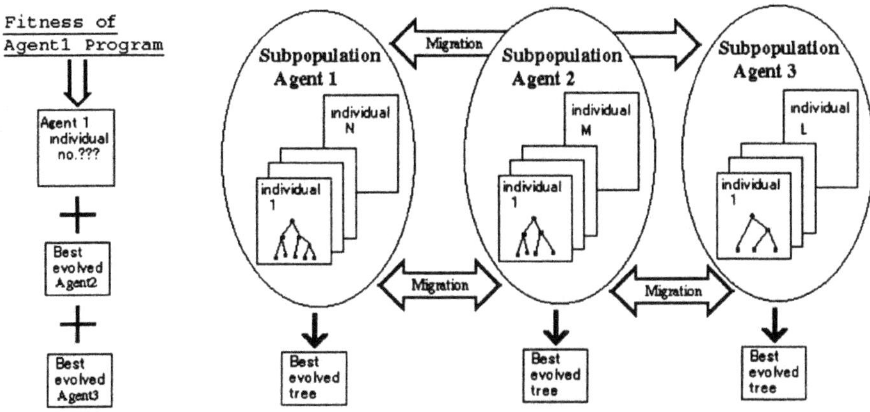

Fig. 2. Co-evolutionary Breeding for Multi-Agent Learning.

the superiority of the co-evolutionary breeding over the traditional strategies, such as the homogeneous breeding[1] and the heterogeneous breeding[2].

The primitive behaviors, such as avoiding obstacles or searching for the goal, are supposed to be common among different agents. These building blocks can be evolved jointly. Therefore, we allow the migration of elite individuals between the agent-type subpopulation. The migration is expected to promote the gene exchange and result in the further improvement of the performance, which will be seen in later experiments.

3 Controlling Effective Introns

Syntactic introns in a GP tree are program code segments that are not reached and non-executed. For instance, in the codes (if true A B) and (or true X), both B and X are not executed. [Soule *et al.*96] used a method of replacing a nested non-functional code by a non-operational code. Consider the following codes:

```
(if A B  (while A C D))
(if_lte A B (if_lte A B E F) G)
```

[1] In the homogeneous breeding strategy, all agents use the same program evolved by GP.

[2] Each agent uses a distinct program in the heterogeneous strategy.

where A, B, C, etc. are any (list of) statements. In the first code, the second argument of the "if" statement, i.e., (while A C D), is never executed, because it is only executed if A is false. In the second code, the statement F is never executed because the "if_lte" condition is satisfied only when A is less than or equal to B. However, it is not easy to check these introns syntactically. It is known to be reducible to the equivalence problem and non-recursive.

There is another type of introns. Consider the following code:

```
(if_obstacle A B C)
```

The statement A in the above code is never executed if the agent is in a room without any obstacles (see Table 1). Thus, the execution of these statements A, B and C is dependent upon the situation. We have often seen this type of introns appear in the evolved GP codes for the robot task.

We introduce the concept of "effective" introns, i.e., non-executed code segments upon the execution. For sake of identification, we attach an execution counter to each terminal or function symbol in a GP tree. This counter is put equal to zero at the outset of the execution. During the evaluation of the tree, the counter is incremented when its symbol is evaluated. For instance, consider the above-mentioned code segments again:

```
(if A[0] B[0] (while A[0] C[0] D[0]))
(if_lte A[0] B[0]
    (if_lte(A[0] B[0] E[0] F[0]) G[0])
```

where the number in the bracket represents the correspondent counter. After the evaluation, suppose that we get the following code with counters incremented:

```
(if A[30] B[30] (while A[0] C[0] D[0]))
(if_lte A[34] B[34]
   (if_lte A[34] B[34] E[34] F[0]) G[0])
```

The symbol whose counter remains zero is regarded as an effective intron, which can be removed by an edit operator. For instance, the statement (while A C D) in the first code and the symbols F and G in the second code can be removed. Note that the concept of effective introns subsumes that one of syntactic introns. Moreover, its definition is dependent upon the evaluating situation. For example, if the symbols A and B in the second code are evaluated dependently upon the situation, i.e., if in some cases A is greater than B or otherwise, then we will have the following results:

```
(if_lte A[34] B[34]
   (if_lte A[24] B[24] E[24] F[0]) G[10])
```

where A is greater than B in 24 cases over 34 cases. In this situation, G is not an intron.

[Smith *et al.*96] discussed the analysis of introns and gave a useful taxonomy of them. Effective introns in our paper correspond to their types 1, 2 and 4. We try to extend their previous researches and establish a controlling method of the above-mentioned effective introns. The next section describes experimental results to show the effectiveness of our approach.

		Controlling Effective Introns	
		×	○
Migration	×	10	23
	○	26	47

Table 2. Numbers of Successful Runs.

4 Experimental Results

This section explains the experimental results with the robot tasks described in Section 2. The chosen GP parameters are as follows: Population size = 512, Maximum generations = 50, and Tournament selection method.

4.1 Navigation Problem

We used six different maps for the training. Some of the training maps are shown in Fig.1(a) and (b). The initial positions of agents are changed in every generation for the training data. The fitness (F) is defined in the following way. In general, the faster the task is finished, the better, i.e., the smaller, the fitness is.

$$F := \begin{cases} 100.0 - 3 \times (\text{Remaining Times}) & \text{Success} \\ 300.0 + \sum_{i=1}^{\#\text{ agents}} \mathrm{D}(Loc_i, Dest_i) & \text{Failure} \end{cases} \quad (1)$$

The GP program of a robot agent is evaluated for a limited number of time steps, i.e., 40 to 50 time steps. If all agents have reached their destination during the evaluation, i.e., the task is completed, then the fitness is reduced with a bonus proportional to the remaining time steps. When the task has not been finished, the fitness is added with a penalty. The penalty is dependent upon the distance between the current agent location and its destination, i.e., $\mathrm{D}(Loc_i, Dest_i)$. The actual fitness of a GP program is the averaged value of the above fitness over all the training maps.

Fig.3(a) shows the experimental result, which plots the fitness values with generations. We compare four different types of GP runs, i.e., GP with/without controlling effective introns, and with/without the migration. The data are averaged over 50 runs. Note that the fitness value of 100.0 is considered as the task complete level. For standard GP runs, the final fitness value was about 140, which is well over the task complete level (see the line labeled as "normal"). In fact, in only ten cases over 50 runs, all four robots were evolved to reach their respective goals. On the other hand, if we controlled the effective introns, the better performance was obtained. When we used the migration as well, the performance was further improved. Table.2 compares the numbers of successful cases over 50 runs.

Fig.4 shows the example behavior of an evolved robot. As can be seen in the figure, some robots behaved in a different way from others. For instance,

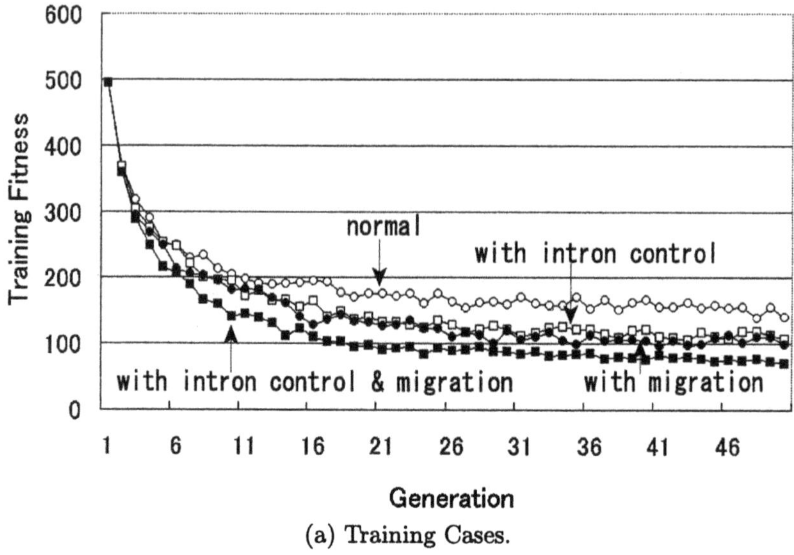

(a) Training Cases.

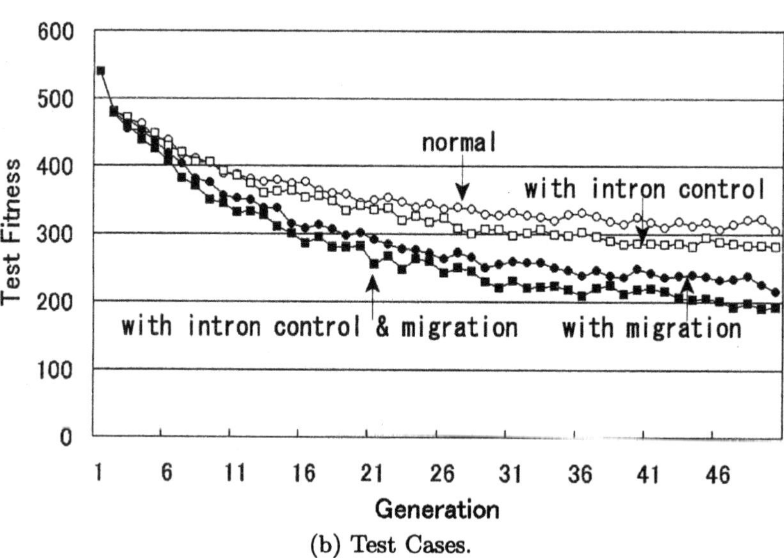

(b) Test Cases.

Fig. 3. Experimental Results (Generation vs. Fitness).

the robot agent marked as an arrow dashed to its goal, i.e., it never gave way even when it came across other agents. Another agent always gave way to other agents. Thus, we can observe that the appropriate job separation has been established for this navigation task.

Fig.5(a) shows the averaged sizes of the best programs with generations. Fig.5(b) plots the intron ratios. We can confirm that the effective introns

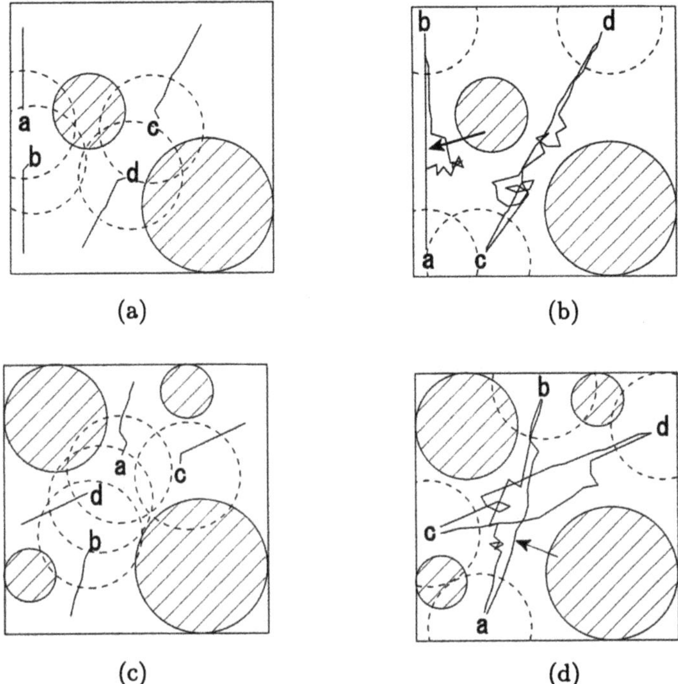

Fig. 4. Acquired Behaviors (Robot Navigation).

were successfully removed by the proposed method, which we believe leads to the above-mentioned improvement.

The robustness is an important feature of a program evolved by GP [Ito *et al.*96]. It is defined as the ability to cope with noisy or unknown situations. In the robot navigation, the robustness could be examined by testing an evolved program for another navigation task. In the pursuit of the robustness, we verified the validity of an evolved program for testing data, which were different from the training data. We used three testing maps. The initial 100 positions were randomly generated every time for sake of testing the generalization performance. Thus, 300 cases in total were tested for the validation. The result is shown in Fig.3(b). As can be seen from the figure, we can confirm the removing method of effective introns, in terms of the robustness.

4.2 Escape Problem

We used four different maps for the training. One of the training maps is shown in Fig.1(c), in which six robot agents are represented as a,b,c etc. The maximum speed of robots are ranked as $a = b < c = d < e = f$. That is, robots e and f move faster than the others. For this task, we introduced a special terminal for identifying the button, i.e., Nearest_Button. We

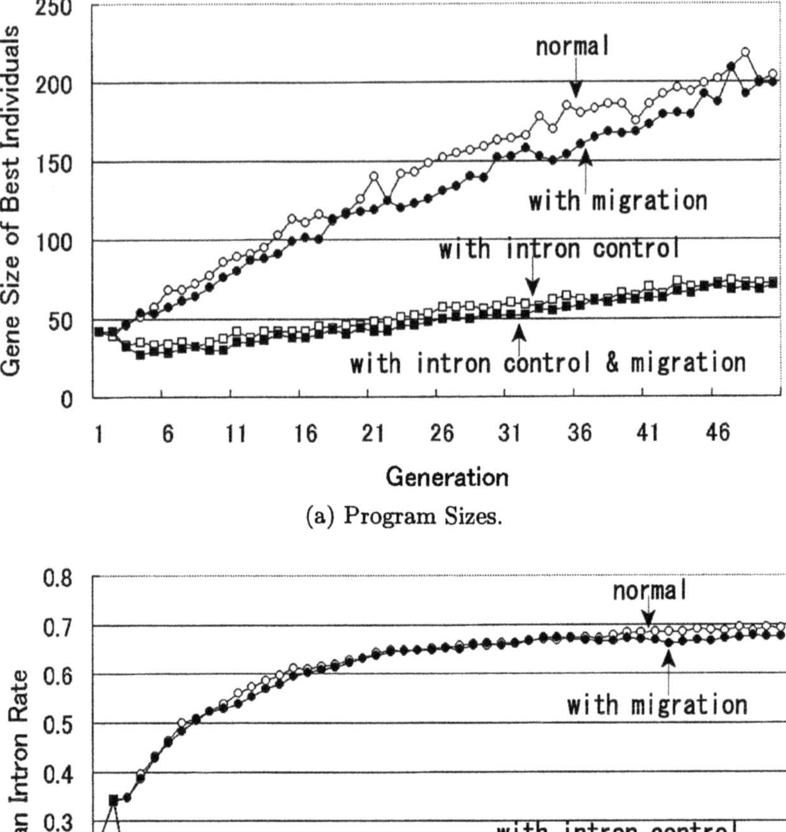

(a) Program Sizes.

(b) Intron Ratios.

Fig. 5. Program Sizes and Introns (Robot Navigation).

have again confirmed the effectiveness of controlling effective introns with this more complicated task (see Fig.6). Fig.7 shows the experimental results, i.e., the example behavior of acquired robot programs. We can observe that faster agents, i.e., e and f in Fig.7(a), bothered to push buttons in spite of being late. In another case, the nearest robots carried out the duty to push buttons (Fig.7(c)). In this way, robot agents have established an effective job separation dependent upon the situation.

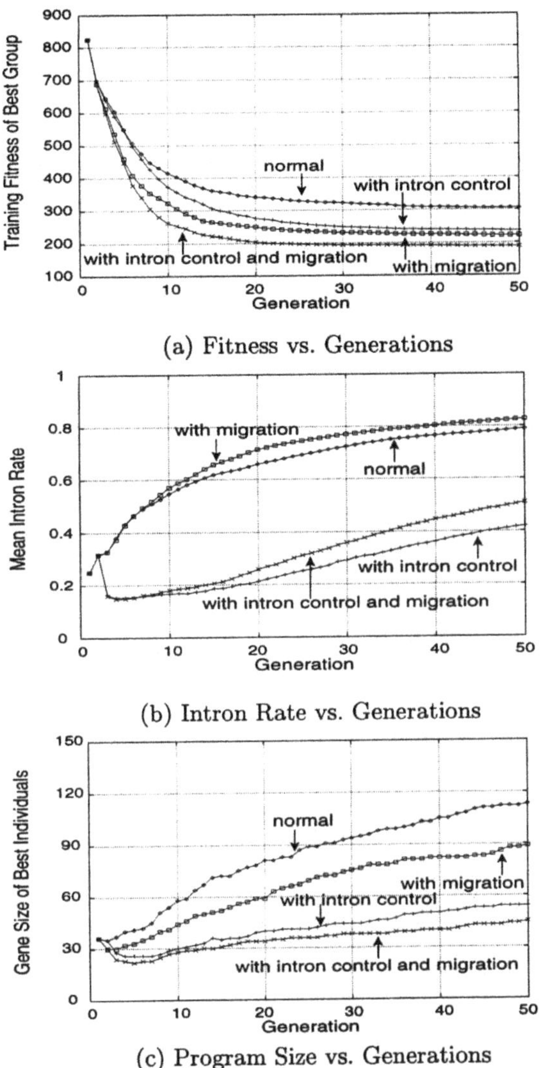

(a) Fitness vs. Generations

(b) Intron Rate vs. Generations

(c) Program Size vs. Generations

Fig. 6. Experimental Results (Escape Problem).

Fig.5(a) shows the averaged sizes of the best programs with generations. Fig.5(b) plots the intron ratios. We can confirm that the effective introns were successfully removed by the proposed method, which, we believe, leads to the above-mentioned improvement.

5 Discussion

In [Angeline98], it was noted that the intron emerged spontaneously from the process of GP evolution and that this emergent property was important for

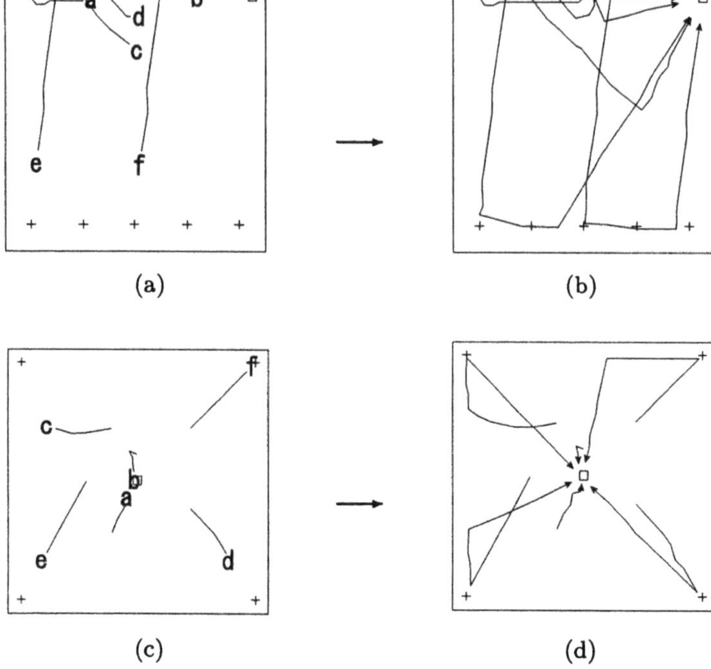

Fig. 7. Example Behaviors (Escape Problem).

successful evolution. There are pros and cons to the emergence of GP introns (see [EC98] and [Banzhaf *et al.*98] for details). During the early and middle part of a run, introns may have beneficial effects so that good building blocks will be able to protect themselves against the damaging effects of crossover. On the other hand, the exponential growth of introns (i.e., bloat) at the end of the run is probably deleterious.

Our experimental results have shown that it is beneficial to remove the introns even at the earlier stage. There was no significant performance difference between (a) the runs with removing introns at each generation and (b) those ones with introns removed in several generations. Moreover, when the introns were removed only in successive generations, the performance was made worse than any other runs. Therefore, we think that the removal of effective introns as often as possible will lead to the success of the multi-agent learning.

The common method for controlling the tree growth in GP is to use the parsimony pressure, i.e., GP individuals are subjected to the selective pressure against length [Soule *et al.*96]. We have conducted comparative experiments with this method for the above navigation task. The used parsimony factor is 0.5, i.e., the fitness is added by the penalty of $0.5 \times$ Tree Size. The experimental results showed that the fitness improvement by the selective pressure was satisfactory at earlier generations, but that the raw fitness value was about 130 at the final generation, which is better than normal GP, i.e., 140 but worse than GP with controlling effective introns, i.e., 107 (see Fig.8(a)). The number of successful runs was 9 over 50 cases. The robustness for testing data was just good like in the normal GP. The averaged size of acquired trees was significantly smaller by the selective pressure (see Figs.8(b) and (c)). We have obtained similar results with other parsimony factors. Strictly speaking, the parsimony pressure, although generates smaller trees, sometimes is able to control the functional codes, i.e. the non-intron parts of the program, and this motivates partially the fact that it does not evolve towards a better solution.

In this paper, we mainly described the method of removing syntactic introns. There is another type of introns, i.e., semantic introns [Angeline98], which are code segments that are executed but have no effect on the overall result. For instance, the codes (+ 0 a) and (not (not x)) include the semantic introns. These introns can be edited and replaced using a predefined template, such as "double not's" or "zero plus" [Koza 92]. Preliminary experiments have shown that editing semantic introns did not any harm or good to our multi-agent GP learning. This is partly due to the fact that these introns seldom occur in our task. We will investigate the role of these introns in our future research.

As future research, we have been applying our method to real-world robots. For instance, we have confirmed that our approach is applicable to the evolution on a real robot simulator, i.e., Webots2.0 (Fig.9(a)). The next step is to evolve real robots, such as Khepera teams (Fig.9(b)).

6 Conclusion

This paper proposed a controlling strategy of effective introns for multi-agent GP learning. Experimental results showed the effectiveness of our approach in the following points: (1) the fitness transition was improved for training, (2) the code growth was effectively reduced, and (3) the robustness of an acquired program was improved.

Our future topics concern the study of this problem on a real robot. We also plan to conduct an experiment in the difficult situations when the workspace is gradually changed with generations.

References

[EC98] Special Issue: Variable-Length Representation and Noncoding Segments for Evolutionary Algorithms, Evolutionary Computation, vol.6, no.4, MIT Press, 1998

[Angeline98] Angeline,P.J., Subtree Crossover Causes Bloat in Proc. of Genetic Programming Conference 1998 (GP98), 1998

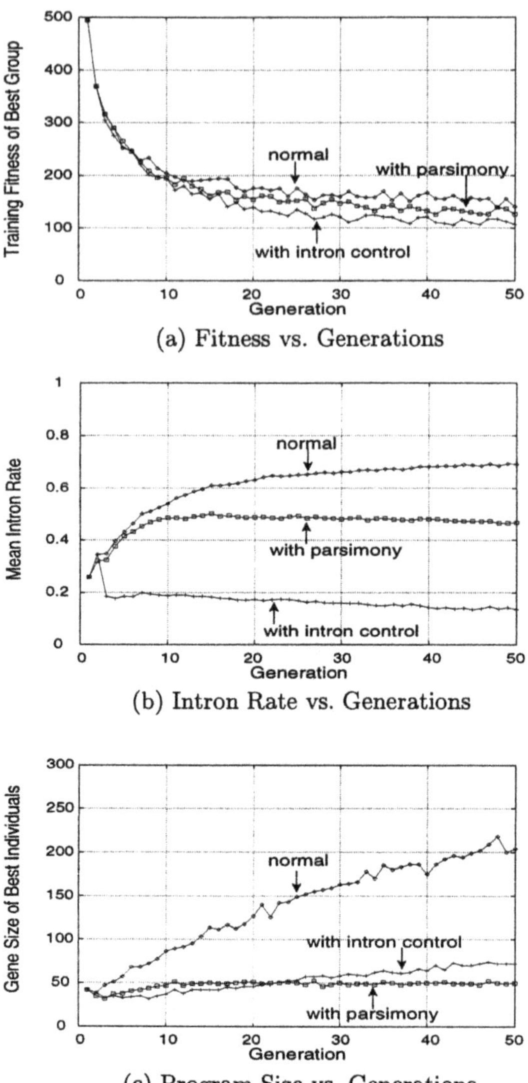

(a) Fitness vs. Generations

(b) Intron Rate vs. Generations

(c) Program Size vs. Generations

Fig. 8. Comparison with Penalty Pressure.

[Banzhaf *et al.*98] Banzhaf,W., Nordin,P., Keller,R.E., and Francone,F.D., Genetic Programming, An Introduction, Morgan Kaufmann, 1998

[Hara *et al.*99] Hara,A., and Nagao,T., Emergence of Cooperative Behavior using ADG; Automatically Defined Groups, in *Proc. of the Genetic and Evolutionary Computation Conference (GECCO99)*, Morgan Kaufmann, 1999

[Haynes *et al.*95] Haynes, T., Wainwright,R., and Sen,S., Evolving a Team, in *Working Notes of the AAAI-95 Fall Symposium on Genetic Programming*, AAAI Press, 1995

[Iba96] Iba,H., Emergent Cooperation for Multiple Agents using Genetic Programming, in *Parallel Problem Solving form Nature IV (PPSN96)*, 1996

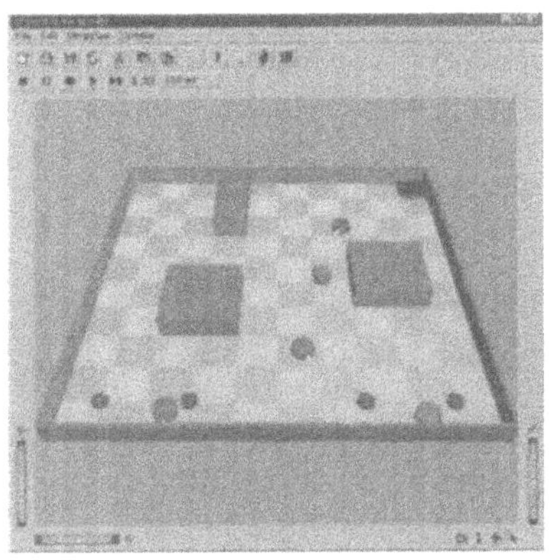

(a) Real Robot Simulation

(b) Khepera Robots Workspace

Fig. 9. Real-world Robot Application.

[Iba98] Iba,H., Evolutionary Learning of Communicating Agents, *Information Sciences*, 108(1-4), 1998

[Ito *et al.*96] Ito,T., Iba,H. and Kimura,M., Robot Programs Generated by Genetic Programming, Japan Advanced Institute of Science and Technology, IS-RR-96-0001I, in *Genetic Programming 96*, 1996

[Koza 92] Koza, J., Genetic Programming, On the Programming of Computers by means of Natural Selection, MIT Press, 1992

[Luke *et al.*96] Luke,S. and Spector,L., Evolving Teamwork and Coordination with Genetic Programming, in Genetic Programming 96, MIT Press, 1996

[Smith *et al.*96] Smith,P.W.H, and Harries,K., Code Growth, Explicitly Defined Introns, and Alternative Selection Schemes, in *Evolutionary Computation*, vol.6, no,4, MIT Press, 1999

[Soule *et al.*96] Soule,T., Foster,J.A., and Dickinson,J., Code Growth in Genetic Programming, in *Genetic Programming 96*, 1996

TalkMine: A Soft Computing Approach to Adaptive Knowledge Recommendation

Luis Mateus Rocha

Los Alamos National Laboratory, MS B256
Los Alamos, NM 87545, USA
e-mail: rocha@lanl.gov
www: http://www.c3.lanl.gov/ rocha

Abstract. We present a soft computing recommendation system named *TalkMine*, to advance adaptive web and digital library technology. *TalkMine* leads different databases or websites to learn new and adapt existing keywords to the categories recognized by its communities of users. It uses distributed artificial intelligence algorithms and soft computing technology. *TalkMine* is currently being implemented for the research library of the Los Alamos National Laboratory under the *Active Recommendation Project* (`http://arp.lanl.gov`).

TalkMine is based on the integration of distributed knowledge networks using Evidence Sets, an extension of fuzzy sets. The identification of the interests of users relies on a process of combining several fuzzy sets into evidence sets, which models an ambiguous "and/or" linguistic expression. The interest of users is further fine-tuned by a human-machine conversation algorithm used for uncertainty reduction. Documents are retrieved according to the inferred user interests. Finally, the retrieval behavior of all users of the system is employed to adapt the knowledge bases of queried information resources. This adaptation allows information resources to respond well to the evolving expectations of users.

In this article the distributed architecture of *TalkMine* is presented together with a description of its implementation in the Active Recommendation Project. In particular, the characterization of information resources as interacting distributed memory banks is presented. Evidence sets and the operations to produce them from several fuzzy sets are detailed. The conversation and adaptation algorithms used by TalkMine to interact automatically with users is described.

Keywords: Recommendation Systems, Information Retrieval, Web-related technologies, Fuzzy Set Theory, Evidence Sets, Measures of Uncertainty, Collaborative Systems, Adaptive Systems, Distributed Artificial Intelligence, Human-machine Interaction, Communities of Agents, Knowledge Representation, Soft Computing.

1 Towards Adaptive Web-Technology Using Soft Computing

1.1 Distributed Information Systems and Information Retrieval

Distributed Information Systems (DIS) are collections of electronic networked *information resources* (e.g. databases) in some kind of interaction with communities of users; examples of such systems are: the Internet, the World Wide Web, corporate intranets, databases, library information retrieval systems, etc. DIS serve large and diverse communities of users by providing access to a large set of heterogeneous electronic information resources. *Information Retrieval* (IR) refers to all the methods and processes for searching relevant information out of information systems (isolated or part of DIS) that contain extremely large numbers of documents. As the complexity and size of both user communities and information resources grows, the fundamental limitations of traditional information retrieval systems have become evident in modern DIS.

Traditional IR systems are based solely on *keywords* that index (semantically characterize) documents and a query language to retrieve documents from centralized databases according to these keywords users need to know how to "pull" relevant information from passive databases. This setup leads to a number of flaws (Rocha and Bollen, 2000), which prevent traditional IR processes in DIS to achieve any kind of interesting coupling with users. The human-machine interaction observed in these systems is particularly rigid: Most cannot pro-actively "push" relevant information to its users about related topics that they may be unaware of, there is typically no mechanism to exchange knowledge, or crossover of relevant information among users and information resources, and there is no mechanism to recombine knowledge in different information resources to infer new linguistic categories of keywords used by evolving communities of users. In other words, traditional IR keeps DIS as static, passive, and isolated repositories of data; no interesting human-machine co-evolution of knowledge or learning is achieved.

1.2 Enabling Evolving DIS with Soft Computing

The limitations of traditional IR and DIS are even more dramatic when contrasted with biological distributed systems such as immune, neural, insect, and social networks. Biological networks function largely in a distributed manner, without recourse to central controllers, while achieving tremendous ability to respond in concerted ways to different environmental necessities. In particular, they are typically endowed with the ability to elicit appropriate responses to specific demands, to transfer and process relevant information across the network, and to adapt to a changing environment by creating novel behaviors (often from recombination of existing ones). These abilities are precisely what has been lacking in IR. Biological networks effectively evolve in an open-ended manner; we are interested in endowing DIS with a similar open-ended capacity to evolve with their users to achieve an open-ended semiosis with them (Rocha, 2000). In biology, open-ended evolution originates from the existence of material building blocks that self-organize non-linearly (e.g. Kauffman, 1993) and are combined via a specification control, such as the genetic system (Rocha, 1998). In contrast, computer systems were constructed precisely with rigid building blocks constrained in such a way as to allow minimum dynamic self-organization and maximum programmability, which results in no inherent evolvability (Conrad, 1990). Therefore, to attain any evolvability in current digital computer systems, we need to program in some "softer" building blocks that can be used to realize the kind of dynamical richness we encounter in biological systems (Rocha and Bollen, 2000).

The ultimate goal of IR is to produce or recommend relevant information to users. It seems obvious that the foundation of any useful recommendation should be first and foremost based on the identification of users and subject matter. In this sense, the goal of recommendation systems can be seen as similar to that of most biological systems, in particular immune systems: to recognize agents (users) and elicit appropriate responses from components of the distributed information network. Furthermore, the information network should learn and adapt to the community of agents (users) it interacts with its environment.

Nevertheless, traditional IR does not identify users and classifies subjects only with unchanging keywords and categories. To build more flexible IR and evolving DIS, we need to design recommendation systems endowed with:

1. A means to recognize *users.*
2. A means to characterize *information resources.*
3. A 2-way means to exchange knowledge between users and information resources: a *conversation* process. As information resources become more and more complex, we cannot expect a simple 1-way query ("pull") to work well. Instead, we need a means to integrate the interests of the user with the knowledge specific to each information resource via an interactive recommendation process ("push").
4. *Adaptation* mechanisms. We also want DIS to adapt to their community of users, as well as to exchange and re-combine knowledge leading to evolvability and creativity.

Below I describe efforts to include these design requirements for recommendation systems using Soft Computing technology. I also discuss how a useful and more natural knowledge management of DIS is achieved with these soft computing designs. Let us start with some background on IR and recommendation systems.

1.3 From IR to Active Recommendation: From "Pull" to "Push"

New approaches to IR have been proposed to improve its inflexible algorithms. *Active recommendation systems*, also known as *Active Collaborative Filtering* (Chislenko, 1998) or *Knowledge Self-Organization* (Johnson et al, 1998) are IR systems which rely on active computational environments that interact with and adapt to their users. They effectively "push" relevant information to users according to previous patterns of IR or individual user profiling.

Recommendation systems are typically based on human-machine interaction mediated by intelligent agents, or other decentralized components, and come in several varieties:

1. In *content-based* recommendation, user profiles are created based on the system's keywords. Documents are recommended to users according to the similarity of their profiles and the similarity of keywords constructed from a semantic distance function obtained from the associations between keywords and documents. Two documents are close when they are classified by many of the same keywords. This is the case of systems such as *InfoFinder* (Krulwich and Burkey, 1996), *NewsWeeder* (Lang, 1995), and many systems developed for the routing task at the TREC Conferences (Harman, 1994).
2. In *collaborative* recommendation no description of the semantics or content of documents is involved, rather recommendations are issued according to a comparison of the profiles of several users that tend to access the same documents. The comparison depends on a distance function between user profiles, defined not by keywords, but on the sets of actual documents retrieved. Two user profiles are close when their users have retrieved many of the same documents. This is the case of systems such as *GroupLens* (Resnick et al, 1994; Kostan et al, 1997), *Bellcore Video Recommender* (Hill et al, 1995), *Ringo* (Shardanad and Maes, 1995). When user feedback is allowed, this type of recommendation is known as *Information Filtering* (Good et al, 1999). For a description of the collaborative recommendation framework see Herlocker et al (1999).
3. In *structural* recommendation, data-mining techniques are employed on the relations among documents and keywords, to discover related documents or documents of particular importance (authorities) in a given information resource. A large portion of work in this area, is concerned with the analysis of the graph structure of Web Hyperlinks (regardless of document keywords), e.g. work pursued under the *CLEVER* Project (Kleinberg, 1998; Chakrabarti et al, 1999), or other graph-theoretic approaches such as Watts' (1999) Small World graphs. A second large area of research is concerned with the semantic relations between documents and keywords, which are analyzed with algebraic techniques such as Singular Value Decomposition, known in IR as Latent Semantic Indexing (LSI) (Berry et al, 1994; Kannan and Vempala, 1999). Documents are recommended to users according to the way they are associated with other documents and/or keywords: the semantic structure of information resources.
4. In *collective* recommendation, the behavior of communities of users is integrated, and utilized to adapt the structure (the pattern of associations) of information resources. This kind of system tracks the paths users follow in the structure of information resources as they retrieve documents. The more certain sets of documents tend to be retrieved together in paths

followed by different users, the closer they become in the structure of the information resource. This type of algorithm employs the distributed behavior of a collection of users to adapt DIS, resulting in systems that learn the interests of their communities of users much in the same way as social insects discover paths based on the pheromone trails left behind by other insects in their colony (Rocha and Bollen, 2000), thus, in time, recommending more and more appropriate documents. This is the case of Adaptive Hypertext systems (Brusilovsky et al, 1998; Bollen and Heylighen, 1998; Eklund, 1998), Knowledge Self-Organization (Johnson et al, 1998; Heylighen, 1999), as well as the work on the collective discovery of linguistic categories (Rocha, 1997a, 2000) detailed below.

Content-based systems depend on single user profiles, and thus cannot effectively recommend documents about previously unrequested content to a specific user. That is, these systems cannot compare and recommend related documents characterized by keywords not previously collected into a given user's profile. Conversely, pure collaborative systems, match only the profiles of users that (to a great extent) have requested exactly the same documents; for instance, different book editions or movie review web sites from different news organizations may be considered distinct documents.

The shortcoming of structural approaches is that they assume that the existing, often static, structure of an information resource contains all the relevant knowledge to be discovered. However, it is often the case that such structure is very poorly designed. On the web in particular, the hypertext links are often not created between important documents, due perhaps to the hurried way in which web sites are created. Indeed, the Web is often more a repository of isolated documents, than a good example of a hypertext fabric. The same applies to the keyword/document relations necessary for LSI.

Collective approaches have the important advantage of adapting to the collective behavior of users, even as it develops in time. This way, a poor initial structure can improve, by creating, strengthening or weakening associations among documents or between documents and keywords. Furthermore, collective recommendation systems can operate without storing individual profiles, thus offering a more private platform for recommendation. Indeed, recommendations are issued according to the adapted structure of the information resources, not according to user profiles. Users can be seen as anonymous social agents. Furthermore, as we shall discuss later, the adapted information resources allow us to capture the knowledge traded by a community of agents. Nonetheless, a disadvantage of collective approaches is that they implement a positive feedback with their communities of users, possibly leading to an excessive adaptation to the interests of a majority of users, thus reducing the diversity of knowledge by recommending only the most retrieved documents in a given area: e.g. the "best of" lists found at Web sites such as *Amazon.com* this is the so-called "curse of averages".

It is clear that good recommendation systems require aspects of all approaches to avoid the shortcomings of each individual one. This is the case, for instance, of *Fab* (Balabanovi and Shoham, 1997) and *Amalthaea* (Moukas and Maes, 1998), which are both content and collaborative recommendation systems. This way they can discover similar users who have not simply retrieved many of the same exact documents, but documents characterized by many of the same keywords. Furthermore, keywords from documents that users have not actually retrieved, may be added to their profiles because they belong to the profiles of other similar users.

Still, neither *Fab* nor *Amalthaea* (nor similar systems) adapt the structure of their information resources with collective user behavior, nor do they use the data-mining techniques of structural algorithms to characterize the knowledge those store. In this sense, they cannot capture the evolving nature of the knowledge of communities of users. In other words, even though they are able to characterize the interests of individual users (both with documents and keywords), the structure of information resources (e.g. Web hyperlink structure or document/keyword matrix) remains unchanged. Furthermore, they rely on individual user profiles, and there is also not an explicit means to discover the knowledge categories that particular communities of users employ. Next I describe the Active Recommendation Project (Rocha and Bollen, 2000) which is building a hybrid Collective/Structural/Content recommendation system designed precisely to tackle these issues. Namely, to adapt information resources to their evolving communities of users, to characterize the knowledge stored in these information resources, and to preserve diversity while not accumulating private user profiles.

2 The Active Recommendation Project

The *Active Recommendation Project*[1] (ARP), part of the Library Without Walls Project, at the Research Library of the Los Alamos National Laboratory is engaged in research and development of recommendation systems for digital libraries. The *information resources* available to ARP are large databases with academic articles. These databases contain bibliographic, citation, and sometimes abstract information about academic articles. Typical databases are *SciSearch©* and *Biosis©*; the first contains articles from scientific journals from several fields collected by ISI (Institute for Scientific Indexing), while the second contains more biologically oriented publications. We do not manipulate directly the records stored in these information resources, rather, we created a repository of XML (about 3 million) records which point us to documents stored in these databases (Rocha and Bollen (2000).

[1] At http://www.c3.lanl.gov/~rocha/lww more information, results, and testbed are available.

2.1 Characterizing the Knowledge Stored in an Information Resource

We have compiled relational information between records[2] and keywords and among records: the *semantics* and the *structure* respectively. The semantics is formalized as a very sparse *Keyword-Record Matrix A*. The structure is formalized as the very sparse *Citation Matrix C*, which is a record-record matrix (details in Rocha and Bollen, 2000). From these matrices, we have calculated additional matrices holding measures of closeness between records and between keywords: the *Inwards Structural Proximity Matrix* or co-citation (Small, 1973), the *Outwards Structural Proximity Matrix* or bibliographic coupling (Kessler, 1963), the *Record Semantic Proximity Matrix* (for any two records it is defined by the number of keywords that qualify both, divided by the number of keywords that qualify either one), and the *Keyword Semantic Proximity Matrix* (for two keywords, it is the number of records they both qualify, over the number of records either one qualifies).

These matrices holding measures of closeness, formally, are proximity relations (Klir and Yuan, 1995; Miyamoto, 1990) because they are reflexive and symmetric fuzzy relations. Their transitive closures are known as similarity relations (Ibid). The collection of this relational information, all the proximity relations as well as A and C, is an expression of the particular knowledge an information resource conveys to its community of users. Notice that distinct information resources typically share a very large set of keywords and records. However, these are organized differently in each resource, leading to different collections of relational information. Indeed, each resource is tailored to a particular community of users, with a distinct history of utilization and deployment of information by its authors and users. For instance, the same keywords will be related differently for distinct resources. Therefore, we refer to the relational information of each information resource as a *Knowledge Context*. We do not mean to imply that information resources possess cognitive abilities. Rather, we note that the way records are organized in information resources is an expression of the knowledge traded by its community of users. Records and keywords are only tokens of the knowledge that is ultimately expressed in the brains of users. A knowledge context simply mirrors some of the collective knowledge relations and distinctions shared by a community of users.

In (Rocha and Bollen, 2000) we have discussed how these proximity relations are used in ARP. However, the ARP recommendation system described in this article (TalkMine) requires only the Keyword Semantic Proximity (KSP) matrix, obtained from A by the following formula:

---

[2] Records contain bibliographical information about published documents. Records can be thought of as unique pointers to documents, thus, for the purposes of this article, the two terms are interchangeable.

Table 1. Keyword Semantic Proximity for 10 most frequent keywords

	cell	studi	system	express	protein	model	activ	human	rat	patient
cell	1.000	0.022	0.019	0.158	0.084	0.017	0.085	0.114	0.068	0.032
studi	0.022	1.000	0.029	0.013	0.017	0.028	0.020	0.020	0.020	0.037
system	0.019	0.029	1.000	0.020	0.017	0.046	0.022	0.014	0.021	0.014
express	0.158	0.013	0.020	1.000	0.126	0.011	0.071	0.103	0.078	0.020
protein	0.084	0.017	0.017	0.126	1.000	0.013	0.070	0.061	0.041	0.014
model	0.017	0.028	0.046	0.011	0.013	1.000	0.016	0.016	0.026	0.005
activ	0.085	0.020	0.022	0.071	0.070	0.016	1.000	0.058	0.053	0.021
human	0.114	0.020	0.014	0.103	0.061	0.016	0.058	1.000	0.029	0.021
rat	0.068	0.020	0.021	0.078	0.041	0.026	0.053	0.029	1.000	0.008
patient	0.032	0.037	0.014	0.020	0.014	0.005	0.021	0.021	0.008	1.000

$$KSP\left(k_i, k_j\right) =$$

$$= \frac{\sum\limits_{k=1}^{m} \left(a_{i,k} \wedge a_{j,k}\right)}{\sum\limits_{k=1}^{m} \left(a_{i,k} \vee a_{j,k}\right)} = \frac{N_{\cap}\left(k_i, k_j\right)}{N_{\cup}\left(k_i, k_j\right)} = \frac{N_{\cap}\left(k_i, k_j\right)}{N\left(k_i\right) + N\left(k_j\right) - N_{\cap}\left(k_i, k_j\right)} \tag{1}$$

The semantic proximity between two keywords, k_i and k_j, depends on the sets of records indexed by either keyword, and the intersection of these sets. $N\left(k_i\right)$ is the number of records keyword k_i indexes, and $N_{\cap}\left(k_i, k_j\right)$ the number of records both keywords index. This last quantity is the number of elements in the intersection of the sets of records that each keyword indexes. Thus, two keywords are near if they tend to index many of the same records. Table I presents the values of KSP for the 10 most common keywords in the ARP repository.

From the inverse of KSP we obtain a distance function between keywords:

$$d\left(k_i, k_j\right) = \frac{1}{KSP\left(k_i, k_j\right)} - 1 \tag{2}$$

d is a distance function because it is a nonnegative, symmetric real-valued function such that $d(k, k) = 0$. It is not an Euclidean metric because it may violate the triangle inequality: $d(k_1, k_2) \leq d(k_1, k_3) + d(k_3, k_2)$ for some keyword k_3. This means that the shortest distance between two keywords may not be the direct link but rather an indirect pathway. Such measures of distance are referred to as semi-metrics (Galvin and Shore, 1991).

2.2 Characterizing Users

Users interact with information resources by retrieving records. We use their retrieval behavior to adapt the respective knowledge contexts of these resources (stored in the proximity relations). But before discussing this interaction, we need to characterize and define the capabilities of users: our agents. The following capabilities are implemented in enhanced "browsers" distributed to users.

1. *Present interests* described by a set of keywords $\{k_1, \cdots, k_p\}$.
2. *History of Information Retrieval (IR).* This history is also organized as a knowledge context as described in 2.1, containing pointers to the records the user has previously accessed, the keywords associated with them, as well as the structure of this set of records. This way, we treat users themselves as information resources with their own specific knowledge contexts defined by their own proximity information.
3. *Communication Protocol.* Users need a 2-way means to communicate with other information resources in order to retrieve relevant information, and to send signals leading to adaptation in all parties involved in the exchange.

Regarding point 2, the history of IR, notice that the same user may query information resources with very distinct sets of interests. For example, one day a user may search databases as a biologist looking for scientific articles, and the next as a sports fan looking for game scores. Therefore, each enhanced browser allows users to define different "*personalities*", each one with its distinct history of IR defined by independent knowledge contexts with distinct proximity data (see Figure 1).

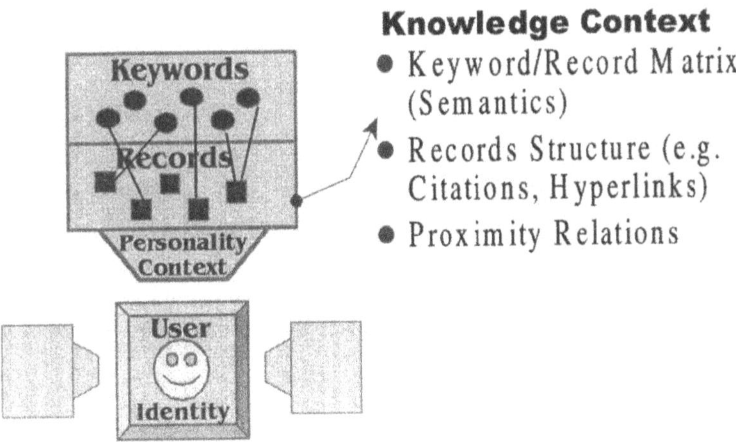

Fig. 1. Each user can have different personalities in enhanced browsers. Each personality is stored as a knowledge context created from previous history of IR. The actual identity of the user can remain private

Because the user history of IR is stored in personal browsers, information resources do not store user profiles. Furthermore, all the collective behavior algorithms used in ARP do not require the identity of users. When users communicate (3) with information resources, what needs to be exchanged is their present interests or query (1), and the relevant proximity data from their own knowledge context (2). In other words, users make a query, and then share the relevant knowledge they have accumulated about their query, their "world-view" or context, from a particular personality, without trading their identity. Next, the recommendation algorithms integrate the user's knowledge context with those of the queried information resources (possibly other users), resulting in appropriate recommendations. Indeed, the algorithms we use define a communication protocol between knowledge contexts, which can be very large databases, web sites, or other users. Thus, the overall architecture of the recommendation systems we use in ARP is highly distributed between information resources and all the users and their browsing personalities (see Figure 2).

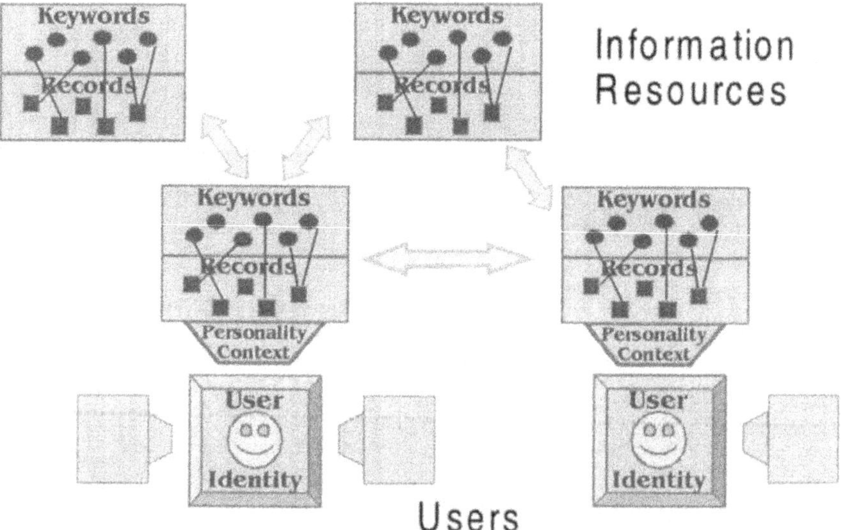

Fig. 2. The algorithms we use in ARP define a distributed architecture based on communication between knowledge contexts from information resources and users alike

The collective behavior of all users is also aggregated to adapt the knowledge contexts of all intervening information resources and users alike. This open-ended learning process (Rocha, 2000) is enabled by the *TalkMine* recommendation system described below.

3 Categories and Distributed Memory

3.1 A Model of Categorization from Distributed Artificial Intelligence

TalkMine is both a content-based and collaborative recommendation system based on a model of linguistic categories (Rocha, 1999), which are created from conversation between users and information resources and used to recombine knowledge as well as adapt it to users. The model of categorization used by *TalkMine* is described in detail in (Rocha, 1997a, 1999, 2000). Basically, as also suggested by Clark (1993), categories are seen as representations of highly transient, context-dependent knowledge arrangements, and not as model of information storage in the brain. In this sense, in human cognition, categories are seen as linguistic constructs used to store temporary associations built up from the integration of knowledge from several neural sub-networks. The categorization process, driven by language and conversation, serves to bridge together several distributed neural networks, associating tokens of knowledge that would not otherwise be associated in the individual networks. Thus, categorization is the chief mechanism to achieve knowledge recombination in distributed networks leading to the production of new knowledge (Rocha, 1999, 2000).

TalkMine applies such a model of categorization of distributed neural networks driven by language and conversation to DIS and recommendation systems. Instead of neural networks, knowledge is stored in information resources, from which we construct the knowledge contexts with respective proximity relations described in section 2. *TalkMine* is used as a conversation protocol to categorize the interests of users according to the knowledge stored in information resources, thus producing appropriate recommendations and adaptation signals.

3.2 Distributed Memory is Stored in Knowledge Contexts

A knowledge context of an information resource (section 2.1) is not a connectionist structure in a strong sense since keywords and records are not distributed as they can be identified in specific nodes of the network (van Gelder, 1991). However, the same keyword indexes many records, the same record is indexed by many keywords, and the same record is typically engaged in a citation (or hyperlink) relation with many other records. Losing or adding a few records or keywords does not significantly change the derived semantic and structural proximity relations (section 2) of a large network. In this sense, the knowledge conveyed by such proximity relations is distributed over the entire network of records and keywords in a highly redundant manner, as required of sparse distributed memory models (Kanerva, 1988). Furthermore, Clark (1993) proposed that connectionist memory devices work by producing metrics that relate the knowledge they store. As discussed in section 2, the distance functions obtained from proximity relations are semi-metrics, which follow all of Clark's requirements (Rocha, 2000). Therefore, we can regard a knowledge context effectively as a distributed memory bank. Below we discuss how such distributed knowledge adapts to communities of users (the environment) with Hebbian type learning.

In the *TalkMine* system we use the KSP relation (formula (1)) from knowledge contexts. It conveys the knowledge stored in an information resource in terms of a measure of proximity among keywords. This proximity relation is unique to each information resource, reflecting the semantic relationships of the records stored in the latter, which in turn echo the knowledge of its community of users and authors. *TalkMine* is a content-based recommendation system because it uses a keywords proximity relation. Next we describe how it is also collaborative by integrating the behavior of users. A related structural algorithm, also being developed in ARP, is described in (Rocha and Bollen, 2000).

4 Evidence Sets: Capturing the Linguistic "And/Or" in Users' Queries

4.1 Evidence Sets Model Categories

TalkMine uses a set structure named *evidence set* (Rocha 1994, 1997a, 1997b, 1999), an extension of a fuzzy set (Zadeh, 1965), to model of linguistic categories. The extension of fuzzy sets is based on the Dempster-Shafer Theory of Evidence (DST) (Shafer, 1976), which is defined in terms of a set function $m : \mathcal{P}(X) \to [0,1]$, referred to as a *basic probability assignment*, such that $m(\emptyset) = 0$ and $\sum_{A \subseteq X} m(A) = 1$. $\mathcal{P}(X)$ denotes the power set of X, and A any subset of X. The value $m(A)$ denotes the proportion of all available evidence which supports the claim that $A \in \mathcal{P}(X)$ contains the actual value of a variable x. DST is based on a pair of nonadditive measures: *belief* (Bel) and *plausibility* (Pl) uniquely obtained from m. Given a basic probability assignment m, Bel and Pl are determined for all $A \in \mathcal{P}(X)$ by the equations:

$$Bel(A) = \sum_{B \subseteq A} m(B),$$

$$Pl(A) = \sum_{B \cap A \neq \emptyset} m(B)$$

the expressions above imply that belief and plausibility are dual measures related by:$Pl(A) = 1 - Bel(\overline{A})$, for all $A \in \mathcal{P}(X)$, where $\overline{A}$ represents the complement of A in X. It is also true that $Bel(A) \leq Pl(A)$ for all $A \in \mathcal{P}(X)$. Notice that "$m(A)$ measures the belief one commits exactly to A, not the total belief that one commits to A." (Shafer, 1976, page 38) $Bel(A)$, the total belief committed to A, is instead given by the sum of all the values of m for all subsets of A.

Any set $A \in \mathcal{P}(X)$ with $m(A) > 0$ is called a *focal element.* A *body of evidence* is defined by the pair $(\mathcal{F}, m)$, where $\mathcal{F}$ represents the set of all focal elements in X, and m the associated basic probability assignment. The set of all bodies of evidence is denoted by $\mathcal{B}(X)$.

An evidence set A of X, is defined for all $x \in X$, by a membership function of the form:

$$A(x) \rightarrow (\mathcal{F}^x, m^x) \in \mathcal{B}\,[0,1]$$

where $\mathcal{B}[0,1]$ is the set of all possible bodies of evidence $(\mathcal{F}^x, m^x)$ on $\mathcal{I}$, the set of all subintervals of $[0,1]$. Such bodies of evidence are defined by a basic probability assignment m^x on $\mathcal{I}$, for every x in X. Thus, evidence sets are set structures which provide interval degrees of membership, weighted by the probability constraint of DST. They are defined by two complementary dimensions: membership and belief. The first represents an interval (type-2) fuzzy degree of membership, and the second a subjective degree of belief on that membership (see Figure 3).

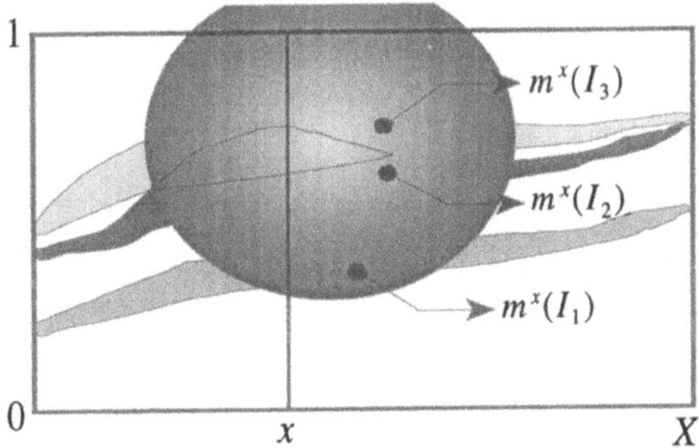

Fig. 3. Evidence set with 3 focal elements for each x

Each interval of membership I_j^x, with its correspondent evidential weight $m^x(I_j^x)$, represents the degree of importance of a particular element x of X in category A *according* to a particular *perspective.* Thus, the membership of each element x of an evidence set A is defined by distinct intervals representing different, possibly conflicting, perspectives. This way, categories are modeled not only as sets of elements with a membership degree (or prototypicality Rocha(1999)), but as sets of elements which may possess different interval membership degrees for different contexts or perspectives on the category.

The basic set operations of complementation, intersection, and union have been defined and establish a belief-constrained approximate reasoning theory of which fuzzy approximate reasoning and traditional set operations are special cases (Rocha 1997a, 1999). Intersection (Union) is based on the minimum (maximum) operator for the limits of each of the intervals of membership of an evidence set. For the purposes of this article, the details of these operations are not required, please consult (Rocha, 1999) for more details.

4.2 The Uncertainty Content of Evidence Sets

Evidence sets are set structures which provide interval degrees of membership, weighted by the probability constraint of DST. Interval Valued Fuzzy Sets (IVFS), fuzzy sets, and crisp sets are all special cases of evidence sets. The membership of an element x in a crisp set is perfectly certain: the element is either a member of the set or not. The membership of an element x in fuzzy set is defined as degree value in the unit interval; this means that the membership is *fuzzy* because the element is a member of the set with degree $A(x)$, and *simultaneously*, is also not a member with complementary degree $1 - A(x)$. The membership of an element x in an IVFS is defined as an interval I contained in the unit interval; this means that the membership is both fuzzy and *nonspecific* (Rocha, 1994, Turksen, 1996), because the element is a member of the set with a nonspecific degree that can vary in the interval I. Finally, membership of an element x in an evidence set is defined as a set of intervals constrained by a probability restriction; this means that the membership is fuzzy, nonspecific, and *conflicting*, since the element is a member of the set with several degrees that vary in each interval with some probability.

To capture the uncertainty content of evidence sets, the uncertainty measures of Klir (1993) were extended from finite to infinite domains (Rocha, 1997b). The total uncertainty, U, of an evidence set A was defined by: $U(A) = (IF(A), IN(A), IS(A))$. The three indices of uncertainty, which vary between 1 and 0, IF (*fuzziness*), IN (*nonspecificity*), and IS (*conflict*) were introduced in (Rocha, 1997a, 1997b), where it was also proven that IN and IS possess good axiomatic properties wanted of information measures. IF is based on Yeager's (1979, 1980) and Klir and Yuan (1995) measure of fuzziness. IN is based on the Hartley measure (Rocha, 1997b), and IS on the Shannon entropy as extended by Klir (1993) into the DST framework. For the purposes of this article, all we need to know is that these measures vary in the unit interval, for full details see (Rocha, 1997b).

4.3 Obtaining an Evidence Set from Fuzzy Sets: The Linguistic "And/Or"

Fundamental to the *TalkMine* algorithm is the integration of information from different sources into an evidence set, representing the category of topics (described by keywords) a user is interested at a particular time. In particular, as described below, these sources of information contribute information as fuzzy sets. This way, we need a procedure for integrating several fuzzy sets into an evidence set.

Turksen (1986) proposed a means to integrate fuzzy sets into IVFS (or type-2 fuzzy sets). He later proposed that every time two fuzzy sets are combined, the uncertainty content of the resulting structure should be of a higher order, namely, the fuzziness of two fuzzy sets should be combined into the fuzziness and nonspecificity of an IVFS (Turksen, 1996). Turksen's Fuzzy Set combination is based on the separation of the disjunctive and conjunctive normal forms of logic compositions in fuzzy logic. A disjunctive normal form (DNF) is formed with the disjunction of some of the four primary conjunctions, and the conjunctive normal form (CNF) is formed with the conjunction of some of the four primary disjunctions, respectively: $A \cap B$, $A \cap \overline{B}$, $\overline{A} \cap B$, $\overline{A} \cap \overline{B}$ and $A \cup B$, $A \cup \overline{B}$, $\overline{A} \cup B$, $\overline{A} \cup \overline{B}$. In two-valued logic the CNF and DNF of a logic composition are equivalent: CNF = DNF. Turksen (1986) observed that in fuzzy logic, for certain families of conjugate pairs of conjunctions and disjunctions, we have instead DNF CNF for some of the fuzzy logic connectives. He proposed that fuzzy logic compositions could be represented by IVFS's given by the interval [DNF, CNF] of the fuzzy set connective chosen (Turksen, 1986). Using Turksen's approach, the union and intersection of two fuzzy sets F_1 and F_2 result in the two following IVFS, respectively:

$$IV^{\cup}(x) = \left[F_1(x) \bigcup_{DNF} F_2(x),\ F_1(x) \bigcup_{CNF} F_2(x) \right] \tag{3}$$

$$IV^{\cap}(x) = \left[F_1(x) \bigcap_{DNF} F_2(x),\ F_1(x) \bigcap_{CNF} F_2(x) \right] \tag{4}$$

where: $A \bigcup_{CNF} B = A \cup B$,
$A \bigcup_{DNF} B = (A \cap B) \cup (A \cap \overline{B}) \cup (\overline{A} \cap B)$,
$A \bigcap_{CNF} B = (A \cup B) \cap (A \cup \overline{B}) \cap (\overline{A} \cup B)$ and $A \bigcap_{DNF} B = A \cap B$,

for any two fuzzy sets A and B, with union and intersection operations chosen from the families of t-norms and t-conorms following the appropriate axiomatic requirements (Klir and Yuan, 1995). In *TalkMine* only the traditional maximum and minimum operators for union and intersection, respectively, are used. Clearly, all other t-norms and t-conorms would also work.

The intervals of membership obtained from the combination of two fuzzy sets can be interpreted as capturing the intrinsic nonspecificity of the combination of fuzzy sets with fuzzy set operators. Due to the introduction of fuzziness, the DNF and CNF do not always coincide. This lack of coincidence reflects precisely the nonspecificity inherent in fuzzy set theory: because we can arrive at different results depending on which normal form we choose, the combination of fuzzy sets is ambiguous. Turksen (1996) suggested that this ambiguity should be treated as nonspecificity and captured by intervals of membership. In this sense, fuzziness "breeds" nonspecificity. Figure 4 depicts the construction of two IVFS from two fuzzy sets F_1 and F_2 according to the procedure described by formulas (3).

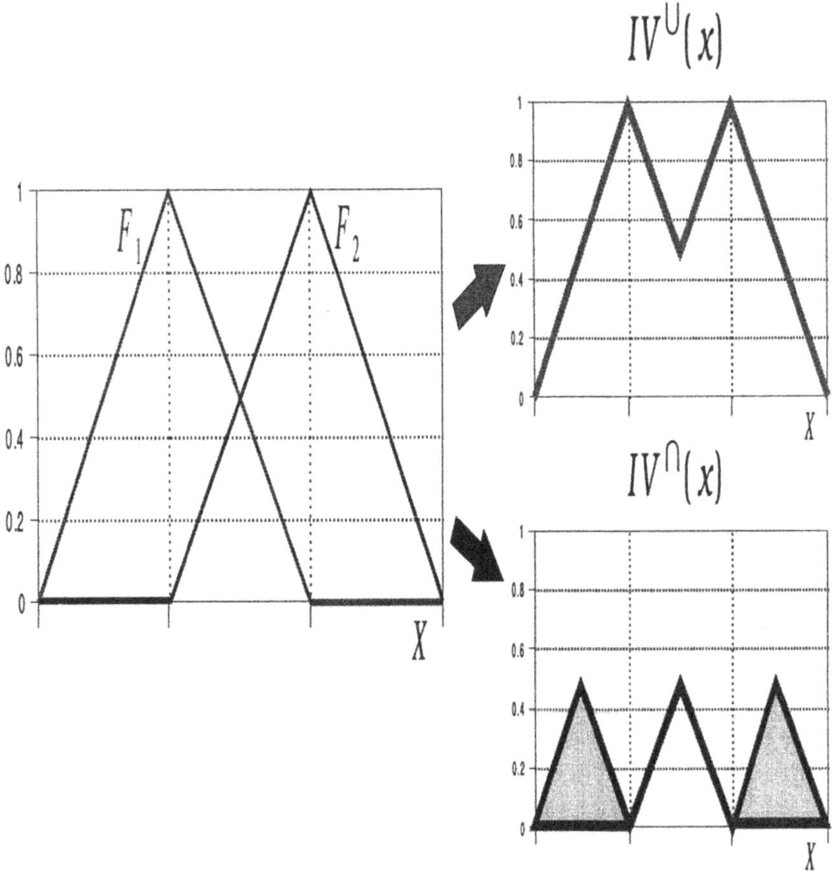

Fig. 4. Combination of two fuzzy sets F_1 and F_2 into IVFS according to formulae 3. The union IVFS $IV^{\cup}$ is a fuzzy set because DNF and CNF coincide, which does not happen for $IV^{\cap}$

Formulae (3) constitute a procedure for calculating the union and intersection IVFS from two fuzzy sets, which in logic terms refer to the "Or" and "And" operators. Thus, $IV^{\cup}$ describes the linguistic expression "F_1 or F_2", while IV describes "F_1 and F_2", capturing both fuzziness and nonspecificity of the particular fuzzy logic operators employed. However, in common language, often "and" is used as an unspecified "and/or". In other words, what we mean by the statement "I am interested in x and y", can actually be seen as an unspecified combination of "x and y" with "x or y". This is particularly relevant for recommendation systems where it is precisely this kind of statement from users that we wish to respond to.

One use of evidence sets is as representations of the integration of both $IV^{\cup}$ and $IV^{\cap}$ into a linguistic category that expresses this ambiguous "and/ or". To make this combination more general, assume that we possess an evidential weight m_1 and m_2 associated with each F_1 and F_2 respectively. These are probabilistic weights ($m_1 + m_2 = 1$) which represent the strength we associate with each fuzzy set being combined. The linguistic expression at stake now becomes "I am interested in x and y, but I value x more/less than y". To combine all this information into an evidence set we use the following procedure:

$$ES(x) = \{\langle IV^{\cup}(x), \min(m_1, m_2)\rangle, \langle IV^{\cap}(x), \max(m_1, m_2)\rangle\} \tag{5}$$

Because $IV^{\cup}$ is the less restrictive combination, obtained by applying the maximum operator, or suitable t-norm to the original fuzzy sets F_1 and F_2, its evidential weight is acquired via the minimum operator of the evidential weights associated with F_1 and F_2. The reverse is true for $IV^{\cap}$. Thus, the evidence set obtained from (4) contains $IV^{\cup}$ with the lowest evidence, and $IV^{\cap}$ with the highest. Linguistically, it describes the ambiguity of the "and/or" by giving the strongest belief weight to "and" and the weakest to "or". It expresses: "I am interested in x and y to a higher degree, but I am also interested in x or y to a lower degree". This introduces the third kind of uncertainty: conflict. Indeed, the ambiguity of "and/or" rests on the conflict between the interest in "and" and the interest in "or". This evidence set captures the three forms of uncertainty discussed in Section 3.3: fuzziness of the original fuzzy sets F_1 and F_2, nonspecificity of $IV^{\cup}$ and $IV^{\cap}$, and conflict between these two as they are included in the same evidence set with distinct evidential weights. Figure 5 depicts an example of the evidence set obtained from F_1 and F_2, as well as its uncertainty content (fuzziness. nonspecificity, and conflict).

Finally, formula (4) can be easily generalized for a combination of n fuzzy sets F_i with probability constrained weights m_i:

$$ES(x) = \left\{\left\langle IV^{\cup}_{F_i/F_j}(x), \frac{\min(m_i, m_j)}{n-1}\right\rangle, \left\langle IV^{\cap}_{F_i/F_j}(x), \frac{\max(m_i, m_j)}{n-1}\right\rangle\right\} \tag{6}$$

This procedure can be used to combine evidence in the form of fuzzy sets from n weighted sources. It produces intervals obtained from the combination

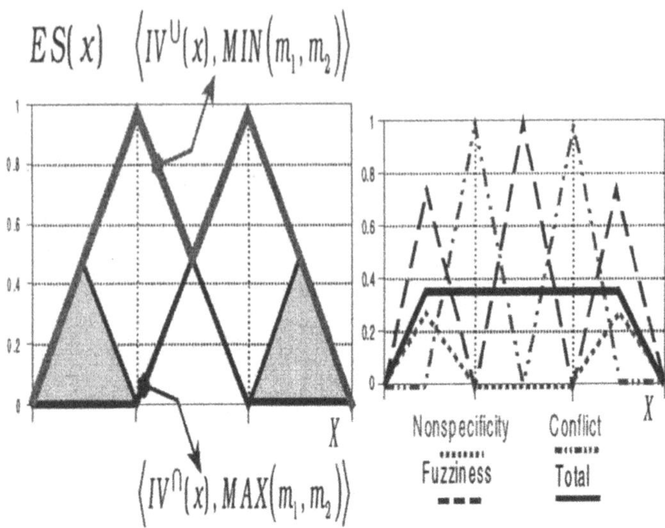

Fig. 5. Evidence set obtained from F_1 and F_2 and respective uncertainty content

of each pair of fuzzy sets with a union and an intersection operator. Intersection is given the highest weight. The evidence set obtained is the ambiguous, common language, "and/or" for n items.

5 *TalkMine*: Integrating Several Sources of Knowledge via Conversation

5.1 Inferring User Interest

The act of recommending appropriate documents to a particular user needs to be based on the integration of information from the user (with her history of retrieval) and from the several information resources being queried. With *TalkMine* in particular, we want to retrieve relevant documents from several information resources with different keyword indexing. Thus, the keywords the user employs in her search, need to be "decoded" into appropriate keywords for each information resource. Indeed, the goal of *TalkMine* is to project the user interests into the distinct knowledge contexts of each information resource, creating a representation of these interests that can capture the perspective of each one of these contexts.

Evidence Sets were precisely defined to model categories (knowledge representations) which can capture different perspectives. As described in Section 2.2, the present interests of each user are described by a set of keywords $\{k_1, \cdots, k_p\}$. Using these keywords and the keyword distance function (2) of the several knowledge contexts involved (one from the user and one from each information resource being queried), the interests of the user, "seen" from the perspectives of the several information resources, can be inferred as an evidence category using (5).

Let us assume that r information resources R_t are involved in addition to the user herself. The set of keywords contained in all the participating information resources is denoted by $\mathcal{K}$. As described in Section 2, each information resource is characterized as a knowledge context containing a KSP relation (1) among keywords from which a distance function d is obtained (cfr. (2)). d_0 is the distance function of the knowledge context of the user, while $d_1...d_r$ are the distance functions from the knowledge contexts of each of the information resources.

Spreading Interest Fuzzy Sets. For each information resource R_t and each keyword k_u in the user's present interests $\{k_1, \cdots, k_p\}$, a *spreading interest fuzzy set* $F_{t,u}$ is calculated using d_t:

$$F_{t,u}(k) = \max\left[e^{\left(-\alpha.d_t(k,k_u)^2\right)}, \varepsilon\right] \forall k \in R_t,\ t = 1\ldots r,\ u = 1\ldots p \quad (7)$$

This fuzzy set contains the keywords of R_t which are closer than to k_u , according to an exponential function of d_t. $F_{t,u}$ spreads the interest of the user in k_u to keywords of R_t that are near according to d_t. The parameter α controls the spread of the exponential function. $F_{t,u}$ represents the set of keywords of R_t which are near or very related to keyword k_u. Because the knowledge context of each R_t contains a different d_t, each $F_{t,u}$ will also be a different fuzzy set for the same k_u, possibly even containing keywords that do not exist in other information resources. There exist a total of $n = r.p$ spreading interest fuzzy sets $F_{t,u}$. Figure 6 depicts a generic $F_{t,u}$.

Combining the Perspectives of Different Knowledge Contexts on the User Interest. Assume now that the present interests of the user $\{k_1, \cdots, k_p\}$ are probabilistically constrained, that is, there is a probability weight associated with each keyword: $\mu_1, \ldots, \mu_p$, such that $\mu_1 + \ldots + \mu_p = 1$. Assume further that the intervening r information resources R_t are also probabilistically constrained with weights: $\nu_1, \ldots, \nu_p$, such that $\nu_1 + \ldots + \nu_p = 1$. Thus, the probabilistic weight of each spreading interest fuzzy set $F_i = F_{t,u}$, where $i = (t-1)p + u$, is $m_i = \nu_t.\mu_u$.

To combine the n fuzzy sets F_i and respective probabilistic weights m_i, formula (5) is employed. This results in an evidence set $ES(k)$ defined on $\mathcal{K}$, which represents the interests of the user inferred from spreading the initial interest set of keywords in the knowledge contexts of the intervening information resources. The inferring process combines each $F_{t,u}$ with the "and/or" linguistic expression entailed by formula (5). Each $F_{t,u}$ contains the keywords related to keyword k_u in the knowledge context of information resource R_t,

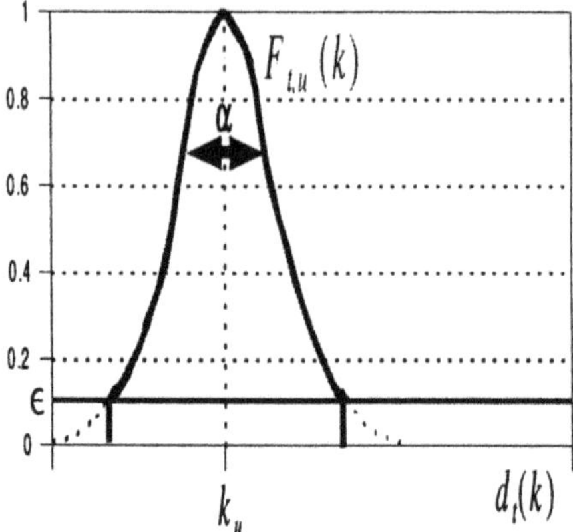

Fig. 6. The exponential membership function of $F_{t,u}(k)$ spreads the interest of a user on keyword k_u to close keywords according to distance function d_t(k) for each information resource R_t

that is, the perspective of R_t on k_u. Thus, $ES(k)$ contains the "and/or" combination of all the perspectives on each keyword $k_u \in \{k_1, \cdots, k_p\}$ from each knowledge context associated with all information resources R_t.

As an example, without loss of generality, consider that the initial interests of an user contain one single keyword k_1, and that the user is querying two distinct information resources R_1 and R_2. Two spreading interest fuzzy sets, F_1 and F_2, are generated using d_1 and d_2 respectively, with probabilistic weights $m_1 = \nu_1$ and $m_2 = \nu_2$. $ES(k)$ is easily obtained straight from formula (4). This evidence set contains the keywords related to k_1 in R_1 "and/or" the keywords related to k_2 in R_2, taking into account the probabilistic weights attributed to R_1 and R_2. F_1 is the perspective of R_1 on k_1 and F_2 the perspective of R_2 on k_1.

5.2 Reducing the Uncertainty of User Interests via Conversation

The evidence set obtained in Section 5.1 with formulas (5) and (6) is a first cut at detecting the interests of a user in a set of information resources. But we can compute a more accurate interest set of keywords using an interactive conversation process between the user and the information resources being queried. Such conversation is an uncertainty reducing process based on Nakamura and Iwai's (1987) IR system, and extended to Evidence Sets by Rocha (1999, 2000).

In addition to the evidence set $ES(k)$ constructed in Section 5.1, a fuzzy set $F_0(k)$ is constructed to contain the keywords of the knowledge context R_0 of the user which are close to the initial interest set $\{k_1, \cdots, k_p\}$ according to distance function d_0. As discussed in Section 2, the user's history of IR is itself characterized as a knowledge context R_0 with its own KSP relation and derived distance function d_0. $F_0(k)$ is given by:

$$F_0(k) = \bigcup_{u=1}^{p} F_{0,u}(k) \tag{8}$$

where $F_{0,u}(k)$ is calculated using formula (6). $F_0(k)$ represents the perspective of the user, from her history of retrieval, on all keywords $\{k_1, \cdots, k_p\}$. Given $ES(k)$ and $F_0(k)$, for a default value of $\alpha = \alpha_0$, the algorithm for *TalkMine* is as follows:

1. Calculate the uncertainty of $ES(k)$ in its forms of fuzziness, nonspecificity, and conflict (see Section 4.2). If total uncertainty is below a predefined small value the process stops, otherwise continue to 2.
2. The most uncertain keyword $k_j \in ES(k)$ is selected.
3. If $k_j \in R_0$, then goto 4 (AUTOMATIC), else goto 6 (ASK).
4. If $F_0(k_j) > 0.5 + \delta$, then goto 7 (YES).
5. If $F_0(k_j) \leq 0.5 - \delta$, then goto 8 (NO), else goto 6 (ASK).
6. ASK user if she is interested in keyword k_j. If answer is yes goto 7 (YES), else goto 8 (NO).
7. An evidence set $YES(k)$ is calculated using the procedure of section 5.1 for a single keyword k_j and all r information resources R_t. The spread of the exponential functions is controlled with parameter α so that answers to previous keywords k_j are preserved. $ES(k)$ is then recalculated as the evidence set union of $YES(k)$ and $ES(k)$ itself.
8. An evidence set $NO(k)$ is calculated as the complement of $YES(k)$ used in 7. $ES(k)$ is then recalculated as the evidence set intersection of $NO(k)$ and $ES(k)$ itself.
9. Goto 1.

The parameter δ controls how much participation is required from the user in this interactive process, and how much is automatically deduced from her own knowledge context used to produce $F_0(k)$. $\delta \in [0, 0.5]$; for $\delta = 0$, all interaction between user and information resources is mostly automatic, as answers are obtained from $F_0(k)$, except when $k_j \notin ES(k)$; for $\delta = 0.5$, all interaction between user and information resources requires explicit answers from the user. If the user chooses not to reply to a question, the answer is taken as NO. Thus, δ allows the user to choose how automatic the question-answering process of *TalkMine* is.

Regarding the change of spread employed in steps 7 and 8 for the construction of the $YES(k)$ and $NO(k)$ evidence sets. A list of the keywords the user (or $F_0(k)$ automatically) has responded YES or NO to is kept. The membership value of these keywords in the final $ES(k)$ produced must be 1 or 0, respectively. Thus, the union and intersections of $ES(k)$ with $YES(k)$ and $NO(k)$ in 7 and 8, must be defined in a such a way as to preserve these values. If the spread obtained with α_0 would alter the desired values, then a new α is employed in formula (6) so that the original values are preserved $\pm\varepsilon$. Because of this change of spreading inference of the $YES(k)$ and $NO(k)$ evidence sets, the sequence of keywords selected by the question-answering process in step 2 affects the final $ES(k)$. That is, the selection of a different keyword may result in a different $ES(k)$.

The final $ES(k)$ obtained with this algorithm is a much less uncertain representation of user interests as projected on the knowledge contexts of the information resources queried, than the initial evidence set obtained in Section 5.1. The conversation algorithm lets the user reduce the uncertainty from the all the perspectives initially available. The initial evidence set produced in Section 5.1 includes all associated keywords in several information resources. The conversation algorithm allows the user and her knowledge context to select only the relevant ones. Thus, the final $ES(k)$ can be seen as a low-uncertainty linguistic category containing those perspectives on the user's initial interest (obtained from the participating information resources) which are relevant to the user and her knowledge context (Rocha, 1999, 2000).

Notice that this category is not stored in any location in the intervening knowledge contexts. It is temporarily constructed by integration of knowledge from several information resources and the interests of the user expressed in the interactive conversational process. Such a category is therefore a temporary container of knowledge integrated from and relevant for the user and the collection of information resources. Thus, this algorithm implements many of the, temporary, "on the hoof" (Clark, 1993) category constructions as discussed in Rocha(2000).

5.3 Recommending Documents

After construction of the final $ES(k)$, *TalkMine* must return to the user documents relevant to this category. Notice that every document n_i defines a crisp subset whose elements are all the keywords $k \in \mathcal{K}$ which index n_i in all the constituent information resources. The similarity between this crisp subset and $ES(k)$ is a measure of the relevance of the document to the interests of the user as described by $ES(k)$. This similarity is defined by different ways of calculating the subsethood (Kosko, 1993) of one set in the other. Details of the actual operations used are presented in Rocha(1999). High values of these similarity measures will result on the system recommending only those documents highly related to the learned category $ES(k)$

5.4 Adapting Knowledge Contexts

From the many $ES(k)$ obtained from the set of users of information resources, we collect information used to adapt the KSP and semantic distance of the respective knowledge contexts. The scheme used to implement this adaptation is very simple: the more certain keywords are associated with each other, by often being simultaneously included with a high degree of membership in the final $ES(k)$, the more the semantic distance between them is reduced. Conversely, if certain keywords are not frequently associated with one another, the distance between them is increased. An easy way to achieve this is to have the values of $N(k_i)$, $N(k_j)$ and $N_\cap(k_i, k_j)$ as defined in formula (1), adaptively altered for each of the constituent r information resources R_t. After $ES(k)$ is constructed and approximated by a fuzzy set $A(x)$, these values are changed according to:

$$N^t(k_i) = N^t(k_i) + w.A(k_i), \; t = 1 \ldots r, \; k_i \in R_0 \cup R_1 \cup \ldots \cup R_r \tag{9}$$

and

$$\begin{aligned} &N_\cap^t(k_i, k_j) = \\ &= N_\cap^t(k_i, k_j) + w.\min\left[A(k_i), A(k_j)\right], \\ &\quad t = 1 \ldots r, \; k_i, k_j \in R_0 \cup R_1 \cup \ldots \cup R_r \end{aligned} \tag{10}$$

where w is the weight ascribed to the individual contribution of each user. The adaptation entailed by (7) and (8) leads the semantic distance of the knowledge contexts involved, to increasingly match the expectations of the community of users with whom they interact. Furthermore, when keywords with high membership in $ES(k)$ are not present in one of the information resources queried, they are added to it with document counts given by formulas (7) and (8). If the simultaneous association of the same keywords keeps occurring, then an information resource that did not previously contain a certain keyword, will have its presence progressively strengthened, even though such keyword does not index any documents stored in this information resource.

6 Collective Evolution of Knowledge with Soft Computing

TalkMine models the construction of linguistic categories. Such "on the hoof" construction of categories triggered by interaction with users, allows several unrelated information resources to be searched simultaneously, temporarily generating categories that are not really stored in any location. The short-term categories bridge together a number of possibly highly unrelated contexts, which in turn creates new associations in the individual information resources that would never occur within their own limited context.

Consider the following example. Two distinct information resources (databases) are searched using *TalkMine*. One database contains the documents (books, articles, etc) of an institution devoted to the study of computational complex adaptive systems (e.g. the library of the *Santa Fe Institute*), and the other the documents of a Philosophy of Biology department. I am interested in the keywords GENETICS and NATURAL SELECTION. If I were to conduct this search a number of times, due to my own interests, the learned category obtained would certainly contain other keywords such as ADAPTIVE COMPUTATION, GENETIC ALGORITHMS, etc. Let me assume that the keyword GENETIC ALGORITHMS does not initially exist in the Philosophy of Biology library. After I conduct this search a number of times, the keyword GENETIC ALGORITHMS is created in this library, even though it does not contain any documents about this topic. However, with my continuing to perform this search over and over again, the keyword GENETIC ALGORITHMS becomes highly associated with GENETICS and NATURAL SELECTION, introducing a new perspective of these keywords. From this point on, users of the Philosophy of Biology library, by entering the keyword Genetic Algorithms would have their own data retrieval system point them to other information resources such as the library of the Santa Fe Institute or/and output documents ranging from "The Origin of Species" to treatises on Neo-Darwinism at which point they would probably bar me from using their networked database!

Given a large number of interacting knowledge contexts from information resources and users (see Figure 2), *TalkMine* is able to create new categories that are not stored in any one location, changing and adapting such knowledge contexts in an open-ended fashion. Open-endedness does not mean that *TalkMine* is able to discern all knowledge negotiated by its user environment, but that it is able to permutate all the semantic information (KSP and d described in Section 2) of the intervening knowledge contexts in an essentially open-ended manner. The categories constructed by *TalkMine* function as a system of collective linguistic recombination of distributed memory banks, capable of transferring knowledge across different contexts and thus creating new knowledge. In this way, *TalkMine* can adapt to an evolving environment and generate new knowledge given a sufficiently diverse set of information resources and users. Readers are encouraged to track the development of this system at `http://arp.lanl.gov`.

TalkMine is a collective recommendation algorithm because it uses the behavior of its users to adapt the knowledge stored in information resources. Each time a user queries several information resources, the category constructed by *TalkMine* is used to adapt those (cfr. Section 5). In this sense, the knowledge contexts (cfr. Section 2) of the intervening information resources becomes itself a representation of the knowledge of the user community. A discussion of this process is left for future work.

TalkMine is a soft computing approach to recommendation systems as it uses Fuzzy Set and Evidence Theories, as well as ideas from Distributed Artificial Intelligence to characterize information resources and model linguistic categories. It establishes a different kind of human-machine interaction in IR, as the machine side rather than passively expecting the user to pull information, effectively pushes relevant knowledge. This pushing is done in the conversation algorithm of *TalkMine*, where the user, or her browser automatically, selects the most relevant subsets of this knowledge. Because the knowledge of communities is represented in adapting information resources, and the interests of individuals are integrated through conversation leading to the construction of linguistic categories and adaptation, *TalkMine* achieves a more natural, biological-like, knowledge management of DIS, capable of coping with the evolving knowledge of user communities.

References

Balabanovi , M. and Y. Shoham (1997)."Content-based, collaborative recommendation." *Communications of the ACM.* March 1997, Vol. 40, No.3, pp. 66-72.

Berry, M.W., S.T. Dumais, and G.W. O'Brien (1995)."Using linear algebra for intelligent information retrieval." *SIAM Review.* Vol. 37, no. 4, pp. 573-595.

Bollen, J. and F. Heylighen (1998)."A system to restructure hypertext networks into valid user models." *The New Review of Hypermedia and Multimedia.* Vol. 4.

Brusilovsky, P., A. Kobsa, and J. Vassileva (Eds.) (1998). *Adaptive Hypertext and Hypermedia Systems.* Kluwer Academic Publishers, Dordrecht, The Netherlands.

Chakrabarti, S. et al (1999)."Mining the Web's link structure." *Computer.* Vol. 32, No.8, pp. 60-67.

Chislenko, Alexander (1998)."Collaborative information filtering and semantic transports." Also available as an electronic publication at: `http://www.lucifer.com/~sasha/articles/ACF.html`.

Clark, Andy (1993). *Associative Engines: Connectionism, Concepts, and Representational Change.* MIT Press.

Conrad, Michael (1990)."The geometry of evolutions." *BioSystems.* Vol. 24, pp.61-81.

Eklund, J. (1998)."The value of adaptivity in hypermedia learning environments: a short review of empirical evidence." In: *Proceedings of the Second Workshop on Adaptive Hypertext and Hypermedia* (Hypertext' 98). P. Brusilovksy and P. de Bra (Eds.). pages 13-21, Pittsburgh, USA, June 1998.

Galvin, F. and S.D. Shore (1991)."Distance functions and topologies." *The American Mathematical Monthly.* Vol. 98, No. 7, pp. 620-623.

Good, N. et al (1999)."Combining collaborative filtering with personal agents for better recommendations." In: *Proceeding of the National Conference on Artificial Intelligence.* Orlando, Florida, July 1999. AAAI, pp. 439-446.

Harman, D. (1994)."Overview of the Third Text Retrieval Conference (TREC-3). ." In: *Proceedings of the Third Text Retrieval Conference.* Gaithersburg, Md, November 1994..

Herlocker, J.L. (1999)."Algorithmic framework for performing collaborative filtering." In: *Proceedings of the Twenty Second International Conference on Research and Development in Information Retrieval.* Berkeley, California, August 1999. ACM, p.. 230-237.

Heylighen, Francis (1999)."Collective Intelligence and its Implementation on the Web: Algorithms to Develop a Collective Mental Map." *Computational & Mathematical Organization Theory.* Vol. 5, no. 3, pp. 253-280.

Hill, W. et al (1995)."Recommending and evaluating choices in a virtual community of use." In: *Conference on Human Factors in Computing Systems* (CHI'95). Denver, May, 1995.

Johnson, N., S. Rasmussen, C. Joslyn, L. Rocha, S. Smith, and M. Kantor (1998)."Symbiotic intelligence: self-organizing knowledge on distributed networks, driven by human interaction." In: *Proceedings of the Sixth International Conference on Artificial Life.* C. Adami, R. K. Belew, H. Kitano, C. E. Taylor (Eds.). MIT Press, pp. 403-407.

Kanerva, P. (1988). *Sparse Distributed Memory.* MIT Press.

Kannan, R. and S. Vempala (1999)."Real-time clustering and ranking of documents on the web." Unpublished Manuscript.

Kauffman, S. (1993). *The Origins of Order: Self-Organization and Selection in Evolution.* Oxford university Press.

Kessler, M.M. (1963)."Bibliographic coupling between scientific papers." *American Documentation.* Vol. 14, pp. 10-25.

Kleinberg, J.M. (1998)."Authoritative sources in a hyperlinked environment." In: *Proc. of the Ninth ACM-SIAM Symposium on Discrete Algorithms.* pp. 668-677.

Klir, G.J. and B. Yuan (1995). *Fuzzy Sets and Fuzzy Logic: Theory and Applications.* Prentice Hall.

Klir, George, J. (1993)."Developments in uncertainty-based information." In: *Advances in Computers.* M. Yovits (Ed.). Vol. 36, pp. 255-332.

Kosko, B. (1992). *Neural Networks and Fuzzy Systems: A Dynamical Systems Approach to Machine Intelligence.* Prentice-Hall.

Kostan, J.A. et al (1997)."GroupLens: applying collaborative filtering to usenet news." *Communications of the ACM.* V. 40, No. 3, pp. 77-87.

Krulwich, B. and C. Burkey (1996)."Learning user information interests through extraction of semantically significant phrases." In: *Proceedings of the AAAI Spring Symposium on Machine Learning in Information Access.* Stanford, California, March 1996.

Lang, K. (1995)."Learning to filter news." In: *Proceedings of the 12th International Conference on Machine Learning.* Tahoe City, California, 1995.

Miyamoto, S. (1990). *Fuzzy Sets in Information Retrieval and Cluster Analysis.* Kluwer.

Moukas, A. and P. Maes (1998)."Amalthaea: an evolving multi-agent information filtering and discovery systems for the WWW." *Autonomous agents and multi-agent systems.* Vol. 1, pp. 59-88.

Nakamura, K. and S. Iwai (1982)."A representation of analogical inference by fuzzy sets and its application to information retrieval systems." In: *Fuzzy Information and Decision Processes.* M.M. Gupta and E. Sanchez (Eds.). North-Holland, pp. 373-386.

Resnick, P. et al (1994)."GroupLens: An open architecture for collaborative filtering of netnews." In: *Proceedings of the ACM Conference on Computer-Supported Cooperative Work.* Chapel Hill, North Carolina, 1994.

Rocha, Luis M. and Johan Bollen (2000)."Biologically motivated distributed designs for adaptive knowledge management." In: *Design Principles for the Immune System and Other Distributed Autonomous Systems.* Cohen I. and L. Segel (Eds.). Santa Fe Institute Series in the Sciences of Complexity. Oxford University Press. In Press.

Rocha, Luis, M. (1994)."Cognitive categorization revisited: extending interval valued fuzzy sets as simulation tools concept combination." *Proc. of the 1994 International Conference of NAFIPS/IFIS/NASA.* IEEE Press, pp. 400-404.

Rocha, Luis M. (1997a). *Evidence Sets and Contextual Genetic Algorithms: Exploring Uncertainty, Context and Embodiment in Cognitive and biological Systems.* Ph.D. Dissertation. State University of New York at Binghamton. UMI Microform 9734528.

Rocha, Luis M. (1997b)."Relative uncertainty and evidence sets: a constructivist framework." *International Journal of General Systems.* Vol. 26, No. 1-2, pp. 35-61.

Rocha, Luis M. (1998)."Selected self-organization and the Semiotics of Evolutionary Systems." In: *Evolutionary Systems: Biological and Epistemological Perspectives on Selection and Self-Organization.* S. Salthe, G. Van de Vijver, and M. Delpos (Eds.). Kluwer Academic Publishers, pp. 341-358..

Rocha, Luis M. (1999)."Evidence sets: modeling subjective categories." *International Journal of General Systems.* Vol. 27, pp. 457-494.

Rocha, Luis M. (2000)."Adaptive Recommendation and Open-Ended Semiosis ." *International Journal of Human-Computer Studies.* (In press).

Shafer, G. (1976). *A Mathematical Theory of Evidence.* Princeton University Press.

Shardanad, U. and P. Maes (1995)."Social information filtering: Algorithms for automating 'word of mouth'." In: *Conference on Human Factors in Computing Systems* (CHI'95). . Denver, May, 1995.

Small, H. (1973)."Co-citation in the scientific literature: a new measure of the relationship between documents." *Journal of the American Society for Information Science.* Vol. 42, pp. 676-684.

Turksen, B. (1986)."Interval valued fuzzy sets based on normal forms." *Fuzzy Sets and Systems.* Vol. 20, pp. 191-210.

Turksen, I.B. (1996)."Non-specificity and interval-valued fuzzy sets." *Fuzzy Sets and Systems.* Vol. 80, pp. 87-100.

van Gelder, Tim (1991)."What is the 'D' in 'PDP': a survey of the concept of distribution." In: *Philosophy and Connectionist Theory.* W. Ramsey et al., Lawrence Erlbaum.

Watts, D. (1999). *Small Worlds: The Dynamics of Networks between Order and Randomness.* Princeton University Press.

Yager, R.R. (1979)."On the measure of fuzziness and negation. Part I: membership in the unit interval." *Internationa Journal of General Systems.* Vol. 5, pp. 221-229.

Yager, R.R. (1980)."On the measure of fuzziness and negation: Part II: lattices." *Information and Control.* Vol. 44, pp. 236-260.

Zadeh, Lofti A. (1965)."Fuzzy Sets." *Information and Control.* Vol. 8, pp. 338-353.

A Soft-Computing Distributed Artificial Intelligence Architecture for Intelligent Buildings

Victor Callaghan[1], Graham Clarke[1], Martin Colley[1], and Hani Hagras[2]

[1] Department of Computer Science, Essex University, Colchester, UK
[2] Department of Computer Science, University of HULL, HULL, UK

Abstract. This paper presents an innovative soft computing architecture based on a combination of DAI (distributed artificial intelligence), fuzzy-genetic driven embedded-agents and IP Internet technology applied to the domain of intelligent-buildings. It describes the nature of intelligent buildings (IB) and embedded-agents, explaining the unique control and learning problems they present. We show how fuzzy-logic techniques can be used to create a behaviour-based multi-agent architecture in intelligent-buildings. We discuss how this approach deals with the highly unpredictable and imprecise nature of the physical world in which the system is situated, and how embedded-agents can be constructed that utilise sensory information to learn to perform tasks related to user comfort, energy conservation, and safety. We explain in detail our machine learning methodology that is based on a novel genetic algorithm mechanism referred to as an associative experience engine (AEE) and present the results of practical experiments. We compare results obtained from the AEE approach to that of the widely known Mendel-Wang method. Finally we explain potential applications for such systems ranging from commercial buildings to living-area control systems for space vehicles and planetary habitation modules.

1 Introduction

The building industry use the term *intelligent*, to describe the way the design, construction and management of a building can ensure that the building is flexible and adaptable, and therefore profitable, over its full life span [Robathan, 89], embracing activities that can be unrelated to computers (eg re-configurable internal walls). The computer industry has a slightly different view, regarding *computers* as an essential component of any *intelligent-buildings*, either focusing on the added functionality derived from networks (e.g. CISCO Internet Home [Sherwin 99]) or the use of artificial intelligence techniques to provide buildings with *capabilities that are comparable to intelligence in humans*. Our work falls into this latter category; the so-called 3rd generation intelligent-buildings [Callaghan 99].

In simplified terms, an intelligent-building works by taking inputs from building sensors (light, temperature, passive infra-red, etc), and uses this to control effectors (heaters, lights, electronically-operated windows, etc) throughout the building. If this system is to be intelligent, as we conceive it, an essential feature must be its ability to *learn from experience*, and hence adapt appropriately. The notion of autonomy is important, as it implies a system that can adapt and *generate its own rules* (rather than being restricted to simple automation). Thus we have proposed a computer science definition – "*An Intelligent-Building is one that utilises computer technology to autonomously govern the building environment so as to optimise user comfort, energy-consumption, safety and work efficiency*". In controlling such a system one is faced with the imprecision of sensors, lack of adequate models of many of the processes and of course the non-deterministic aspects of dealing with the human occupants and their needs. Such problems are well known and there have been various attempts to address them. The most significant of these approaches has been the pioneering work on behaviour-based systems from researchers such as Rodney Brooks [Brooks 91 and Luc Steels [Steels 95]] who have had considerable success in the field of mobile robots.

In our work we embed agents into computer based building devices and use networks to allow them to cooperate and be remotely accessed. We refer to these as *embedded-agents* as they are inseparably integrated into products. The computationally small footprint of computers making up building devices places severe constraints on the AI solutions that are possible. In the remainder of this paper we discuss these issues further and present one such solution based on the use of a hierarchical fuzzy-genetic agent and a hierarchical distributed agent architecture.

1.1 The Challenge of IB Control

A classical control application in a building might be a controller varying heat output in relation to a sensed temperature. Such a single parameter control system would be well suited to traditional PID, fuzzy-logic and even mechanical systems, such as thermostats. Clearly, using an agent would be overkill if all it did were to replace a thermostat! Thus, the value of an IB agent must lie in other aspects. In our current model this is seen as residing in:

(a) The agent's ability to learn and predict a person's needs and automatically adjust the system to meet them (we call this *particularisation*).
(b) The agent's ability to do such learning and prediction based on a wide set of parameters.

This latter aspect of an IB agent is crucial. In other words an IB agent needs the ability to modify effectors for environmental variables like heat and light etc on the basis of a *complex multi-dimensional input vector*, the dynamics of which we can't specify in advance. For example, an IB agent may have to contend with circumstances such as that where the agent's actions are contested "unpredictably" by the occupant who is also reacting to the changes in the environment, thereby misleading the cause-effect learning and introducing some non-determinism into the model (see Figure 1a). We refer to this as *Human Transformation.* A more complex situation is that where an agent or person adjusting one apparently independent control loop (e.g. reducing light level) which may cause a person to change behaviour (e.g. sit down) which in turn may result in them effecting another apparently independent control loop (e.g. raising heat). We refer to this effect as human cross-coupling (see Figure 1b).

Figure 1c illustrates a similar cross coupling as in Figure 1b, except via multi agents acting within a single environment (i.e. action of agent alters world, altered world provokes a reaction from a second agent that may change world which in turn may cause reaction from original agent). Clearly agents that only look at single sensor channels are unable to take these wider issues into account. Thus, the whole control problem is made considerably more difficult by the inclusion of essentiality non-deterministic and highly individual occupants within the control loop plus the need to deal with large and highly dynamic input vectors. When viewed in such terms it is possible to see why simple controllers are unable to deal satisfactorily with the problem.

1.2 The Challenge of IB Learning

Learning in intelligent buildings mostly takes the form of identifying cause-effect relationships based on building occupant actions in response to changes in the environment. The learning mechanism needs to be able to interpret these cause-effect relationships based on the combinational states and temporal sequences of numerous input vectors. The agent uses these relationships as part of a mechanism to serve the occupant's needs by taking pre-emptive actions. For efficient and robust learning, it is necessary to have mechanisms to identify, combine or resolve similar or contradictory events. IB based learning is focused around the actions of people. People are highly individual and to some degree idiosyncratic (i.e. partially unpredictable). Hence, to better serve individual needs, the learning needs to emphasise particularisation (as opposed to generalisation) and provide some learning inertia to cope with erratic events (e.g. erroneous or one-off actions). Thus, for example, generalisation is used more sparingly in IB learning, to contain rule size to available resources, rather than minimising rule sets to the lowest possible number. Buildings are, by and large, occupied by people who for a variety of reasons (e.g. time, interest, skills etc) would not wish, or be able to cope with much interaction with the building systems. Thus, in general, learning should, as far as possible, be non-intrusive and transparent to the occupants (i.e. requiring minimal involvement from the occupants). IB agents are sensor rich and it is difficult to be prescriptive about which sensor parameter set would lead to the most effective learning of any particular action. Thus, to maximise the opportunity for the agent to find an optimum input vector set, whilst containing the processing overloads, the ideal agent would be able to learn to focus

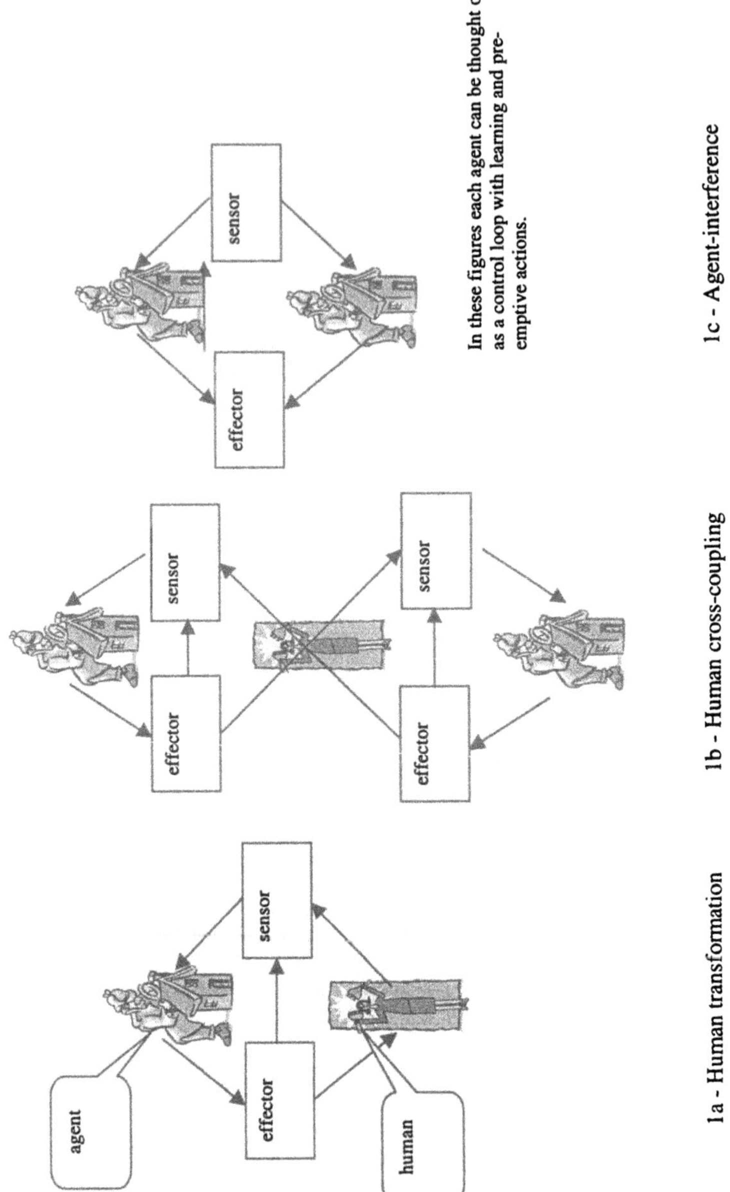

Fig. 1. Some Sources of Non-Determinism In IB Based Embedded-Agents

on a sub-set of the most relevant inputs. Thus, minimally constrained approaches, that maximise agent-learning opportunities, are favoured. Finally, the computationally compact nature of agents in IB (e.g. limited memory) has an effect that permeates all aspects of learning such as altering the extent of particularisation versus generalisation or the granularity of similarity clustering.

1.3 Why Use Robotic Techniques in Intelligent Buildings?

At a simple level, it can be seen that modern buildings have strong physical similarities to machines, in that they contain a myriad of mechanical, electrical, electronic, computing and communications devices. As building services become increasingly sophisticated they contain ever more sensors (to gain information about the environment within the building), effectors (to make changes to conditions within the building), computer based devices (to increase automation) and networks (to facilitate remote control and more efficient management).

We contend that there are enough similarities between machines (particularly mobile robots), and buildings to justify such techniques being applied to building control systems to make them behave more intelligently. For example, both are dealing with a highly dynamic, unpredictable world, in which people and items move about, natural phenomena occur, and people may behave idiosyncratically or even irrationally. As has been shown by other researchers [Brooks 91] this situation makes it almost impossible to model the world, or to plan in advance for every possible occurrence (making traditional model-based control techniques particularly difficult to apply).

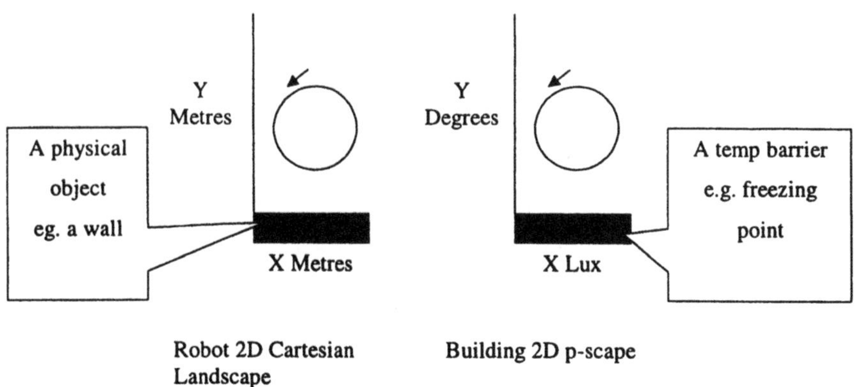

Fig. 2. Agent Navigation Spaces

Further similarities are revealed when we consider how the intelligent mechanisms of both systems work. A machine such as a mobile robot activates effectors in response to sensor information, and in doing so moves safely and efficiently from one point in Cartesian space to another. Work at Essex has shown that buildings may be regarded as "navigating" safely and efficiently through analogous landscapes to robots - "*sensory maps*" (s-maps). To illustrate the principle, a highly simplified 2D illustration of these maps is provided in Figure 2. From this it is possible to view a building as navigating like a mobile-robot within a constrained world populated by distinctive features. In robotic machines (and by analogy in IBs), these distinctive features are used to trigger distinct behaviours, with the interaction of behaviours and distinctive features giving rise to the emergent intelligent behaviour that provides pseudo reasoning and planning. At the end of this paper, in the section devoted to future work, these "s-maps" are considered as a possible means of enabling learning without interaction with the user

Both practical and market-driven factors require building control systems to have a small computational footprint (i.e. to be small and relatively cheap). Hence in intelligent-buildings, centralised, traditional AI, with bulky planners and reasoning systems, becomes less attractive and using techniques from mobile robots techniques, offers more promise.

Thus, from the considerations above we contend that buildings might be regarded as machines or even "*robots that we live inside*".

2 Distributed Architecture

As people's work or leisure is usually *room-based* (i.e. different activities take place in different rooms) and rooms are often devoted to specific purposes, we argue that both the physical and logical unit of a building is therefore a room. We have accordingly chosen to distribute control at room-level This mirrors the architect's perception of the functionality of the building. Thus, each room contains an *embedded-agent*, which is responsible, via sensors and effectors for the local control of that room as shown in Figure 1. All embedded-agents are connected via a high level network (IP-ethernet in our case), allowing collaboration or sharing of information to take place where appropriate [Sharples 99]. Within a room, devices such as sensors and effectors are connected together using a building services network (Lontalk in our case). Internet networks (ethernet-TCP/IP) have advantages over existing building services networks in that they are much higher bandwidth (10-100Mb/s versus 1Mb/s) and are in widespread use (with attendant economies of scale). However, they generally suffer the disadvantage of being non-deterministic and having bulky computational overheads (i.e. support for functions not often needed in building service). Currently there is much work underway to bring Internet network technologies into building services. In our approach we address this dilemma by utilising a hierarchy with the agent forming the bridge between Lonworks at the lower level and IP at the higher level; thus allowing us to benefit from the best aspects of both worlds while the technology and market is developing. This DAI architecture is illustrated in Figure 3. Other work we have undertaken, beyond the scope of this paper, extends to mobile and body based agents [Callaghan 2000].

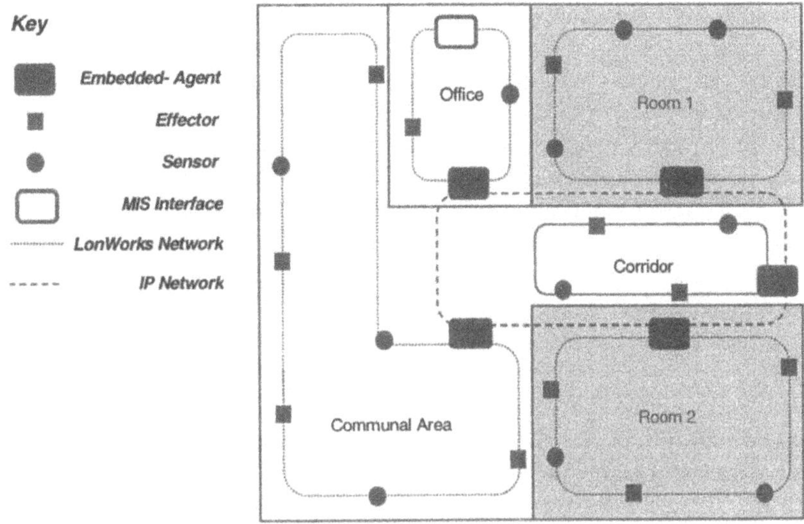

Fig. 3. The DAI Building-Wide Architecture (Simplified Example)

As far as we are aware, this approach differs significantly to that adopted by other researchers working on interactive intelligent environments and related agent architectures for IB. Examples of such work [Coen 97] include research in Sweden [Davisson 98] that utilises multi-agent principles to control an Intelligent Building. Their primary goal is energy-efficiency, and although their system does adjust the heating and light level to suit individual preferences, these settings must be pre-defined. Their agents are built from traditional AI (i.e. not behaviour based) and their work does not address issues, such as occupant based learning. The system, so far implemented in simulation only, managed to achieve energy savings of 40being controlled manually by occupants. A group in Colorado [Mozer 98] are using a soft computing approach - neural networks - focusing solely on the intelligent control of lighting within a building, by anticipating when particular *zones* (regions in a room) will be occupied or unoccupied. Their system, implemented in a building with a real occupant, also achieved a significant energy reduction, although this was sometimes at the expense of the occupant's comfort. They use a centralised control architecture which differs from our multi-agent approach and which intrinsically seeks a generalised solution rather than a *particularised* solution, as is the case for us. A third group based at the MIT Artificial Intelligence Lab in Massachusetts is working on an Intelligent Room project. They employ a mix of cameras, microphones and multiplexer to enable people to interface with room-based systems in a natural way using speech, gesture, movements, and context information [Brooks 97]. This primary focus on facility of the user interface differs to our work where ideally the agent remains more or less invisible to the user of the building.

Distributed computing, programming and communication models such as MEX [Lehikoinen 99], Java (including Jini and JavaSpaces, JAFMAS, JATLite etc) [Jeon 2000] KQML/FIPA [Labrou 99] offer important infrastructure support for distributed agent systems. Java is proving particularly popular and useful in programming such systems due to its focus on network support, in part driven by its role as a main Internet and Web programming tool. The HIVE project at MIT [Minar 99] is an example of a particularly forward-looking distributed agent model. The model differs to ours principally in respect that their agents are soft (rather than our hard embedded-agents) with access to hard devices being via coded objects referred to shadows. The soft agents reside on servers (eg PCs) which thereby de-emphasis minimalist aspects of agent design which is a central focus of our work. A particularly attractive feature of the HIVE model is the ad-hoc nature of the multi-agent agent structures supported and that it can be integrated with standard services such as Java derivatives. Whilst the HIVE work is not at a point that we could adopt it into this work, we are hoping it will evolve to become an option for us. Agent communication languages form another essential component in the overall framework. In traditional soft agent work the most widely used standards are KQML and FIPA. A consequence of being designed for non-minimal agents is that they attract a large computational footprint that makes them unsuitable for compact embedded-agents. To overcome this problem we propose using a Distributed Intelligent Building Agent Language (DIBAL) being developed at the University of Essex, that has been tailored to the needs of intelligent-building based embedded-agents. The main feature of DIBAL is that has a versatile hierarchical tagged data format, which provides highly compact representation [Cayci 2000].

3 The Embedded-Agents

Nikola Kasabov offers useful criteria for intelligent systems, based on seven requirements [Kasabov 98]. They include fast learning from large data sets, on-line incremental adaptation, accommodation of new knowledge, memory based, interaction with environment (and other systems), adequate representation and an ability to analyse their own performance. In our agent design, we aim to meet as many of these criteria as we can. The internal architecture of the embedded-agents we use is illustrated in Figure 4. It is based on the behaviour-based approach, pioneered by Brooks, and composed of many simple co-operating units [Brooks 91]. This approach has produced very promising results when applied to the control of robots, which, as we explained above, can include intelligent-buildings. Controlling a large integrated building system requires a complicated control function because it involves both a large input and output space and the need to deal with many imprecise and unpredictable factors, including people. This function can be made more manageable by breaking down the space for analysis into multiple behaviours, each of which responds to specific types of situations, and then integrating their recommendations.

3.1 Embedded-Agent Control Architecture

Our work is broadly situated within the behaviour based architecture work, pioneered by Brooks, consisting of many simple co-operating sub-control units [Brooks 91]. This has produced very promising results when applied to the control of robots [Hagras 99a, Hagras 99b, Hagras 2000a, Hagras 2000b], which we argue includes IB. We have extended this work to include a double hierarchy of behaviours (implemented as fuzzy controllers) and learning (implemented using genetic algorithms).

We use a room-based DAI decomposition with each agent having behaviours consisting of two groups of meta-functions. The first group are fixed (pre-programmed) behaviours which are not subject to adaptation and consist of; a *Safety behaviour* (this ensures environmental conditions are always at a safe level), an *Emergency behaviour* (reactions to fire, burglary etc), and an *Economy behaviour* (this ensures that energy is not wasted). The second group of meta-functions are dynamic behaviours which the system seeks to learn from the occupant based on his/her actions; the main one being a *Comfort behaviour* which attempts to set the room to a state that matches examples of the occupants previous preferences. These dynamic meta-functions have an adaptable rule base, which learns from the room occupant's behaviour. The management of these dynamic behaviours offers the main challenge to our research due to there numerous, dynamic, imprecise and uncertain nature.

Fuzzy logic offers a framework for representing imprecise and uncertain knowledge. It has similarities to the way people make decisions as it uses a mode of approximate reasoning, which allows it to deal with vague and incomplete information. In addition fuzzy controllers exhibit robustness with regard to noise and variations of system parameters. However, it is often difficult to determine parameters for fuzzy systems. In most fuzzy systems, the fuzzy rules were determined and tuned through trial and error by human operators. It normally takes many iterations to determine and tune them. As the number of input variables increases (IBs have very large numbers of rules due to particularisation) the number of rules increases disproportionately, which can cause difficulty in matching and choosing between large numbers of rules.

In our approach we implement each behaviour as a fuzzy process and then use higher level fuzzy process to co-ordinate them. The resultant architecture takes the form of a hierarchical tree structure form (see Figure 3). This approach has the following advantages:

- It simplifies the design of the embedded-agent, reducing the number of rules to be determined (in previous work we have given examples of rules reduction of two orders of magnitude via the use of hierarchies).
- It uses the benefits of fuzzy logic to deal with imprecision and uncertainty.
- It provides a flexible structure where new behaviours can be added (eg comfort behaviours) or modified easily.
- It utilises a continuous activation scheme for behaviour coordination which provides a smoother response than switched schema

The learning process involves the creation of Comfort behaviours. This is done *interactively* using reinforcement where the controller takes actions and monitors these actions to see if they satisfy the occupant or not, until a degree of satisfaction is achieved. This process would be acceptable in a hotel or apartment block but would probably require the intervention of a care assistant in housing for the elderly or those with learning difficulties. The behaviours, resident inside the agent, take their input from a variety of sensors in the room (such as occupancy, internal illumination level, external illumination level, internal temperature, external temperature etc), and adjust device outputs (such as heating, lighting, blinds, etc) according to pre-determined, but settable, levels. The complexities of training and negotiating satisfactory values for multiple use rooms would depend upon having a reliable means of identifying different users.

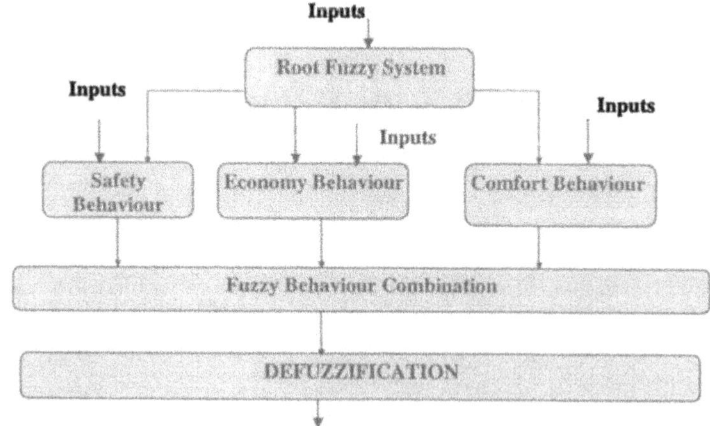

Fig. 4. The Hierarchical Fuzzy Logic System

In our prototype system each agent has six inputs made up of four environmental variables - a Room Temperature (RTEMP), the External Temperature (ONTEMP), the Room Illumination (RILLUM) and the External Illumination (ONILLUM) each of which have the fuzzy membership functions shown in Figure 5. Each input is represented by three fuzzy sets, as this was the minimum number that gave satisfactory results. The two remaining inputs to the system are a room occupancy indicator and an emergency alarm flag. The system has two outputs; Room Heater (RH) setting and a Room Illuminator (RI) setting which have the membership functions shown in Figure 6. Seven fuzzy sets were found to be the minimum needed to provide satisfactory results. Whenever an alarm input is activated the Emergency behaviour becomes dominant and the room illumination is switch to max and heat is switched off (a pre-determined plan). The Economy behaviour is active to a fuzzy degree dependent on occupancy, outside temperature and light. Behaviour is fuzzily co-ordinated as shown in Figure 7.

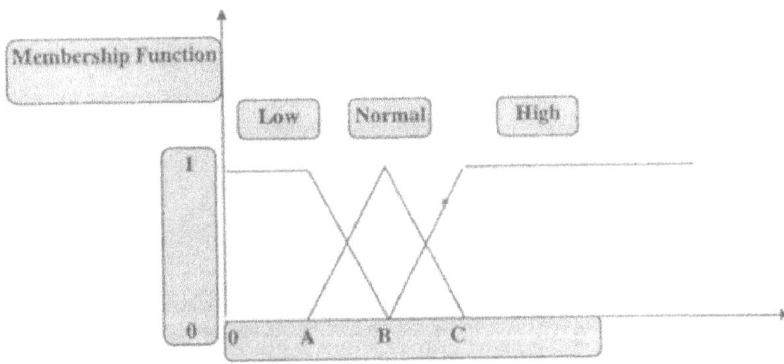

Fig. 5. Input membership functions for RTEMP and ONTEMP $A = 10°$, $B = 20°$, $C = 30°$, for RILLUM and ONILLUM. A= 300 Lux, B= 400 Lux, C= 500 Lux

Each behaviour uses a singleton fuzzifier, triangular membership functions, product inference, max-product composition and height defuzzification. The selected techniques were chosen due to their computational simplicity. The equation that maps the system input to output is given by:

$$Y_t = \frac{\Sigma_{p=1}^{M} y_p \Pi_{i=1}^{G} \alpha_{Aip}}{\Sigma_{p=1}^{M} \Pi_{i=1}^{G} \alpha_{Aip}} \tag{1}$$

In this equation M is the total number of rules, y is the crisp output for each rule, ($\Pi_{i=1}^{G} \alpha_{Aip}$ is the product of the membership functions of each rule input and G is the number of inputs. In this hierarchical architecture

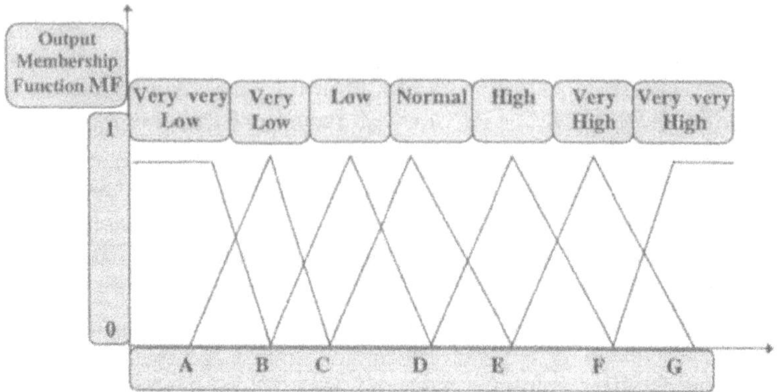

Fig. 6. Output membership functions for: RI A= 0 %, B= 20 %, C= 35 %, D=40 %, E=50 %, F=70 %, G=100 % RH A=0 %, B=30 %, C=40 %, D=50 % , E= 70 %, F=85 %, G=100 %

we utilise a fuzzy operator to combine the preferences of different behaviour into a collective preference. Command fusion is decomposed into two steps: preference combination, decision and in the case of using fuzzy numbers for preferences, product-sum combination and height defuzzification. The total control output C is [Saffiotti 97]:

$$C = \frac{\Sigma_i(BW_i * C_i)}{\Sigma_i BW_i} \tag{2}$$

In Equation (2) i = economy, comfort, Ci is the behaviour command output (room temperature). BWi is the behaviour weight. The behaviour weights are calculated dynamically taking into account the context of the agent. In Figure 2 each behaviour is treated as an independent fuzzy controller, which is fuzzily combined to provide a single output, which is then deffuzzified to give the final crisp output. The fuzzy values form an input to context rules, which directly govern when, which, and to what extent behaviours are fired, depending on fuzzy membership functions in Figure 7. The default rule we use is:

```
IF ONTEMP IS HIGH AND ONILLUM IS HIGH AND THE ROOM IS
OCCUPIED THEN ECONOMY.
IF ONTEMP IS LOW AND ONILLUM IS LOW THEN COMFORT
IF THE ROOM IS VACANT THEN RH IS LOW AND RI IS LOW
```

The final output is a mix of the different behaviour outputs, each weighted by the degree of its importance, and the final output is calculated using Equation (2).

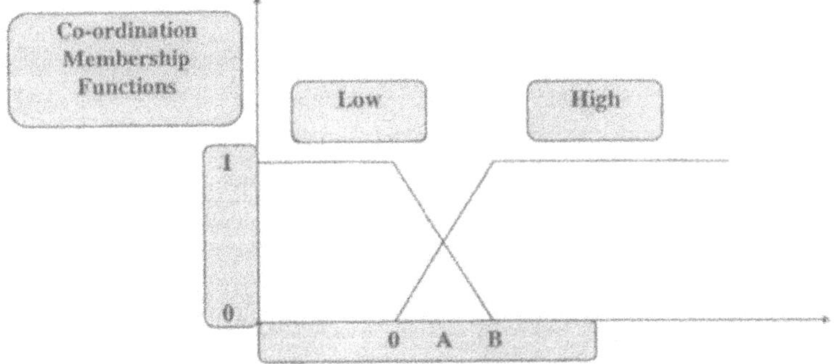

Fig. 7. Co-ordination parameters for ONILLUM A= 350 Lux and B= 400 Lux, for ONTEMP $A = 15°$ and $B = 25°$

3.2 Embedded-Agent Learning Architecture

It is clear that, in order for an agent to autonomously particularise its service to an individual, some form of learning is essential.

In our agent learning takes the form of adapting the dynamic Comfort behaviour's rule base, according to the occupants actions. To do this we utilise an evolutionary computing mechanism based on a novel hierarchical genetic algorithm (GA) technique which modifies the fuzzy controller rule-sets through interaction with the environment and user.

The hub of the GA learning architecture is what we refer to as an *Associative Experience Engine* [British patent 99-10539.7]. Each behaviour is a fuzzy logic controller (FLC) that has two parameters that can be modified; a Rule Base (RB) and its associated *Membership Functions* (MF). In our learning we will modify the rule-base. The architecture, as adapted for IB embedded-agents, is given in Figure 8. The behaviours receive their inputs from sensors and provide outputs to the actuators via the *co-ordinator* that weights their effect. When the system fails to have the desired response (e.g an occupant manually changes an effector setting), the learning cycle begins.

When a learning cycle is initiated, the most active behaviour (i.e. that most responsible for the agent behaviour) is provided to the *Learning Focus* from the *Co-ordinator* (the fuzzy engine which weights contributions to the outputs), which uses the information to point at the rule-set to be modified (i.e. learnt) or exchanged. Initially, the Contextual Prompter (which gets a characterisation of the situation, an experience, from the Co-ordinator) is used to make comparison to see whether there is a suitable behaviour rule set in the *Experience Bank*. If there is a suitable experience, it is used. When the past experiences do not satisfy the occupant's needs we use the best-fit experiences to reduce the search space by pointing to a better starting point,

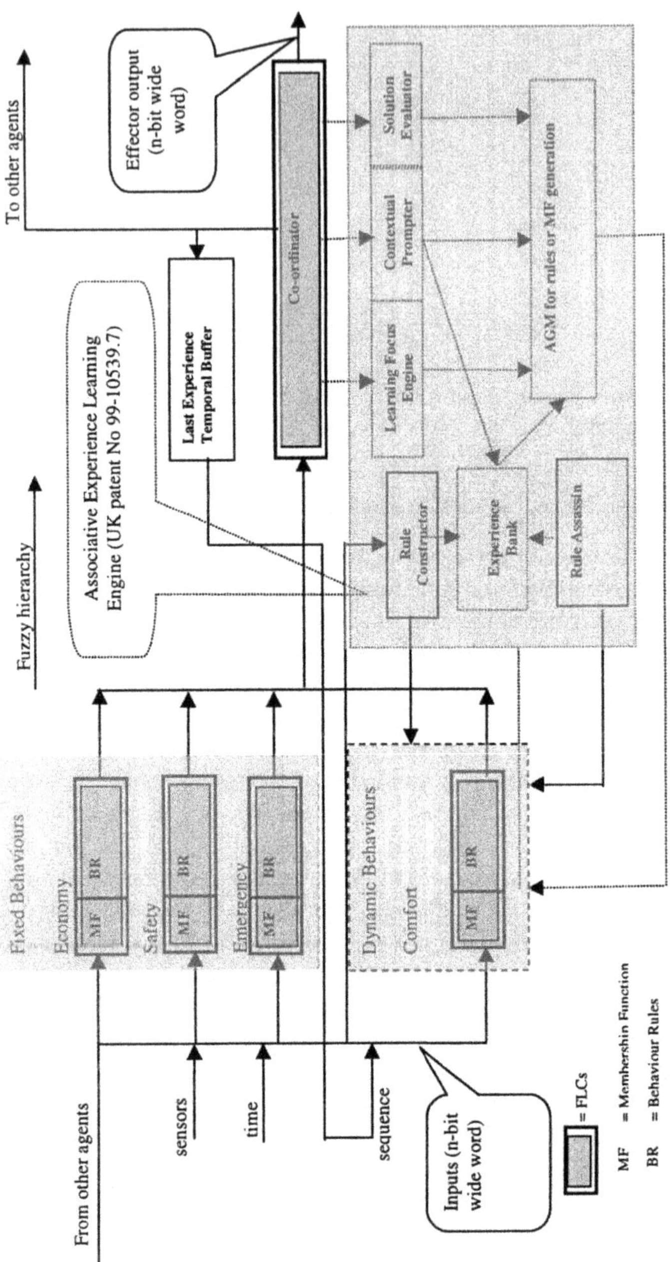

Fig. 8. The Embedded-Agent Architecture

which is the experience with the largest fitness. We then fire an *Adaptive Genetic Mechanism* (AGM) using adaptive learning parameters to speed the search for new solutions. The AGM is constrained to produce new solutions in a certain range defined by the *Contextual Prompter* to avoid the AGM searching options where solutions are unlikely to be found. By using these mechanisms we narrow the AGM search space massively, thus improving its efficiency. After generating new solutions the system tests the new solution and gives it fitness through the *Solution Evaluator.* The AGM provides new options via operators such as crossover and mutation until a satisfactory solution is achieved.

The system then remains with this set of active rules (an experience) until the occupant's behaviour indicates a change of preference (e.g. has developed a new habit), signalled by a manual change to one of the effectors when the learning process described above is repeated. In the case of a new occupant in the room the *Contextual Prompter* gets and activates the most suitable rule base from the *Experience Bank* or if this proves unsuitable the system re-starts the learning cycle above. The *Solution Evaluator* assigns each stored rule base in the *Experience Bank* a fitness value. When the *Experience Bank* is full, we have to delete some experiences. To assist with this the *Rule Assassin* determines which rules are removed according to their importance (as set by the *Solution Evaluator*). The *Last Experience Temporal Buffer* feeds back to the inputs a compressed form of the $n - 1$ state, thereby providing a mechanism to deal with temporal sequences.

Multi-Agent operation is supported by making this compressed information available to the wider network. The compressed data takes the form of which behaviours are active (and to what degree). The general philosophy we have adopted is that data from remote agents is simply treated in the same way as all other sensor data. As with any data, the processing agent decides for itself which information is relevant to any particular decision. Thus, multi-agent processing is implicit to this paradigm, which regards remote agents as simply more sensors. We have found that receiving high level processed information from remote agents, such as "the room is occupied" is more useful than being given the low level sensor information from the remote agent that gave rise to the high-level characterisation. This is because the compressed form both relieves agent processing overheads and reduces network loading. Inter-agent communication also requires appropriate networking and programming infrastructure together with standardised agent communication languages. This is a large and complex subject beyond the scope of this paper but we refer interested readers to our work concerned with intelligent-building and agent communication languages [Cayci 2000].

¿From a users viewpoint the system functions interactively as follows. A user is asked to select his preference for any given programmable setting. The system then tries to adapt its rules to achieve this setting. The user is prompted to confirm or deny his satisfaction with the result. If the occupant is dissatisfied the system tries to re-adjust the rules. If the user is satisfied, the current rule set is accepted. Experiments to date show the *experience engine* achieves a satisfactory solution in a small number of iterations. Our experiments show this takes an average of twenty-one iterations. As we mentioned earlier this process would probably have to be undertaken by a care assistant for some groups of occupants. In the next section we will explain the techniques in more detail

4 The Associative Experience Learning Engine in Detail

Most automated fuzzy controller design employing conventional GAs use simulation to overcome problem of lengthy training periods caused by the testing of numerous generations of possible solutions [e.g. Fukuda 99, Linkens 95, Bonarini 96, Hoffmann 98]. As explained above, we employ a combination of domain constraints and environmental cues to reduce the search space and thereby substantially speed up the GA process, eliminating the need for simulation. The following paragraphs explain these methods in detail.

4.1 Identifying Poorly Performing Rules

The rule-base is initialised to have all the outputs switched off. The GA population consists of all the rules consequents contributing to an action, which is usually a small number of rules. As is the case for classifier systems, in order to preserve the system performance, the GA is allowed to replace a subset of the classifiers (the rules in this case). The worst m classifiers are replaced by the m new classifiers created by the application of the GA on the population [Dorigo 93]. The new rules are tested by the combined action of the performance and apportionment of credit mechanisms. We will replace all the rules that participated in this action for a given input.

In the learning phase, the agent is introduced to different situations (e.g. low temperature and illumination both inside and outside the room), and the agent, guided by the occupant, attempts to discover the rules needed for each situation. The learning system consists of learning different situations. The model to be learnt is small, as is the search space, and in each situation only small number of rules will be fired. In our agent model, control is dominated by activity physically close to the agent. Knowledge of remote agents (and their activity), and information *from* remote agents is less important and smaller in quantity (e.g. only information on active behaviours is passed on). The accent on local models at all levels implies the possibility of learning by focusing at each step on a small part of the search space only, thus reducing interaction among partial solutions. The interaction among local models, due to the intersection of neighbouring fuzzy sets means local learning reflects on global performance [Bonarini 96[mjc1]]. Moreover, the smooth transition among the different controllers implemented by fuzzy rules implies robustness with respect to data noise. Thus, we can have global results coming from the combination of local models, and smooth transition between close models. Also dividing the learning into local situations can reduce the number of learnt rules. For example, in one situation we started learning with 81 rules, and the agent discovered that during its interactive training with the occupant, it needed only 49 rules.

4.2 Fitness Determination and Credit Assignment

The system fitness is determined by the Solution Evaluator and is evaluated by how much the system satisfies the room occupant's desired target value (such as desired temperature) in a specific situation and how it reduced the normalised absolute deviation (d) from the normal value. This is given by:

$$d = \frac{|normal\ value - deviated\ value|}{max\ deviation} \tag{3}$$

Here, the normal value will correspond to that desired by the occupant. The deviated value corresponds to the actual measured value. The maximum deviation is the theoretical maximum that can occur. Hence the fitness of the solution may be found from the difference $d_1 - d_2$, where d_2 is the normalised absolute deviation before introducing a new solution and d_1 is the normalised absolute deviation following the new solution. The deviation is measured using the physical sensors, which gives the agent the ability to adapt to the imprecision and the noise found in the real sensors rather than relying on estimates from previous simulations. The fitness of each rule for a given situation is calculated as follows. The crisp output Y_t can be written as in (1). If the agent has two output variables, then we have Y_{t_1} and Y_{t_2}. The normalised contribution of each rule p output (Y_{p_1}, Y_{p_2}) to the total output Y_{t_1} and Y_{t_2} can be denoted by S_{r_1}, S_{r_2} where S_{r_1} and S_{r_2} is given by:

$$S_{r_1} = \frac{Y_{p_1} \Pi_{i=1}^{G} \alpha_{Aip}}{\frac{\Sigma_{i=1}^{m} \Pi_{i=1}^{G} \alpha_{Aip}}{Y_{t_1}}} \tag{4}$$

$$S_{r_2} = \frac{Y_{p_2} \Pi_{i=1}^{G} \alpha_{Aip}}{\frac{\Sigma_{i=1}^{m} \Pi_{i=1}^{G} \alpha_{Aip}}{Y_{t_2}}} \tag{5}$$

We then calculate each rule's contribution to the final action $S_c = \frac{S_{r_1} + S_{r_2}}{2}$. Then the most effective rules are those that have the greatest values of S_c. The fitness of the rule in a given solution is supplied by the Solution Evaluator and is given by:

$$S_{r_t} = Constant + (d_1 - d_2) * S_c \tag{6}$$

$d_1 - d_2$ is the deviation improvement or degradation caused by the adjusted rule-base produced by the algorithm. If there is improvement in the deviation, then the rules that have contributed most will be given more fitness to boost their actions. If there is degradation then the rules that contributed more must be punished by reducing their fitness w.r.t to other rules giving other useful actions an opportunity to produce better solutions.

4.3 Memory Based Mechanisms

Zhou [Zhou 90] presented the CSM (Classifier System with Memory) system that addressed the problem of long versus short-term memory (i.e. how to use past experiences to ease the problem solving activity in novel situations). Zhou's approach was to build a system in which short and long-term memory are simultaneously present. The short-term memory is simply the standard set of rules found in every learning classifier system (the fuzzy rule base in our case). The long-term memory is a set of rule clusters, in which every rule cluster represents a generalised version of problem solving expertise acquired in previous problem solving activity. Each time the agent is presented a problem it starts the learning procedures trying to use long-term experience by means of an appropriate initialisation mechanism. Thereafter, the system works as a standard classifier system (except for some minor changes) until an acceptable level of performance has been achieved. It is at this point that a generalising process takes control and compresses the acquired knowledge into a cluster of rules that are stored for later use in the long-term memory.

In our system, when the agent begins learning it has no previous experience and the *Experience Bank* is empty. But as it begins GA enabled learning, it begins filling the memory with different rule bases, each associated to different users. Each stored rule base consists of rules and the actions (consequents) that were learnt by the GA. With a new user, after monitoring the user's action for a period the agent matches the rules fired during this time to sets of rule bases for different users stored in the *Experience Bank*. The system tries to identify which rule base is appropriate to the user on the basis of actions taken by him during this time, and the rule base containing the most similar actions to the occupants is chosen as a starting point for learning and adaptation.

Each time the agent is presented with a situation to solve, it begins checking if the consequents of firing the rules from a rule base extracted from the *Experience Bank* suits the new user or not. If these rules are suitable for the user then they are used for the Comfort behaviours. If some actions are not suitable for the user, the system begins identifying the poorly performing rules as described in Section (4.1), then it fires the Adaptive Genetic Mechanisms (AGM) to change these rules. This action helps to speed up the genetic search as it starts from the search from the best known point in the search space instead of starting randomly. In this way the system does not need the "matcher calculations" used by [Zhou 90]. This is because we do not use the binary message coding, or "don't care", conditions but instead utilise perfect matches; hence we don't need the generaliser. The clusters are arranged in a queue starting from the most recent experiences.

Problems occur as the system begins accumulating experience that exceeds the physical memory limits. This implies that we must delete some of the stored information as the acquired experience increase. Clearly not all experiences are of equal value. One that are frequently used or difficult to learn are clearly of more value that others. Thus, for every rule base cluster we attach a *difficulty counter* to count the number of iterations taken by the agent to find a suitable rule base for a given user, we also attach a *frequency counter* to count how often they have been retrieved. The *degree of importance* of each rule base cluster is calculated by the *Experience Survival Valuer* and is given by the product of the *frequency counter* and the *difficulty counter*. This approach tries to keep the rules that have required a lot of effort to learn (due to the difficulty of the situation) and also the rules that are used frequently. When there is no more room in the *Experience Bank*, the rule base cluster that had the least *degree of importance* is selected for removal. If two rule base clusters share the same importance degree, tie breaking is resolved by a least-recently-used strategy. Thus an *age parameter* is also needed for each rule base cluster. We can also operate the *Experience Survival Valuer* in an "Assassin Mode". In this mode it periodically, decrements the frequency counter by one (e.g. once a day etc) thereby proactively forcing death on little used rules or ageing out rules.

4.4 Producing New Solutions

If the rule base extracted from the *Experience Bank* is not suitable for the user, the GA starts its search for new solutions (i.e. new rules). The fitness of each rule in the population is proportional to its contribution in the final action. If the proposed action by the new solution results in an improvement in performance then the rules that have contributed most will have their fitness increased more than the rules that have contributed less in this situation (and vice-versa for negative results). This allows us to move away from points in the search space that cause no improvement (or even degradation) in the performance. The parents for any new solution are chosen proportional to their fitness using the roulette-wheel selection process together with genetic operations of crossover and mutation. The proposed system can be viewed as a double hierarchy system in which the fuzzy behaviours are organised in hierarchical form. The learning algorithm can also be seen as a hierarchy. At the higher level we have a population of solutions stored in the *Experience Bank*. If the stored experiences leads to a solution then the search ends. If none of these stored experiences leads to a solution then each of these experiences acquires a fitness assigned by the *Experience Assessor* that finds how many rules in the stored rule-base are similar to the user's action in the test period. At this lower level the highest fitness experience is used as a starting position for the GA.

The Adaptive Genetic Mechanism (AGM) is the rule discovery component for our system (as in the classifier system). We used Srinivas method [Srinivas 96] to adapt the control parameters (mutation and crossover probabilities). The strategy used for adapting the control parameters depends on the specification of the performance of the GA. In a non-static environment (which is our case), where the optimal solution changes with time, the GA should also possess the capacity to track optimal solutions. The adaptation strategy needs to vary the control parameters appropriately whenever the GA is not able to find the optimum. It is essential for GAs to have two characteristics for optimisation. The first characteristic is the capacity to converge to an optimum (local or global) after locating the region containing the optimum. The second characteristic is the capacity to explore new regions of the solution space in search of the global optimum. In order to vary P_c (crossover probability) and P_m (mutation probability) adaptively, for preventing premature convergence of the GA, it is essential to be able to identify whether the GA is converging to an optimum. One possible way of detecting convergence is to observe the average fitness value f' of the population in relation to the maximum fitness value f_{max} of the population. $f_{max} - f'$ is likely to be less for a population that has converged to an optimum solution than that for a population scattered in the solution space. The equations that determine P_c, P_m are given by:

$$P_c = \begin{cases} (f_{max} - f'')/(f_{max} - f') & \text{when } f'' \geq f' \\ 1 & \text{when } f'' < f' \end{cases} \tag{7}$$

$$P_m = \begin{cases} (f_{max} - f)/f_{max} - f') & \text{when } f \geq f' \\ 0.5 & \text{when } f < f' \end{cases} \tag{8}$$

Where f'' is the larger of the fitness values of the solutions to be crossed, f is the fitness of the individual solutions. The method means that we have pc and pm for each chromosome. We chose a one-point crossover for computational simplicity and real time performance. In [Srinivas 96] this method was superior to the simple GA and gave a rapid convergence rate of 8:1. We use this adaptive method for finding the values of crossover and mutation probabilities. We use an elite strategy, meaning that the best individual is automatically promoted to the next generation, and used to generate new populations. We also use constrained GA search, in the form of a *contextual prompter* based on the occupant's needs. For example, if a temperature is too high for the room occupant then the AGM will be constrained so as not to suggest solutions involving increasing the temperature. In this way we can minimise the search space of the GA and achieve faster conversion.

In order to justify these techniques we have conducted various Comfort behaviour leaning experiments using both open and constrained Adaptive GA (AGA) operation plus Simple GA (SGA) with constrained operation. The results are shown in Figure 9.

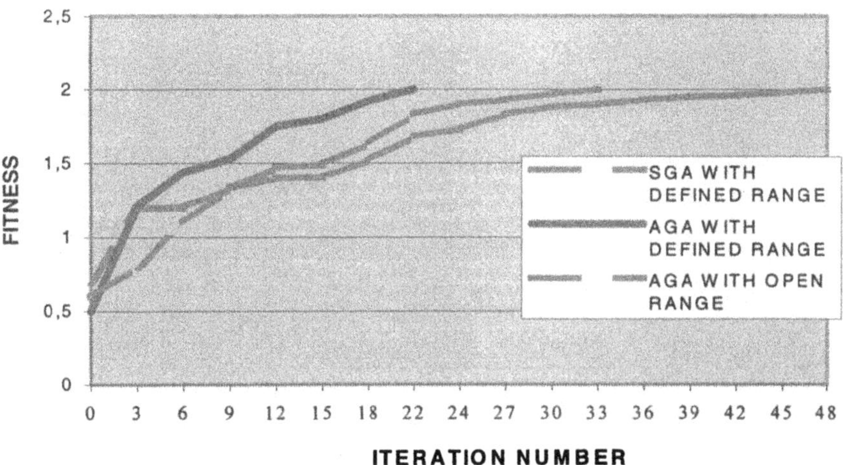

Fig. 9. The best fitness plotted against the number of iterations for different GA learning

The SGA was tried with different parameters in the range [0.5, 1.0] for p_c and [0.001 0.1] for pm. The best performance was found to occur at p_c =0.7 and p_m =0.002 (see Figure 8). It was found that constrained AGA converges to a solution in average of 22 iterations. The AGA with open operation converged after larger number of iterations (33 iterations in average), as it needs longer to explore the search space and determine its limits. The SGA with defined limits, p_c =0.7 and p_m =0.002, converged to a solution after an average of 48 iterations. These experiments show the constrained GA methodology results in the quicker convergence. We use binary coding in the GA. For each rule there are two actions, room heating and illumination. As we have 7 output membership function, we decode each action by three bits as follows, Very Very Low is 000, Very Low is 001, Low 010, Normal is 011, High is 100 Very High 101 Very Very High 110. By doing this we have a chromosome length of 6 bits.

Figure 10 illustrates GA operation where actions of rule number 5 and rule number 7 of the comfort behaviour are chosen for reproduction by roulette wheel selection due their high fitness. They have contributed more with their actions to improvement, or contributed less to degradation. The adaptive crossover and mutation probabilities have been applied to both chromosomes. The resultant offspring were used to replace the consequents of rules 1 and rule 2, which were blamed more than the others for the unsatisfactory responses.

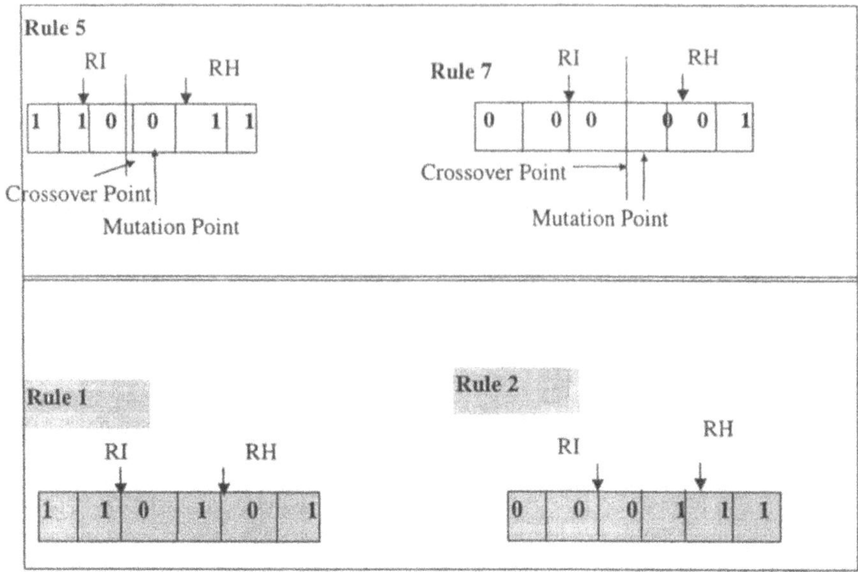

Fig. 10. GA process example: rule 5 and rule 7 (selected due to higher fitness) generate new actions for rules 1 and2

5 Experimental Results

In our preliminary experiments we have used an IB agent based on a 68000 Motorola processor, see photo 1. The agent is equipped with light and heat sensors and effectors in the form of a heater and a light source. The room is subject to various conditions such as multiple occupancy, differing levels of natural light/temperature, varying times of day and different human preferences. Whilst we used a real physical agent and sensors, in order to accelerate the passage of time the agent was operated in an emulation mode, where the sensors were subjected to controlled stimulation thereby allowing days to be cycled in hours. The agent shown in Figure (11) was tried, under different conditions such as hot, sunny days and cold, dull days.

Economy behaviour seeks to minimise heat and light when the room is vacated. Safety behaviour prevents the heat going below a minimum safe level (e.g. zero degrees that would result in pipes freezing). The Comfort behaviour generation mechanism proactively serves the needs and desires of the human occupant(s). Where necessary (e.g. setting up the system) the agent interacts with occupants.

The rules generated are presented in Table (1). Whilst operating the AEE method the agent proved itself able to rapidly deduce appropriate rules (an average of 21 iterations). It was noted that the method also optimised the number of rules by using only rules demonstrated to be important to the

Fig. 11. The Prototype IB Agent

room occupant. The AEE optimised the number of rules from an expected 34 = 81 rule base to only 49 rules.

To provide a benchmark for the AEE we implanted and evaluated the performance of an IB embedded-agent using the Mendel-Wang fuzzy rule learning method (which outperforms the ANFIS network). The Mendel-Wang approach learns by constructing fuzzy rules from input and output values. This is a widely known method, which will not be described here but can be found in Mendel-Wang's own papers [Mendel 92].

The rules generated by Mendel-Wang are presented in Table (1) where they can be compared to the AEE method. Although both systems appear to give comparable results, the AEE system out-performs Mendel-Wang in at least one important aspect; Mendel-Wang uses essentially off-line learning, in which each learning cycle needs to repeat from the beginning, requiring both the initial training set together with any newly acquired data. In contrast the AEE method directly interacts with the user in an essentially on-line way, continuing the learning cycle from an advanced point rather than starting afresh making it much faster. Thus the AEE system works by cause-effect actions in the form of fuzzy rules, based on the occupant's actions. The advantage of this is that the system responds and adapts to the users needs interactively.

Techniques, such as Mendel-Wang, have the disadvantage that the interface with the user is based on the provision of a set of desired values rather than simply interacting with the user to obtain a satisfactory result. Whilst the user may eventually acquire a feel for what figures to supply to get the right result, but even if a computer program was used to assist, the process is far from intuitive. Thus, although the rules extracted by the AEE method are similar to the Mendel-Wang rules, the difference is that with AEE learning the occupant can interact directly with the agent until satisfied with the actual settings.

Table (1): The rule base learnt by the AEE and Mendel-Wang methods.

				AEE		Medel-Wang	
RTEMP	ONTEMP	RILLUM	ONLLUM	RH	RL	RH	RL
L	L	L	L	V H	H	V V H	V H
L	L	L	N	V V H	V V H	V H	V H
L	L	N	L	V H	N	V H	N
L	L	N	N	N	N	N	N
L	L	N	H	V H	V L	V H	V L
L	L	H	L	H	V L	V H	V L
L	L	H	N	H	V V L	V H	V V L
L	L	H	H	H	V V L	V H	L
L	N	L	L	N	V V H	N	V H
L	N	L	N	N	N	N	H
L	N	N	L	V V H	V L	V V H	V L
L	N	N	N	H	V L	V H	V V L
L	N	N	H	H	V V L	V H	V L
L	N	H	L	V H	L	V V H	V L
L	N	H	N	N	V V L	H	V L
L	N	H	H	V H	V V L	V V H	L
L	H	L	L	N	V H	V V H	V H
L	H	L	N	V V H	H	V V H	H
L	H	N	L	H	N	V V H	H
L	H	N	N	V V L	V L	V V L	V L
L	H	N	H	V V L	V L	V V L	V L
L	H	H	N	V V L	V L	V V L	V L
L	H	H	H	V V L	V L	V V L	V L
N	L	L	L	N	H	N	H
N	L	L	N	N	V V H	H	H
N	L	N	L	N	N	N	N
N	L	N	N	N	N	H	H
N	L	N	H	V V L	V L	V V L	L
N	L	H	N	L	N	V V L	L
N	L	H	H	V V L	V L	V L	N
N	N	L	L	V L	V H	V V L	V V H
N	N	N	L	L	N	V L	H
N	N	N	N	V	L	V V L	V V L
N	N	N	H	V V L	L	V L	V V L
N	N	H	N	L	V L	V V L	L
N	N	H	H	V L	L	V V L	L
N	H	L	L	V V L	H	V V L	N
N	H	H	H	V V L	V L	V V L	V L
H	L	L	L	V L	H	V L	V H
N	H	H	H	V V L	V L	V V L	V L
H	L	L	L	V L	H	V L	V H
H	L	N	L	V L	V V H	V L	V H
H	L	N	N	V V L	L	V L	V L
H	L	N	H	N	V V L	N	V L
H	L	H	N	N	L	V V L	L
H	L	H	H	V L	L	V L	L
H	N	L	L	N	H	V L	H
H	N	N	L	L	V H	V L	V H
H	N	N	N	V V L	L	L	V L
H	N	N	H	V V L	V L	V V L	L
H	N	H	H	V V L	V L	L	V V L

6 Conclusion

6.1 Summary

In this paper we have introduced innovative fuzzy-genetic distributed agent architecture for intelligent buildings. We have outlined the difficult and unique control and learning problem that IB based agents need to cope with, in particular, dealing with large numbers of sensory inputs which display complex dynamics due to interactions with the environment, people and other agents.

We have also described a novel soft-computing architecture that solves this problem and is based on the use of hierarchical fuzzy controls. The fuzzy controllers form a behaviour-based architecture comprising three fixed behaviours - the Safety, Emergency and Economy behaviours and a dynamic (adaptable) rule-set that forms what we term a Comfort behaviour.

We have explained the importance of learning in IB agents and in particular the emphasis on particularisation rather than generalisation that is required to tailor the agents activities to the individual needs of differing occupants, moods and occasions. To address this challenge we have described a novel constrained GA learning methodology (Associative Experience Engine - AEE) that uses both past experiences and contextual information to find solutions more efficiently. In practical experiments we have conducted we found that AEE based agents interactively learn optimised rule bases for the comfort behaviour in approximately 21 iterations. In a comparative study to the Mendel-Wang method we showed that the AEE could produce similar rules and had the significant advantage of being able to interactively adapt to environmental (occupant driven) changes. Other notable characteristics are incremental rules processing (adding rules as more about the problem and solution is discovered), memory based exemplar processing (including short and long term processing such as aging) and self-analysis in terms of behaviour, error or success.

6.2 Future Work

Our current work is aimed at (1) establishing a standard communication framework for distributed embedded-agents (e.g. DIBAL), (2) development of better simulation/emulation tools for distributed embedded-agents, (3) the application of emerging technologies (eg embedded-internet, Mex, Java, Jini, JavaSpaces etc) and (4) exploring the use of alternative agent architectures (e.g. neural networks, Fuzzy Neural Networks, Instance Based etc). Concerning the associative experience engine, whilst it has allowed us make some significant progress towards meeting the challenges we set ourselves in sections 1.1 and 1.2 above, we clearly have work left to achieve the ideal embedded-agent for intelligent-buildings. Our original and continuing goal is a system that learns from the occupant without the need for any explicit input (i.e. non-intrusive online learning). Our current experimental system requires explicit interaction in order to develop its rules. We need a system that is capable of carrying out a recalculation of the appropriate rule base after the trigger of occupant intervention (i.e. changing an effector setting) without having to engage the occupant in the process. This would make the learning process totally transparent to the occupant.

We are exploring various possibilities for giving the AEE such a non-intrusive learning capability. We are currently investigating a mechanism we refer to as *Incremental Synchronous Learning (ISL)* which would work as follows: when an occupant changes an effector setting manually, the system would respond by immediately carrying out the action, setting the building to the requested state and generating a new rule based on that instance. In a manner comparable to the use of the AGM in the experimental system such a change of behaviour would initiate a learning sequence. In this case the learning sequence would be the equivalent of one iteration of the experimental system. At this point any further action would be suspended until there was another interaction with the occupant. That is, there would be no forced interactions with the occupant but rather the occupants spontaneous interactions would be used to trigger a simple learning process. It is hoped that such a modification to the system would allow the system to learn in the same way as the experimental prototype but unobtrusively by spreading the iterations over an extended period using the natural interactions of the user with the system. Thus for example, considering a temperature controller, each day the occupant might make an adjustment to the system (i.e. one learning iteration) thereby completing a learning cycle in an average of 21 days (according to our experimental data) which we would argue would be a most acceptable time for an agent to learn to particularise it services to a person (given in a manual system the user will always need command the system, whereas in the agent-assisted system the manual load upon the occupant reduces over time). In addition to providing a non-intrusive learning mechanism, this approach also places the user in prime control as it unfailingly and immediately responds to his command.

Another method we intend to examine is how s-maps (see section 1.2) might be used as an intermediate representation (i.e. a target system behaviour template) against which the AGM might explore actions to develop a new set of rules without having to interact with the occupant (i.e. it interacts with the template in a virtual space). This would be done as a background task (off-line learning in the strict sense), with the existing rules, including the newly acquired rule, in operation until they could be replaced by the newly learnt rules based upon the changes to the navigation spaces that the independent action of the occupant has occasioned. This should lead to the acceleration of learning to the same sort of speed as the prototype system but without the need for explicit occupant interaction.

With respect to applications, our interest include situations as diverse as mobile phones, wearable agents, through white/black goods to space-based transport and habitats.

Acknowledgements: We are pleased to acknowledge the contribution of Malcolm Lear (Essex University) who built the agent hardware, sensors and test rig. We would also like to thank, Anthony Pounds-Cornish, Sue Sharples, Gillian Kearney, Robin Dowling and Filiz Cayci with whom we have had many stimulating discussions on embedded-agent architectures. Finally, we would like to express our gratitude to Martin Henson for his assistance in translating the original WORD version of this paper into Latex.

References

[Bonarini 96] A. Bonarini, F. Basso, " Learning Behaviors Implemented As Fuzzy Logic And Reinforcement Learning", 2nd Online Workshop On Evolutionary Computation, 1996.
[Brooks 91] R Brooks, "Intelligence Without Representation", Artificial Intelligence 47, pp139-159, 1991.
[Brooks 97] R. Brooks, "Intelligent Room Project", Proc 2nd Int'l Cognitive Technology Conference, Japan 1997.
[Callaghan 2000] Callaghan V, Clarke, G, "Buildings As Intelligent Autonomous Systems: A Model for Integrating Personal and Building Agents", Proc. 6th International Conference on Intelligent Autonomous Systems, Venice, Italy; July 25 - 27, 2000.
[Cayci 2000] Cayci F, Callaghan V, Clarke G, "DIBAL - A Distributed Intelligent Building Agent Language", Proc. 6th International Conference on Information Systems Analysis and Synthesis, Orlando, Florida, July 2000.
[Coen 97] M.H.Coen, "Building Brains for Rooms: Designing Distributed Software Agents", Proc. Ninth Innovative Applications of AI Conference, AAAI Press, 1997.
[Davisson 98] P. Davisson "Energy Saving and Value Added Services; Controlling Intelligent-Buildings Using a Multi-Agent System Approach" in DA/DSM Europe DistribuTECH, PennWell, 1998.
[Dorigo 93] M. Dorigo, "Genetics-Based Machine Learning And Behaviour Based Robotics: A New Synthesis", IEEE transactions on Systems, Man, Cybernetics, pp. 141-154, 1993.
[Fukuda 99] T. Fukuda , N. Kubota , "An Intelligent Robotic System Based On Fuzzy Approach", Proceedings of the IEEE, Vol. 87, No. 9, pp.1448-1470, September 1999.
[Hagras 99a] H.Hagras, V Callaghan, M Colley, "A Fuzzy-Genetic Based Embedded-Agent Approach to Learning and Control in Agricultural Autonomous Vehicles", IEEE International Conference on Robotics and Automation, pp. 1005-1010, Detroit- U.S.A, May 1999.
[Hagras 99b] H.Hagras, V Callaghan, M Colley, "Online Learning of Fuzzy Behaviours using Genetic Algorithms and Real-Time Interaction with the Environment", IEEE International Conference on Fuzzy Systems, Seoul-Korea, pp. 668-672, August 1999.
[Hagras 2000a] Hagras H, Callaghan V, Colley M, "Online Learning Of Fuzzy Behaviour Co-Ordination For Autonomous Agents Using Genetic Algorithms And Real-Time Interaction With The Environment" IEEE International Conference on Fuzzy Systems in San Antonio, Texas, USA, 7-10 May 2000.

[Hagras 2000b] Hagras H, Callaghan V, Colley M, "On-Line Learning Of The Sensors Fuzzy Membership Functions In Autonomous Mobile Robots", IEEE International Congress on Robotics and Automation, San Francisco, April 2000.

[Hoffmann 98] F. Hoffmann, "Incremental Tuning Of Fuzzy Controllers By Means Of Evolution Strategy", GP-98 Conference, pp. 550-556, Madison, Wisconsin, 1998.

[Jeon 2000] Jeon H, Petrie C, Cutkosky M.R, "JATLite: A Java Agent Infrastructure with Message Routing", University of Stanford, IEEE Internet Computing, March/April 2000.

[Kasabov 98] Kasabov N "The ECOS Framework and the ECO Learning Method for Evolving Connectionist Systems", J. Advanced Computational Intelligence, Vol 2, No 6, 1998.

[Labrou 99] Labrou Y, Finin T, Peng Y, "The Current Landscape Of Agent Communication Languages", IEEE Intelligent Systems, Vol. 14, No. 2, March/ April 1999.

[Lehikoinen 99] J. Lehikoinen, J. Holopainen, M. Salmimaa, and A. Aldrovandi "MEX: A Distributed Software Architecture for Wearable Computers" 3rd International Symposium on Wearable Computers, San Francisco, California 18-19 October 1999.

[Linkens 95] G.Linkens, O. Nyongeso, "Genetic Algorithms For Fuzzy Control, Part II: Online System Development And Application", IEE proceedings Control theory applications, Vol.142, pp.177-185, 1995.

[Minar 99] M Nelson, M Gray, O Roup, R Krikorian, P Maes "HIVE: Distributed Agents For Networking Things", Proc. First International Symposium on Agent Systems and Applications and Third International Symposium on Mobile Agents, Rancho Las Palmas Marriott's Resort and Spa, Palm Springs, California, October 3 - 6 1999.

[Mozer 98] M. Mozer "The Neural Network House: An Environment That Adapts To Its Inhabitants", Proc of American Association for Artificial Intelligence Spring Symposium on Intelligent Environments, pp110-114, AAAI Press, 1998.

[Robathan, 89] P. ROBATHAN, "Intelligent Buildings Guide", Intelligent Buildings Group and IBC Technical Services Limited, 1989.

[Saffiotti 97] A. Saffiotti, "Fuzzy Logic In Autonomous Robotics: Behaviour Co-Ordination", Proc. 6th IEEE International Conference on Fuzzy Systems, Vol.1, pp. 573-578, Barcelona, Spain, 1997.

[Sharples 99] S. Sharples, V. Callaghan, G. Clarke, "A Multi-Agent Architecture for Intelligent Building Sensing and Control" International Sensor Review Journal, May 1999.

[Srinivas 96] M. Srinivas, L. Patnaik, "Adaptation In Genetic Algorithms", Genetic Algorithms For Pattern Recognition", (Eds Pal and Wang), CRC press, pp. 45-64, 1996.

[Steels 95] L. Steels, "When Are Robots Intelligent Autonomous Agents", Journal of Robotics and Autonomous Systems, Vol. 15, pp.3-9, 1995.
[Mendel 92] J. Mendel, L. Wang, "Generating Fuzzy Rules by Learning Through Examples", IEEE Trans. on Systems, Man and Cybernetics, Vol. 22, pp. 1414-1427, December 1992.
[Sherwin 99] Sherwin A "Internet House Offers a Life of Virtual Luxury", The Times, p10, 3rd Nov 1999.
[Zhou 90] H. Zhou, " A Computational Model of Cumulative Learning", Machine Learning Journal, pp. 383-406, 1990.
[mjc1]Reference is to Bonarini 1996, Not as listed in text.

Towards a Multiagent Design Principle: Analyzing an Organizational-Learning Oriented Classifier System

Keiki Takadama[1], Takao Terano[2], Katsunori Shimohara[3], Koichi Hori[4], and Shinichi Nakasuka[5]

[1] ATR International,
2-2-2 Hikaridai, Seika-cho, Soraku-gun
Kyoto 619-0288, Japan
E-mail: keiki@isd.atr.co.jp

[2] University of Tsukuba
3-29-1, Otsuka, Bunkyo-ku
Tokyo 112-0012, Japan
E-mail: terano@gssm.otsuka.tsukuba.ac.jp

[3] ATR International
2-2-2 Hikaridai, Seika-cho, Soraku-gun
Kyoto 619-0288, Japan
E-mail: katsu@isd.atr.co.jp

[4] University of Tokyo
4-6-1 Komaba, Meguro-ku
Tokyo 153-8904, Japan
E-mail: hori@ai.rcast.u-tokyo.ac.jp

[5] University of Tokyo
7-3-1 Bunkyo-ku
Tokyo 113-8656 Japan
E-mail: nakasuka@space.t.u-tokyo.ac.jp

Abstract. This paper addresses a big issue of a multiagent design principle by exploring our model in terms of its *generality*, *scalability*, and *performance*. To investigate these aspects in our model, we apply it into another domain, analyze its characteristics in large-scale problems, and compare its performance with that one of conventional models. Intensive simulations on a complex domain problem reveal the following implications: (1) our model shows its effectiveness in another domain, maintains its effectiveness in large-scale problems, and achieve a better performance than conventional models; (2) three key elements derived from our model have the potential to be important and essential factors towards multiagent design principles; and (3) the interpretation of general concepts from a computational viewpoint is one of the useful ways of addressing multiagent design principles.
Keywords: multiagent design, learning agents, learning classifier system, organizational learning

1 Introduction

In complex and dynamic environments where multiple autonomous agents interact with each other, how do we design these agents to obtain desired results? This is a big issue requiring clarification for both practical and engineering uses. To find a solution for this problem, a lot of research on multiagents [Gasser 88,Weiss 99] has been reported in recent years. Some examples include a communication design in a multiagent environment [Balch 95], a framework for team behaviors [Collinot 96], and primitive behaviors for adaptive group behaviors [Mataric 95]. These approaches, however, mainly focus on an architecture of a multiagent system and do not directly support a particular internal design of an agent (such as the aspect of *learning*). Considering the fact that this kind of an internal design has a big influence on deciding the collective performance, we cannot omit to analyze the influence of internal designs on multiagent systems.

To address this issue, our previous research investigated what kinds of elements are needed to improve the collective performance from the aspect of learning [Takadama 99]. Concretely, we focused on *organizational learning (OL)* [Argyris 78,Cohen 95] for organization and management science. We analyzed characteristics of a multiagent model that introduced the concept of OL using *soft computing* methods [Zadeh]. We selected OL and a soft computing approach because the former directly addresses the issue of collective learning and the latter provides useful techniques for designing an internal model of an agent. Specifically, in our previous research, we carried out an intensive analysis of our multiagent model, comparing the results with those ones of human experts on Printed Circuit Boards (PCBs) re-design problems in the Computer Aided Design (CAD) domain. From the analysis, we found that our implementation of OL from the computational viewpoint contributes to find good solutions at small computational costs and also found that three key elements derived from the implementation of OL are essential components for designing good learning agents.

However, the effectiveness of both the implementation of OL and the three key elements are shown only in a few typical boards in the CAD domain. From this fact, the following essential questions still remain towards multiagent design principles: (1) do both the implementation of OL and the three key elements show their effectiveness in other domains? (2) Do they keep their effectiveness as the problem scale becomes large? Moreover, (3) do they lead to a higher performance than conventional models? To answer these questions, this paper empirically applies our multiagent model into another domain, experimentally investigates its characteristics in large-scale problems, and computationally compares its performance with that of conventional models. Through the above experiments, this paper discusses a perspective of a multiagent design principle from the viewpoint of both our implementation of OL and the three key elements.

This paper is organized as follows. Section 2 starts by describing OL, and Section 3 explains our multiagent model and key elements in a multiagent design derived from the model. An example for analyzing our model in another domain is given in Section 4. Section 5 gives simulations and experimental results on scalability and comparisons with conventional models. A multiagent design principle is discussed through an analysis of the experimental results in Section 6, and our conclusions are finally made in Section 7.

2 Organizational Learning

2.1 Four Loop Learning in Organizational Learning

Organizational learning (OL) has been studied in the context of organization and management science and is roughly characterized as activities that improve the organizational performance which cannot be achieved at an individual level. In particular, OL consists of the following four kinds of learning [Argyris 78,Kim 93].

- **Individual single-loop learning** improves the performance within an individual norm.
- **Individual double-loop learning** improves the performance through the change of an individual norm itself.
- **Organizational single-loop learning** improves the performance within an organizational norm.
- **Organizational double-loop learning** improves the performance through the change of an organizational norm itself.

2.2 Reinterpretation of Four Loop Learning

The categorization in the previous section stipulates that (1) there are individual and organizational levels in learning, and (2) each learning can be classified as a single or double type. However, the term *norm* [1] in the above learning has not been defined clearly from a computational viewpoint. Therefore, this paper starts by assuming the norms as follows.

- **Individual norm** is implemented by individual knowledge.
- **Organizational norm** is implemented by organizational knowledge.

Next, the two types of knowledge in the above implementation are assumed as follows.

- **Individual knowledge** is implemented by a rule set.
- **Organizational knowledge** is implemented by a set of individual knowledge (rule set).

[1] For instance, a routine and a weltanschauung are examples of an individual norm and an organizational norm, respectively.

These assumptions may seem to define only parts of organizational learning, but they come from the consideration that individual (or organizational) norms are kind of behaviors established in an individual (or an organization) and these behaviors are derived from individual (or organizational) knowledge. By clarifying such norms through the above assumptions, new results which cannot be derived from the conventional definitions can potentially be found. Based on this claim, this paper defines *computational organizational learning* as "learning that includes four kinds of computationally interpreted loop learning."

3 Multiagent Model and Key Elements in its Design

3.1 Organizational-learning Oriented Classifier System

An Organizational-learning oriented Classifier System (OCS) [Takadama 99] is an extension of Learning Classifier Systems (LCSs) [Goldberg 89] to a multiagent architecture introducing the concept of OL. Specifically, OCS addresses a multiagent environment that includes imprecision, uncertainty and partial truth, by integrating complementary mechanisms like those found in soft computing, and thus OCS can be roughly considered as a kind of soft computing architecture. In detail, four kinds of computationally interpreted loop learning mechanisms are complementary integrated in OCS to implement the concept of OL.

○ **Agents**

In OCS, agents are implemented by their own LCSs, which are extended to introduce the concept of OL. In order to solve problems that cannot be solved at an individual level, agents divide given problems by acquiring their own appropriate *functions* through interaction with other agents. According to this method of problem solving, the *aim* of the agents is defined as finding appropriate *functions*. Furthermore, these functions are acquired through changes in agents' *if–then* rules and changes in the strength values[2] of rules, and thus a *function* is defined as a rule set in OCS.

○ **Architecture**

As shown in Figure 1, OCS is composed of many agents, and each agent has the same architecture that includes the following components.

< **Problem Solver** >

- **Detector** and **Effector** translate a part of an environment state into an internal state of an agent and derive actions based on this internal state [Russell 95], respectively.

[2] The term strength in this paper is defined as the value or weight of rules.

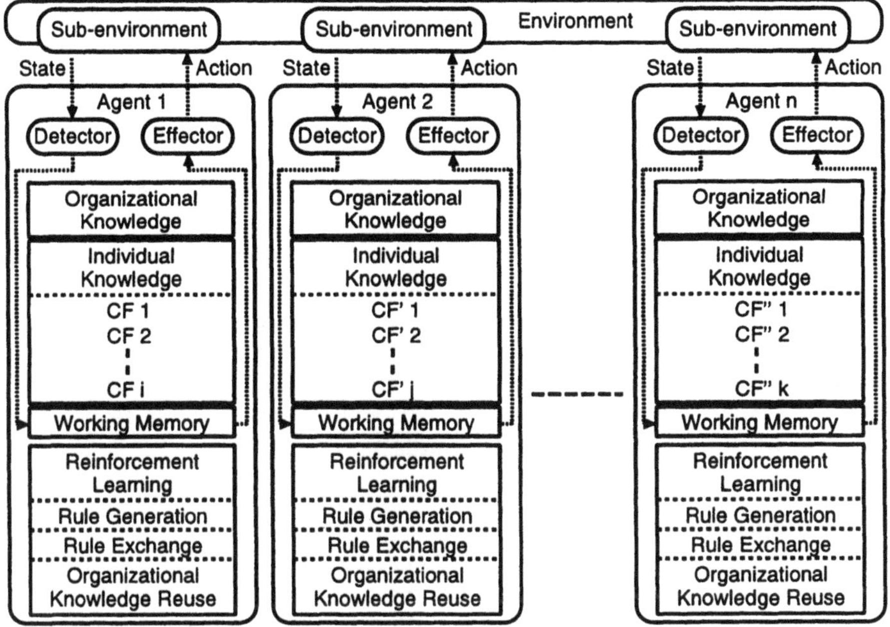

Fig. 1. OCS Architecture

< Memory >

- **Organizational knowledge memory** stores a set comprising each agent's rule set as organizational knowledge. In OCS, this knowledge is shared by all agents and represents knowledge on the function acquisition of agents, which is based on the role assignment without a hierarchical framework.
- **Individual knowledge memory** stores a rule set (a set of CFs (classifiers)) as individual knowledge. In OCS, agents independently store different CFs that are composed of *if-then* rules with a strength factor. In particular, one primitive action is included in a *then* part.
- **Working memory** stores the recognition results of sub-environmental states and also stores the internal states of actions of fired rules.

< Mechanisms >

- **Reinforcement learning, rule generation, rule exchange, and organizational knowledge reuse mechanisms** are computationally interpreted from the four kinds of learning in OL (The details will be described later). The mechanisms are improved by simple and ordinary techniques, avoiding the specific or elaborate ones.

○ Learning in OCS

(1) Reinforcement learning mechanism

In OCS, the reinforcement learning (RL) mechanism enables agents to acquire their own appropriate actions that are required to solve given problems. In particular, RL supports the learning of the appropriate order of fired rules by changing the strength values of the rules. Since this mechanism improves the problem solving efficiency at an individual level (not by creating/deleting but) by utilizing rules while changing the order of the fired ones, it works as one kind of "individual single-loop learning," which is interpreted to improve the performance within individual rules in computational organizational learning. Specifically, this mechanism works as shown in Figure 2–1, and OCS employs a *profit sharing* method [Grefenstette 88], which reinforces the sequence of all rules when agents obtain some rewards.[3]

(2) Rule generation mechanism

The rule generation mechanism in OCS creates new rules when none of the stored rules matches the current environmental state as shown in Figure 2–2. In particular, when the number of rules is MAX_CF (maximum number of rules), the rule with the lowest strength value is removed and a new rule is generated. Since this mechanism improves the problem solving range at an individual level by creating/deleting rules, it works as one kind of "individual double-loop learning," which is interpreted to improve the performance through the changes of the same individual rules in computational organizational learning.

In the process of rule generation, the condition (if) part of a rule is created to reflect the current situation, the action (then) part is determined randomly, and the strength value of the rule is set to the initial value. Furthermore, the strength value of the fired rule (*e.g.*, the No. i rule) is temporarily decreased as $ST(i) = ST(i) - SC(i)$, where $ST(i)$ indicates the strength of the No. i rule and $SC(i)$ indicates the selected number of the No. i rule. In particular, $SC(i)$ is counted when the No. i rule is fired and is reset to 0 when the situation changes. With this mechanism, the strength value of fired rules is decreased as long as the situation does not change like in deadlocked situations where the same rules are selected repeatedly. Then, these rules become candidates to be replaced by new rules, while the strength value of these rules is recovered when the situation changes.

(3) Rule exchange mechanism

In OCS, agents exchange rules with other agents at a particular time interval (GA_STEP [4]) in order to solve given problems that cannot be solved at an individual level as shown in Figure 2–3. Since this mechanism improves the

[3] The detailed credit assignment in OCS was proposed in [Takadama 98].

[4] This step is defined in section 4.2.

```
procedure reinforcement learning
  begin
    if problem is solved then
      for all agents do
        fired rules are reinforced;
  end
```

Figure 2–1

```
procedure rule generation
  begin
    for all agents do
      if no matched rules then
        begin
          if number of rules = MAX_CF then
            a rule with the lowest strength value is deleted;
          a new rule is created;
          a strength value of the new rule is set to an initial one;
        end
  end
```

Figure 2–2

```
procedure rule exchange
  begin
    if mod (step, GA_STEP)=0 then
      for all pairs of agents do
        for (number of rules)×GENERATION_GAP rules do
          if a lowest strength value of rule ≤ BORDER_ST then
            begin
              a rule with a low strength value is replaced by a rule
                with a high strength value between two agents;
              a strength value of the replaced rule is reset to an
                initial one;
            end
  end
```

Figure 2–3

```
procedure organizational knowledge reuse
  begin
    if iteration = 0 then
      stored organizational knowledge is utilized;
    else if solution is the best then
      begin
        if organizational knowledge is stored then
          stored organizational knowledge is deleted;
        current organizational knowledge is stored;
      end
  end
```

Figure 2–4

Fig. 2. Algorithms of Four Learning Mechanisms

problem solving efficiency at the organizational level not by creating/deleting a set comprising each agent's rule set but by utilizing it among the agents, this mechanism works as one kind of "organizational single-loop learning," which is interpreted to improve the performance within a set comprising each agent's individual rules in computational organizational learning.

In this mechanism, a particular number ((the number of rules) × `GENERATION_GAP` [5]) of rules with low strength values are replaced by rules with high strength values between two arbitrary agents. For example, when agents X and Y are selected as shown in Figure 3, the CFs in each agent are sorted by order of their strength values (upper CFs have high strength values). After this sorting, $CF_{j-2} \sim CF_j$ and $CF'_{k-2} \sim CF'_k$ in this case are replaced by $CF'_1 \sim CF'_3$ and $CF_1 \sim CF_3$, respectively. However, rules that have higher strength values than a particular value (`BORDER_ST`) are not replaced to avoid unnecessary crossover operations. The strength values of replaced rules are reset to their initial values. This is because effective rules in some agents are not always effective for other agents in multiagent environments.

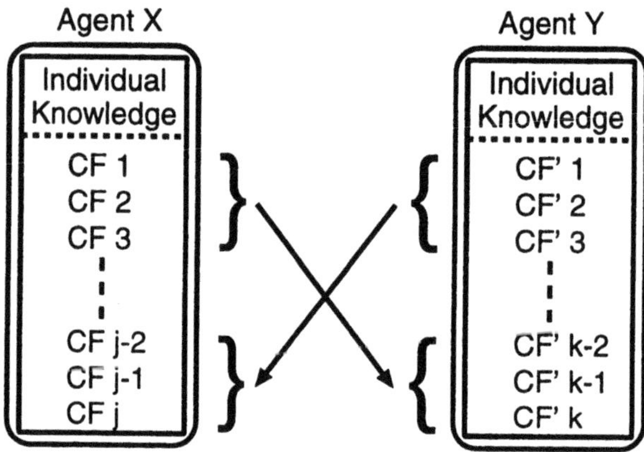

Fig. 3. Rule Exchange

(4) Organizational knowledge reuse mechanism

Finally, agents in OCS store a set comprising each agent's rule set (individual knowledge) as knowledge on the function acquisition when they most effectively solve given problems.[6] After storing this knowledge, agents reuse it when solving the same types of problems, such as an identical problem

[5] The ratio of removed rules.

[6] Since the efficiency depends upon the problems, it is difficult to generally define the efficiency. However, as one of the methods, agents are able to solve a given

starting with different random seeds or an identical small or large problem. Here, considering the situation in which n agents most effectively solve certain problems, a set comprising each agent's rule set is stored as shown in Figure 4 and agents later reuse the best of the rule sets in the same problem solving. This set is called organizational knowledge and it is updated through problem solving as shown in Figure 2–4. Since this mechanism improves the problem solving range at an organizational level by creating/deleting organizational knowledge, it works as one kind of "organizational double-loop learning," which is interpreted to improve the performance through changes of a set comprising each agent's individual rules itself in computational organizational learning.

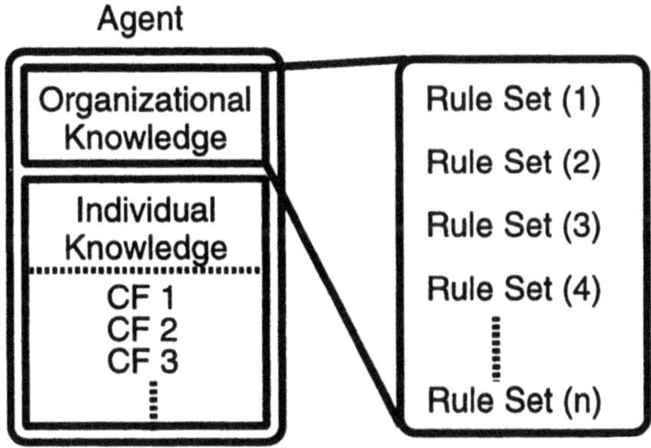

Fig. 4. Organizational Knowledge Reuse

As a concrete characteristic of this mechanism, organizational knowledge in OCS is represented by {RS (1), RS (2), $\cdots$, RS (n)}, where RS(x) is the rule set for the x-th agent and n is the total number of agents in the organization. Since this knowledge is composed of rule sets that indicate a function of each agent, the organizational knowledge represents the function acquisition of all the agents, which is based on the role assignment without a hierarchical framework. Other characteristics of this mechanism are summarized as follows: (a) each agent at the current stage of OCS does not store the entire individual rule sets of all the other agents independently, but shares the rule sets of all agents with other agents; (b) agents cannot use both individual and organizational knowledge at the same time, because the former knowledge is modified by each agent *during* problem solving while the latter knowledge is stored or reused by all agent *after* or *before* problem solving. This indicates that the organizational knowledge alone is utilized, instead of the initial indi-

problem most effectively by measuring a "good solution" or a "small computational cost."

vidual knowledge generated randomly; and (c) the organizational knowledge is different from ordinary effective knowledge in a single LCS, because the former knowledge represents the function acquisition and is used in the unit of *multiple agents*, while the latter knowledge is utilized in the unit of *one agent.*

○ **Relationships among the four learning mechanisms**
The total algorithm of OCS follows the procedure shown in Figure 5. Briefly, organizational knowledge is reused if it is stored before agents solve a problem, and both the rule generation and rule exchange mechanisms are executed until the problem is solved. After the problem solving, both the reinforcement learning and organizational knowledge reuse mechanisms are executed, and agents continue to solve the same problem from the same initial situation until the solution converges.

```
procedure OCS
  begin
    iteration=0;
    organizational knowledge reuse;
    while solution is not converged do
      begin
        step=0;
        while problem is not solved do
          begin
            rule generation;
            rule exchange;
            step=step+1;
          end
        iteration=iteration+1;
        reinforcement learning;
        organizational knowledge reuse;
      end
  end
```

Fig. 5. Algorithms of OCS

○ **Supplemental setup**
In addition to the above mechanisms, OCS is set up as follows. A particular number (FIRST_CF) of rules in each agent is generated randomly in advance, and the strength values of all the rules are set to the same initial value.

3.2 Key Elements in Multiagent Design

Using OCS, our previous research found that the integration of the four kinds of learning mechanisms in OL is effective in terms of both solution and computational cost [Takadama 99] and also found that its effectiveness is supported by the following three key elements: (1) indispensable different dimensions in learning mechanisms, (2) meta-level interaction (*i.e.*, interaction among the learning mechanisms in OCS) in addition to interaction among agents, and (3) the combination of exploration at an individual level and exploitation at an organizational level. These three elements are effective because they respectively (1) make up for the defects of the other single learning mechanism, (2) overcome the limitations of the effects derived from the interaction among agents, and (3) solve the trade-off problem between exploration and exploitation by an appropriate balance of the learning mechanisms.

4 Pentomino Tiling Problem

4.1 Problem Description

As different kinds of a problem in the previous research, we employ a pentomino tiling problem. A pentomino is a figure that combines five squares as shown in Figure 6 (a), and its tiling problem is to appropriately place the pentominos while minimizing the area that encloses all the pentominos without any overlap. We select this domain because (1) this problem can be considered as a multiagent problem when one pentomino is assumed to be one agent; (2) it is easy to increase/decrease the number of pentominos; (3) the minimum solution is known as shown in Figure 6 (b); and (4) the effects of both our implementation of OL and the three key elements in the multiagent design can be measured in terms of solution and computational cost. Here, our implementation of OL means an integration of four computationally implemented loop-learning mechanisms in OCS.

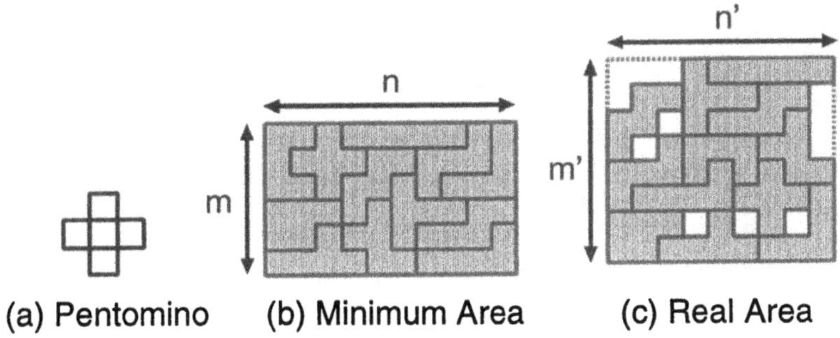

Fig. 6. Pentominos

4.2 Pentomino Design and Problem Setting

In the task, each pentomino is designed as an agent in OCS and learns to acquire an appropriate sequence of actions that minimizes the area enclosing all pentominos without any overlap. In detail, the pentominos have 17 primitive actions including stay, move, and rotate, and the pentominos get a turn in order to execute their primitive actions. In a concrete problem setting, all the pentominos are initially placed randomly without considering any overlap, and thus many pentominos actually overlap with others. After this initial placement, the pentominos start to perform some primitive actions to reduce such overlap while minimizing the area that encloses all of them. When the size of this area converges without any overlap, all the pentominos evaluate their own sequences of actions according to the size of the area. Then, the pentominos restart from the initial placement to acquire more appropriate sequences of actions to find a smaller area. In this cycle, one *step* is counted when all pentominos perform one primitive action, and one *iteration* is counted when the size of the area converges without overlap.

4.3 Index of Evaluation

In this task, the following two indices are evaluated:

$$Solution = (Real\ area)/(Minimum\ area) \tag{1}$$

$$Computational\ cost = \sum_{i=1}^{n} step(i) \tag{2}$$

The first index (*solution*) evaluates the area enclosing all pentominos and shows how the current area, like that shown in Fig 6 (c), is small compared with the minimum area in Fig. 6 (b). The next index (*computational cost*) calculates the accumulated steps. In this equation, "*step* (i)" and "n" indicate the steps counted in i iterations and the number of final iterations, respectively.

4.4 Rule Set Design and Task Environment

The rule sets in the pentomino tiling problem are designed as follows. Note that the rule below indicates an individual rule of agents.

- The condition part of CF (classifier) has the following four parts.
  1. Previous action (17 types)
  2. A flag distinguishing whether a pentomino is overlapped or not (1 or 0)
  3. A flag distinguishing whether a pentomino is totally enclosed by other pentominos or not (1 or 0)
  4. A flag distinguishing whether a pentomino removes an overlapping area within a certain time or not (1 or 0)

- The action part of CF indicates primitive behaviors (17 types).

According to this design, one example of 210# 6 in CF shows that *if* `a previous action is the 2nd action` and `there is overlap` and `the pentomino is not enclosed`, *then* `act on the 6th action`. In this case, the mark of # indicates "don't care."

5 Simulation

To ensure and extend the effectiveness of both our implementation of OL (*i.e.*, the integration of four computationally implemented loop-learning mechanisms in OCS) and the three key elements in the multiagent design, this section addresses the issues of (1) another domain, (2) large-scale problems, and (3) a comparison with conventional LCSs. In detail, we employ the pentomino tiling problem as a problem in another domain, investigate the performance of OCS in large-scale problems, and compare the results of OCS with those of conventional LCSs. Note that our simulations on large-scale problems and comparison of conventional LCSs are performed in the pentomino tiling problem.

5.1 Large-Scale Problem

○ Experimental design
As the large-scale problems, the following four cases were tested with 24 ($= 2 \times 12$), 48 ($= 4 \times 12$), 96 ($= 8 \times 12$), 192 ($= 16 \times 12$), and 384 ($= 32 \times 12$) pentominos in the pentomino tiling problem. The reason for selecting the above numbers of pentominos is because the minimum area is known when the number of pentominos is a multiple of 12 as shown in Figure 6 (b). Due to these selections, pentominos of the same type as in Figure 6 (b) are used in the above tests. For example, two pentominos of the same type are used in 24 pentominos.

- **Case 1:** RGXK
- **Case 2:** RGX (RGXK-K)
- **Case 3:** RGK (RGXK-X)
- **Case 4:** GXK (RGXK-R)

In the above cases, R, G, X, and K indicate the mechanisms of **R**einforcement learning, rule **G**eneration, rule e**X**change, and Organizational **K**nowledge reuse, respectively. These learning mechanisms are computationally implemented from the concept of OL as described in section 2. In particular, RGXK indicates the case where all four mechanisms are included and RGX indicates the case where the organizational knowledge reuse mechanism is removed from RGXK. Note that RXK, where the G mechanism is removed from RGXK, is omitted in this simulation. This is because pentominos without the rule generation mechanism cannot create new rules which are needed to solve the given problems.

○ **Experimental setup**
In the pentomino tiling problem, organizational knowledge and parameters in OCS are designed as follows.

- **Organizational knowledge** in this simulation is created as a set comprising each rule set of pentominos that is acquired by 12 pentominos in a pre-simulation, and this knowledge is reused as the initial rule sets of the 24, 48, 96, 192, and 384 pentominos. From this creation of organizational knowledge, the initial rule sets are neither pre-programmed nor randomly generated. As the way of utilizing this knowledge by the y numbers of pentominos, an equation can be roughly written as follows, where $RS_y(x)$ indicates the rule set of the x-th pentomino whose total number is y. In this simulation, y is either 24, 48, 96, 192, or 384.

$$RS_y(x) \leftarrow RS_{12}(mod((x-1), 12) + 1), \;\; x = 1, \cdots, y$$

- **Parameters** in OCS, except for the population size, are set as shown in Table 1. Note that we found that the tendency of the results does not change drastically with the parameter setting.

○ **Experimental results**
Figures 7 (a) and (b) show results of *solution* ((real area)/(minimum area)) and *computational cost* (sum of steps), respectively. These indices are indicated in the vertical axes, and the number of pentominos, represented in a unit of a multiple of 12, is indicated in the horizontal axes. FILL indicates a result in which all pentominos are placed by minimizing the area in one try. We employ FILL for measuring an ability of the integration of the learning mechanisms through a comparison with the result of FILL. comparing with other mechanisms. In the experiment, the results of FILL and all others are averaged from 100 and five situations with different random seeds, respectively. In the case of using the organizational knowledge reuse mechanism, the steps needed to acquire the organizational knowledge are added to the results. From these figures, we find the following characteristics.

- RGXK is the only method that finds good solutions with small computational costs.
- The effectiveness of RGXK is maintained even when the problem size becomes large.

5.2 Comparison with Conventional LCSs

○ **Experimental design and setup**
Next, as a comparison to conventional LCSs, the following three cases are tested in the same pentomino tiling problem with 24 pentominos. We select the Michigan approach [Holland 78] and Pittsburgh approach [Smith 83] as our targets to compare because both approaches are standard in the context of LCS literature.

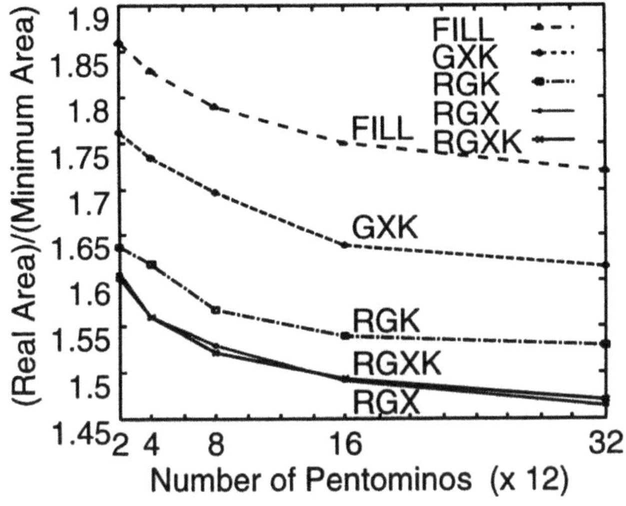

(a) **Solution: (Real area)/(Minimum area)**

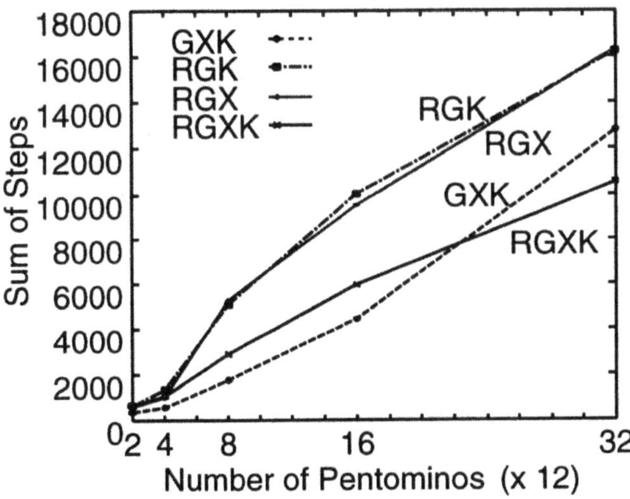

(b) **Computational Cost: Sum of Steps**

Fig. 7. Solution and Computational Cost

- **Case 1:** Michigan Approach
- **Case 2:** Pittsburgh Approach
- **Case 3:** OCS

The experimental setups of the Michigan approach, the Pittsburgh approach, and OCS are shown in Table 1. Note that we found the tendency of the results does not change drastically with the parameter setting.

Table 1. Variables in Michigan, Pittsburgh, and OCS

	Michigan	Pittsburgh	OCS
Population size	1 LCS	24 LCSs	
FIRST_CF	30		
MAX_CF	50		
GA_STEP	20 steps	1 iteration	20 steps
Crossover	1 point crossover		rule exchange
GENERATION_GAP	0.1		
BORDER_ST	—		-50
Mutation	1 bit change		—
Mutation rate	0.05		—
Inversion rate	—	0.05	—
Credit assignment	profit sharing	—	profit sharing

† FIRST_CF, MAX_CF, GA_STEP, GENERATION_GAP, and BORDER_ST, respectively, indicate the number of initial rules of each pentomino, the maximum number of rules of each pentomino, the interval steps in GA operations, the ratio of operated rules, and the lowest strength of the rule not for removal.

○ Experimental results

Figure 8 shows results of both *solution* and *computational cost* in the Michigan approach, the Pittsburgh approach, and OCS. In this experiment, all results are averaged from five situations with different random seeds. The steps needed to acquire the organizational knowledge are added to the results in OCS, and the *computational cost* in the Pittsburgh approach is adjusted by multiplying p, which is the number of LCSs. The reason for the multiplication is because the same problem is solved by each LCS at the same iteration in the Pittsburgh approach. From this figure, we find the following characteristics.

- The computational cost in the Michigan approach is small, but the solution itself is not good.
- The solution in the Pittsburgh approach is quite good, but requires a huge computational cost.

- In comparison with the above results, the solution of OCS is almost the same as that of the Pittsburgh approach, and has the smallest computational cost.

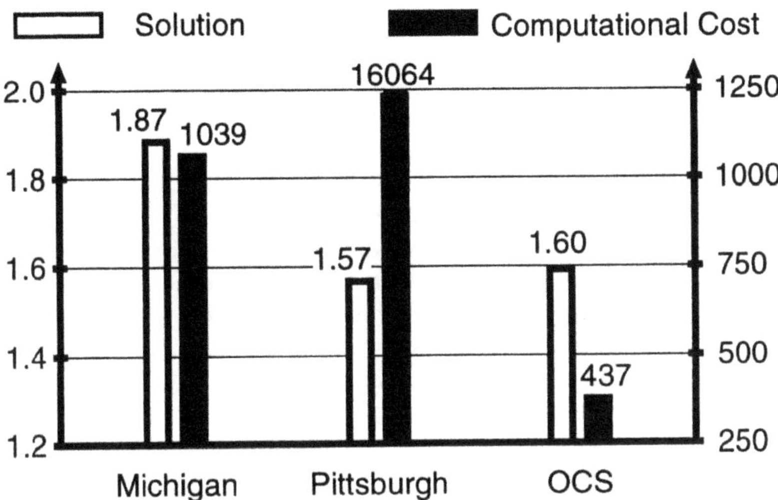

Fig. 8. Solution and Computational Cost: Comparison of Michigan, Pittsburgh, and OCS

6 Discussion

6.1 Analysis: Implementation of OL

○ Other Domains

Through the simulations on large-scale problems and comparisons with conventional LCSs in the pentomino tiling problem, the results show that the integration of the four learning mechanisms in OCS finds good solutions with small computation costs. This indicates that our way of implementing the concept of OL from the computational viewpoint is effective not only in the Printed Circuit Boards (PCBs) re-design problems in the previous research but also in the pentomino tiling problem. Although this effectiveness is simply shown only in two problems, the simulation results suggest an applicability of our implementation of OL in a lot of other domains.

○ Large-Scale Problems

From the result of the simulation on the large-scale problem in Figure 7, we find that the integration of the four learning mechanisms (RGXK in Figure

7) finds good solutions with small computational costs even when the number of pentominos increases by a factor of two. This indicates that our way of implementing the concept of OL from the computational viewpoint is effective without depending on the problem scale. In particular, considering the fact that either the solution or computational cost becomes worse when one of the learning mechanisms is missing, our implementation of OL is an important factor in improving the collective performance in large-scale problems.

So, why is our implementation of OL effective in large-scale problems where the environment changes more dynamically and frequently than in small-scale problems? The reasons are shown as follows: (1) the reinforcement learning mechanism provides an adaptation capability by seeking better rewards according to the changes of an environment; (2) the rule generation mechanism enables agents to adapt to a changing environment by creating new rules that match the environment; (3) the rule exchange mechanism reduces the cases of changes to an environment by quickly solving given problems through the exchange of necessary rules for problem solving; and (4) the organizational knowledge reuse mechanism, finally, restrains the changes of an environment by effectively limiting large search ranges through the reuse of the organizational knowledge.

To summarize the above features, the RG (reinforcement learning and rule generation) mechanisms adapt to a changing environment and the XK (rule exchange and organizational knowledge reuse) mechanisms restrain the changes of an environment. In particular, the adaptation to a changing environment by the RG mechanisms contributes to explore good solutions as shown in Figure 7 (a), while the restraint on the changes of an environment by the XK mechanisms contributes to reduce computational costs as shown in Figure 7 (b). From the above analysis, the integration of the four learning mechanisms is sufficiently useful for practical and engineering domains because the effectiveness of our implementation of OL is maintained even when the problem size becomes larger.

○ Comparison with Conventional LCSs

The results of the simulations on the comparisons with conventional LCSs shown in Figure 8 tell us that OCS finds better solutions at smaller computational costs than the Michigan and Pittsburgh approaches. This indicates that our way of implementing the concept of OL from the computational viewpoint is useful for providing a higher performance than that of conventional LCSs. In particular, considering the fact that OCS is composed of the four learning mechanisms, our implementation of OL is an important factor in improving the collective performance.

So, why is our implementation of OL effective in comparison with conventional LCSs? This is because some of the learning mechanisms in OL are missing both in the Michigan and Pittsburgh approaches whereas OCS includes all four of them. Concretely, the Michigan approach includes individual single-loop learning (reinforcement learning) and individual double-loop learning (crossover and mutation)[7], but the other two mechanisms are missing. The Pittsburgh approach, on the other hand, includes individual single- and double-loop learning (inversion and mutation) and organizational single-loop learning (crossover), but lacks organizational double-loop learning. In particular, the lack of the rule exchange mechanism in the organizational single-loop learning of the Michigan approach prevents the solution from improving. This is because pentominos in the Michigan approach cannot acquire their own appropriate rules independently, which is required to find good solutions through cooperation among pentominos. Furthermore, the lack of the organizational knowledge reuse mechanism in the organizational double-loop learning of both the Michigan and Pittsburgh approaches requires large computational costs. This is because pentominos in both the Michigan and Pittsburgh approaches do not have an architecture for utilizing pre-learned rules, which contribute to reduce the computational costs. From these analyses, the integration of the four learning mechanisms in OCS is important for overcoming limitations in the performance of conventional LCSs.

6.2 Towards a Multiagent Design Principle

From the above discussion, the integration of the four learning mechanisms provides the following possibilities: "generality" to show a good performance in other domains, "scalability" to maintain the same level of performance in large-scale problems, and "a high performance" that is better than that in conventional LCSs. Note that the above three advantages can be easily obtained just by integrating the four learning mechanisms even if each mechanism is simple and ordinary. From this feature, our implementation of OL can improve the collective performance in multiagent problems.

However, our implementation of OL is only related to a guideline for designing a LCS architecture and has not yet arrived at a guideline for designing general multiagent systems. From this fact, the previous research investigated what kinds of elements are important and essential factors for general guidelines and found that the following three key elements support the effectiveness of our implementation of OL [Takadama 99]: (a) indispensable different dimensions in learning mechanisms, (b) meta-level interaction (*i.e.*, interaction among the learning mechanisms) in addition to interaction among agents, and (c) the combination of exploration at an individual level and exploitation at an organizational level. By using these three key elements, the following guidelines are provided for designing multiagent systems: (a) the indispensable number of learning mechanisms should be introduced into systems to work with different dimensions; (b) the interaction among the learning mechanism is carefully implemented when introducing the learning

[7] The crossover and mutation in the Michigan approach contribute to create new rules but do not work at an organizational level.

mechanisms, because this meta-level interaction determines the characteristics of the interaction among agents; and (c) the learning mechanisms must be designed to be divided into exploration-oriented and exploitation-oriented types, in which the former learning mechanisms must be designed to address the problem solving at an individual level while the latter ones must be designed to address the problem solving at an organizational level.

From these guidelines, we can notice important aspects in designing multiagent systems. However, the three key elements were not very powerful for the design guidelines at the time of the previous research, because they were derived only from a certain specific result. Therefore, simulations in another domain, large-scale problems, and comparisons with conventional LCSs extend the valid range of the design guidelines in terms of "generality", "scalability", and "performance". From this extension, the three key elements are potentially useful multiagent design principles. Furthermore, owing to this potential, the three key elements come to provide clearer reasons why either the solution or computational cost becomes worse when one of the learning mechanisms is missing in the simulations of the large-scale problem (Figure 7) and the comparisons with conventional LCSs (Figure 8). Some brief considerations for the simulation results are summarized as follows: (a) the defect caused by removing one learning mechanism cannot be covered by the remaining learning mechanisms, even if the remaining learning mechanisms play their own roles in different dimensions; (b) the appropriate execution order of learning mechanisms, which is one of the interaction among learning mechanisms, is broken by omitting one learning mechanism; and (c) the appropriate balance between exploration and exploitation in a search process is lost by removing one learning mechanism.

From the above capability of the design guidelines, we have arrived at the conclusion that (1) the three key elements are important and essential factors towards multiagent design principles and (2) an interpretation of general concepts (such as *organizational learning*) from a computational viewpoint is one of the useful ways of addressing multiagent design principles.

7 Conclusion

This paper deals with the issue of a multiagent design principle by exploring the proposed model in terms of its *generality*, *scalability*, and *performance*. Concretely, this paper applied OCS to pentomino tiling problems as another problem, investigated the performance of OCS in large-scale problems, and compared both the solutions and computational costs of OCS with the conventional LCSs. Although the results in this paper do not cover the entire problem solving range, (1) our implementation of OL, which includes the integration of four learning mechanisms, (a) shows its effectiveness in other domains, (b) maintains its effectiveness in large-scale problems, and (c) achieves a better performance than conventional LCSs. We also found the following possibilities that (2) the three key elements derived from our implementation of OL are important and essential factors towards multiagent design principles; and (3) the interpretation of general concepts such as *organizational learning* from a computational viewpoint is one of the useful ways of addressing multiagent design principles.

Future researches will include: (1) an exploration of the multiagent design principle from other viewpoints (other than the viewpoint of OL); and (2) further experiments with other examples to strengthen the multiagent design principle.

References

[Argyris 78] C. Argyris and D.A. Schön: *Organizational Learning*, Addison-Wesley, 1978.

[Balch 95] T.R. Balch and R.C. Arkin: "Communication in Reactive Multiagent Robotic Systems", *Autonomous Robots*, Vol. 1, No. 1, pp. 27–52, 1995.

[Cohen 95] M.D. Cohen and L.S. Sproull: *Organizational Learning*, SAGE Publications, 1995.

[Collinot 96] A. Collinot, A. Drogoul, and P. Benhamou: "Agent Oriented Design of a Soccer Robot Team", *The Second International Conference on Multi-Agent Systems (ICMAS '96)*, pp. 41–47, 1996.

[Gasser 88] L. Gasser and A. Bond: *Readings in Distributed Artificial Intelligence*, Morgan Kaufman Publishers, 1988.

[Goldberg 89] D.E. Goldberg: *Genetic Algorithms in Search, Optimization, and Machine Learning*, Addison-Wesley, 1989.

[Grefenstette 88] J.J. Grefenstette: "Credit Assignment in Rule Discovery Systems Based on Genetic Algorithms," *Machine Learning*, Vol. 3. pp. 225–245, 1988.

[Holland 78] J.H. Holland and J. Reitman: "Cognitive Systems Based on Adaptive Algorithms," in *Pattern Directed Inference System*, D.A. Waterman and F. Hayes-Roth (Eds.), Academic Press, 1978.

[Kim 93] D. Kim: "The Link Between Individual and Organizational Learning," *Sloan Management Review*, Fall, pp. 37–50, 1993.

[Mataric 95] M.J. Mataric: "Designing and Understanding Adaptive Group Behavior," *Adaptive Behavior*, Vol. 4, No. 1, pp. 51–80, 1995.

[Russell 95] S.J. Russell and P. Norving: *Artificial Intelligence: A Modern Approach*, Prentice-Hall International, 1995.

[Smith 83] S.F. Smith: "Flexible Learning of Problem Solving Heuristics through Adaptive Search," *1983 International Joint Conference on Artificial Intelligence (IJCAI '83)*, pp. 422–425, 1983.

[Takadama 98] K. Takadama, S. Nakasuka, and T. Terano: "Multiagent Reinforcement Learning with Organizational-Learning Oriented Classifier System," *IEEE 1998 International Conference On Evolutionary Computation (ICEC '98)*, pp. 63–68, 1998.

[Takadama 99] K. Takadama, T. Terano, K. Shimohara, K. Hori and S. Nakasuka: "Making Organizational Learning Operational: Implication from Learning Classifier System," *Computational and Mathematical Organization Theory (CMOT)*, Kluwer Academic Publishers, Vol. 5, No. 3, pp. 229–252, 1999.

[Weiss 99] G. Weiss: *Multiagent Systems – Modern Approach to Distributed Artificial Intelligence* –, The MIT Press, 1999.

[Zadeh] L.A. Zadeh: "What is Soft Computing?", in Berkeley Initiative in Soft Computing (BISC) web site (http://www.cs.berkeley.edu/projects/Bisc/bisc.wel-come.html).

A Human-Centered Approach for Intelligent Internet Applications

Ernesto Damiani[1], Rajiv Khosla[2], and Somkiat Kitjongthawonkul[2]

[1] Universitá di Milano, Polo Didattico e di Ricerca di Crema, Italy
[2] LaTrobe University, Department of Computer Science and Computer Engineering, Melbourne, Australia

Abstract. Intelligent agents are being increasingly used on the Internet to provide various kinds of support to the Internet users. *Task level* support is aimed at modeling the user's tasks and problem solving models. In this work, we focus on design and application of intelligent agents for providing task level support in Internet-based applications via an *Electronic Broker*. Our Broker is used to locate the desired information or product for its user and acts as a mediator between the information providers or on-line suppliers and the user/customer. The operation of the intelligent electronic broker is demonstrated through a sample application, namely, the purchase of hardware adapters on the Internet.

1 Introduction

Intelligent agents (and in general software agents) are increasingly being used on the Internet to provide *clerical*, *tool* and *task* level support to the Internet users. The clerical support is being provided in terms of fetching and depositing data across different machines on the Internet. Tool support is being provided in terms of applying various soft and hard computing technologies like neural networks, fuzzy logic, genetic algorithms and knowledge based systems for searching, mining and manipulating data on the Internet. Finally, task level support is being provided in terms of modeling user's tasks and problem solving models. Given the increasing quantity of on-line suppliers and multimedia information/products on the Internet, general-purpose Internet search engines seem wholly unfit to this task. In this work we focus on design and application of intelligent agents for providing task level support in Internet-based applications. Task level support involves the search phase of Internet applications and is provided in the form of an *Electronic Broker* . The electronic broker is used to locate the desired information or product for its user and acts as a mediator between the information providers or on-line suppliers and the user/customer. The application of the intelligent electronic broker is demonstrated through a Internet based applications, namely, purchase of hardware adapters on the Internet.

The paper is organized as follows. Section 2 briefly surveys of various intelligent technologies (e.g., knowledge based systems, fuzzy logic, neural networks and genetic algorithms) from an application perspective. Section

3 outlines five layers of an intelligent agent based distributed architecture for Internet applications. Section 4 outlines the overall electronic brokerage framework for the hardware adapter application. Section 5 describes the application of the intelligent agent based distributed architecture in the hardware adapter application. Finally, Section 6 concludes the paper and outlines the mapping of the intelligent distributed agent based distributed architecture for Internet applications in the hardware adapters application domain.

2 Intelligent Technologies and Hybrid Configurations

The purpose of this Section is twofold. Firstly, we want to introduce to the reader the range of intelligent technologies, which are being used on the Internet (among other aspects) for facilitating search, building domain ontologies . Secondly, the introduction to these technologies helps us to explain the task-centered approach adopted by us for modeling intelligent agents. The four most commonly used intelligent methodologies in the Nineties are symbolic knowledge based systems (e.g. expert systems), artificial neural networks, fuzzy systems and genetic algorithms. Symbolic knowledge based systems have served varied purposes in industry and commerce during the last three decades. The most widely used versions being expert systems which have found their way into industry and commerce, including manufacturing, planning, scheduling, design, diagnosis, sales and finance. In these applications, the unitary architecture of production rules, normally enhanced by frames or objects, has been used to capture human expertise and to solve different problems. The different knowledge representation techniques like semantic networks, frames, scripts and objects have been able to capture some of the ways in which humans utilize knowledge. However, practitioners have also identified some of the limitations of symbolic knowledge based systems. These include among others, slow and constricted knowledge acquisition processes, inability to properly deal with imprecision in data, inability to process incomplete information, combinatorial explosion of rules, retrieval problems in recovering relevant past cases, and inability to reason under time constraints on occasions. People deal every day with imprecision and fuzziness in data. This imprecision may be represented by linguistic statements. A number of fuzzy systems have been built based on fuzzy concepts and imprecise reasoning. Fuzzy systems have been used in a number of areas including control of trains in Japan, sales predictions, and stock market risk analysis. A major disadvantage of fuzzy systems and expert systems is their heavy reliance on human experts for knowledge acquisition. This knowledge may be in the form of rules used to solve a problem and/or the shape of the membership functions used for modeling a fuzzy concept. Besides the knowledge acquisition problem, these systems are restricted in terms of their adaptive and learning capabilities. The limitations in knowledge based systems and fuzzy systems have been primarily responsible for the resurgence of artificial neural networks . In the financial sector, neural networks are used for prediction and modeling of markets, signature analysis, automatic reading of handwritten characters (checks), assessment of credit worthiness and selection of investments. In the telecommunication sector, applications can be found in signal analysis, noise elimination and data compression. Similarly, in the environment sector, neural networks have been used for risk evaluation, chemical analysis, weather forecasting and resource management. Other applications can be found in quality control, production planning and load forecasting in power systems. In these applications, the inherent parallelism in artificial neural networks and their capacity to learn, process incomplete information and generalize has been exploited. However, the stand-alone approaches of artificial neural networks have exposed some limitations such as the problems associated with lack of structured knowledge representation, inability to interact with conventional symbolic databases and inability to explain the reasons for conclusions reached. Their inability to explain their conclusions has limited their applicability to high-risk domains (e.g. real-time alarm processing). Another major limitation associated with neural networks is the problem of scalability. For large and complex problems, difficulties exist in training the networks and also in assessing their generalization capabilities. Optimization of manufacturing processes is another area where intelligent methodologies like artificial neural networks and genetic algorithms have been used. Genetic algorithms are being used for solving scheduling and control problems in industry. They have also been successfully used for optimization of symbolic, fuzzy and neural network based intelligent systems because of their modeling convenience. One of the problems associated with genetic algorithms is that they are computationally expensive, which can restrict their on-line use in real-time systems where time and space are at a premium. In fact, real-time systems add another dimension to the problems associated with the various intelligent methodologies. These problems are largely associated with the time and space constraints of real-time systems. Some examples of real-time systems are command and control systems, process control systems, flight control and alarm processing systems. These computational and practical issues associated with the four intelligent methodologies have made the practitioners and researchers look at ways of hybridizing the different intelligent methodologies from an applications viewpoint. However, the evolution of hybrid systems is not only an outcome of the practical problems encountered by these intelligent methodologies but is also an outcome of deliberative, fuzzy, reactive, self-organizing and evolutionary aspects of the human information processing system [16]. Intelligent hybrid systems can be grouped into three classes, namely, fusion systems, transformation systems, combination systems [10]. In fusion systems ([27], [17], [20], [22], [23]), the representation and/or information processing features of intelligent methodology A are fused into the representation structure of another intelligent methodology B. In this way, the intelligent methodology B augments its information processing in a manner that can cope with different levels of intelligence and information processing. From a practical viewpoint, this augmentation can be seen as a way by which an intelligent methodology addresses its weaknesses and exploits its existing strengths to solve a particular real-world problem. The hybrid systems based on the fusion approach revolve around artificial neural networks and genetic algorithms. In artificial neural network based fusion systems, representation and/or information processing features of other intelligent methodologies like symbolic knowledge based systems and fuzzy systems are fused into artificial neural networks. Genetic algorithm based fusion systems involve fusion of intelligent methodologies like knowledge based systems, fuzzy systems, and artificial neural networks. Transformation systems ([19], [21]) are used to transform one form of representation into another. They are used to alleviate the knowledge acquisition problem by transforming distributed or continuous representations into discrete representations. From a practical perspective, they are used in situations where knowledge required to accomplish the task is not available and one intelligent methodology depends upon another intelligent methodology for its reasoning or processing. For example, neural nets are used for transforming numerical/continuous data into symbolic rules which can then be used by a symbolic knowledge based system for further processing. Transformation systems have also been used for knowledge discovery and data mining [10]. Combination systems ([25], [18], [26], [25]) involve explicit hybridization. Instead of fusion, they model the different levels of information processing and intelligence by using intelligent methodologies that best model a particular level. Intelligent combination systems, unlike fusion systems, retain the separate identity of each intelligent methodology within a module. These systems involve a modular arrangement of two or more intelligent methodologies to solve real-world problems. These three different classes of intelligent hybrid systems and their industrial applications have been researched and reported in [10]. The concepts of fusion, transformation, and combination have been used in different situations or tasks, and by applying a top-down and/or bottom-up knowledge engineering strategy. All these hybrid architectures have a number of advantages in that the hybrid arrangement is able to successfully accomplish tasks in various situations. However, these hybrid architectures also suffer from some drawbacks. These drawbacks can be explained in terms of the quality of solution and range of tasks covered as shown in Figure 1. Fusion and transformation architectures on their own do not capture all aspects of human cognition related to problem solving. For example, fusion architectures result in conversion of explicit knowledge into implicit knowledge, and as a result lose on the declarative aspects of problem solving. Thus, they are restricted in terms of the range of tasks covered by them. The transformation architectures with bottom-up strategy get into problems with increasing task complexity. Therefore the quality of solution suffers when there is heavy overlap between variables, where the rules are very complicated, the quality of data is poor, or data is noisy. Also, because they lack explicit reasoning, the range of tasks covered by them becomes restricted. The combination architectures cover a range of tasks because of their inherent flexibility in terms of selection of two or more intelligent methodologies. However, because of lack of (or minimal) knowledge transfer among different modules the quality of solution suffers for the very reasons the fusion and transformation architectures are used. As fusion, transformation, and combination architectures have been motivated by and developed for different problem solving tasks/situations, it is useful to associate these architectures in a manner so as to maximize the quality as well as range of tasks that can be covered. These class of systems are called associative systems (or associative hybrid systems) as shown in Figure 1

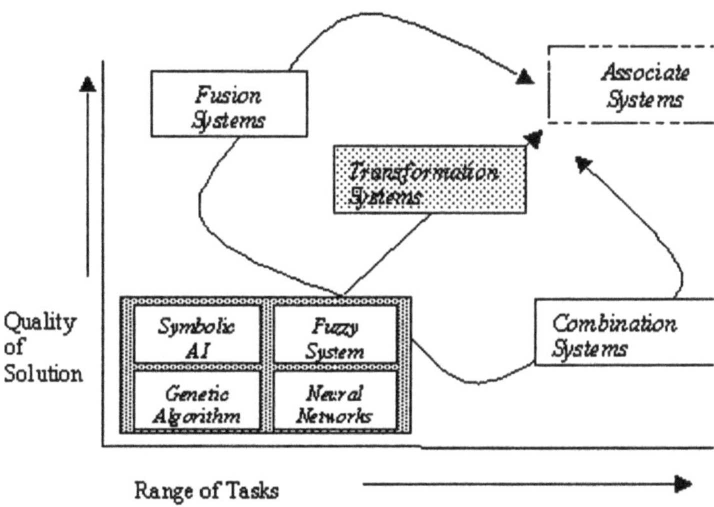

Fig. 1. Intelligent task-centered associative systems

The groundwork related to associative hybrid systems has been reported and explored in a book by [10] and other publications ([11], [28], [29], [30]). As may be apparent from Figure 1, associative systems consider the four intelligent technologies and their hybrid configurations, namely, fusion, transformation, and combination as technological primitives that are used to accomplish tasks. The selection of these technological primitives is contingent upon satisfaction of task constraints (e.g. presence/absence of domain knowledge, noisy incomplete data, learning, adaptation, etc.) which in Figure 1 have been grouped under the quality of solution dimension. In summary, it can seen from the discussion in this Section that intelligent associative systems have evolved from a technology-centered approach where stand-alone intelligent technologies (e.g. neural networks, fuzzy logic, etc.) have been used for building intelligent systems to a task-centered approach where various intelligent technologies are used as primitives rather than prime drivers for building intelligent systems. The task-centered approach is problem driven and is human-centered as it employs various intelligent technologies and their hybrid configurations based on satisfaction of pragmatic task constraints. This approach intends not only to model user/stakeholder tasks and capture deliberate, fuzzy, reactive, self-organizing and evolutionary aspects of human information processing through use of various intelligent technological artifacts but also accounts for epistemological limitations which humans and computers have through satisfaction of various pragmatic task constraints. More aspects underpinning this approach are discussed and described in [10] and [15]. The agent-based electronic broker architecture described in this paper is based on this approach.

3 Human-Centered Intelligent Distributed Multi-Agent Framework

This Section builds upon Section 2 by developing a human-centered intelligent distributed multi-agent framework for Internet applications. For that matter, this Section is divided into parts. The first part outlines the conceptual or knowledge level of the framework. The second part outlines the computational level of the framework.

3.1 Knowledge Level

In Section 2 we established a need for a human-centered (as against technology-centered) approach for harnessing the strengths of various soft and hard intelligent technologies. We said that the human-centered approach is primarily problem driven and is based on user/stakeholder tasks. The selection of one or more intelligent technologies is contingent upon satisfaction of pragmatic task constraints including epistemological limitations of humans and computers. Keeping these perspectives and numerous others (eg., cognitive science, neurobiology, learning, etc..) in view ([10], [15]) we have conceptualized the tasks employed by managers, engineers and other stakeholders while solving complex problems into five information processing phases. The tasks have been studied in the context of using computers to solve complex problems. Table 1 shows some of the tasks in each phase and the corresponding intelligent technologies and their hybrid configurations employed for accomplishing the tasks. The five phases and the tasks in these phases have been empirically validated by applying them on a range of real world problems including alarm processing, sales recruitment and benchmarking, face recognition and annotation, medical image retrieval, medical diagnosis, intelligent computer games, and others ([10], [15]). A more comprehensive description of the knowledge level can be found in [15].

In the third column of Table 1 we have used two abbreviated terms: *TD* and *BU*. *TD* stands for *Top-Down knowledge engineering strategy* and BU

Table 1. Summary of some generic tasks in the five information processing phases

PHASE	TASKS	HYBRID CONFIGURATION
Preprocessing	Input conditioning	Transformation (BU)
Decomposition	Abstract concept decomposition	Combination (TD and/or BU)
Control	Domain dependent decision	Fusion (TD or BU)
Decision	Specific decision instances	Fusion (TD or BU)
Postprocessing	Decision validation	Fusion (TD or BU)

stands for Bottom-UP knowledge engineering strategy respectively. The TD strategy assumes that the domain knowledge is available and the use of a hybrid configuration is based on that assumption.

Likewise, the BU strategy assumes that domain knowledge required by a particular technology in stand-alone or hybrid configuration is not available. In such a case the stand-alone or hybrid configuration is used to learn or extract domain knowledge from raw data. Besides, the definition of information processing phases, tasks, intelligent technologies and their hybrid configurations, the ontology of the knowledge level also consists of goals of each phase, task constraints, external representations of the domain (based on psychological scales like nominal, ordinal and interval) and internal representations (e.g. continuous values of a neural network, rules, mathematical computation, etc.), perceptual representing dimensions. All these aspects of the knowledge level ontology are encapsulated in a problem solving adapter construct. Thus the knowledge level ontology is defined in the form of five problem solving adapters, namely, pre-processing adapter, decomposition adapter, control adapter, decision adapter and post-processing adapter.

The sequence in which the five problem solving adapters are used depends upon the decision ladder employed by the user in the domain of application. More details on the ontology are described in [15] and [10].

3.2 Computational Level

In order to define the computational level of the framework, we integrate the knowledge level ontology model and intelligent technology with software artifact models like the object-oriented model, the agent model, the distributed process model and the Internet technology based `XML/XTL` model as shown in Figure 2. These software artifact models are integrated from a computational viewpoint as well as with a view to harness their software modeling strengths from an intuitive point of view [10]. The final result of this integration is the distributed agent framework shown in Figure 3.

The framework consists of five layers, namely:

- The *object layer*, which defines the data architecture or structural content in the context of the work activity, the software agent layer, which helps to define the distributed processing constructs, and the XML/XTL based

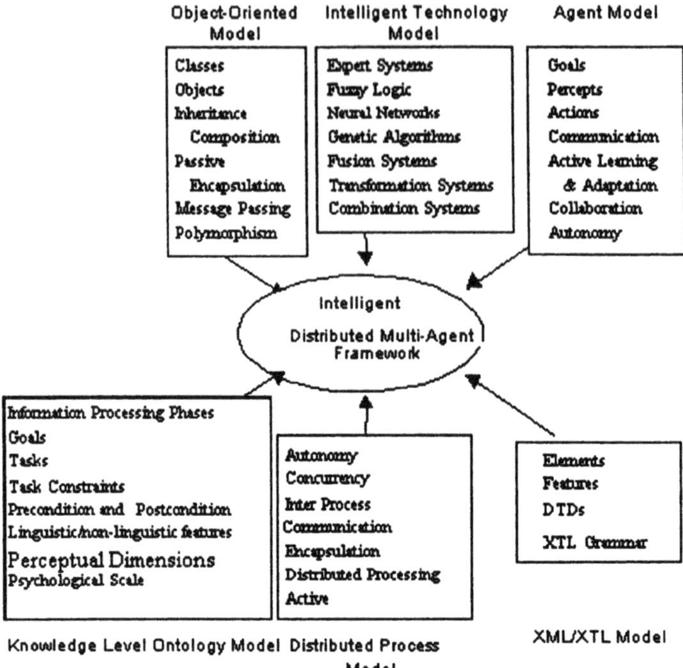

Fig. 2. Integration of knowledge level ontology model and intelligent technology model with software artefact models

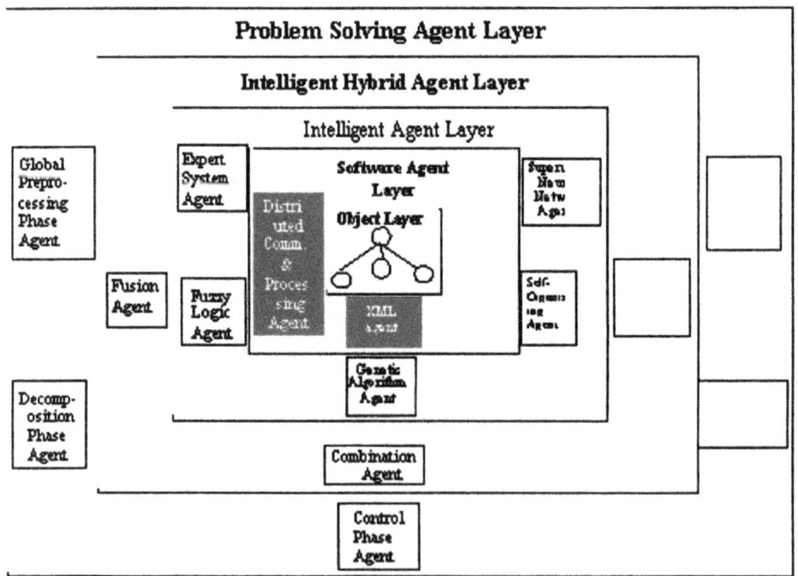

Fig. 3. Five Layers of the intelligent distributed multi-agent framework

constructs used for transforming task and psychological scale constructs of the problem solving adapters into an XML representation for Internet based applications.
- The *intelligent agent layer*, which defines the constructs for intelligent technologies [15].
- The *hybrid layer*, which defines constructs for intelligent fusion, combination and transformation technologies.
- The problem solving agent layer defines the constructs related to the problem solving adapters outlined in Section 2.

The five layers facilitate a component based approach for agent based software design. The generic agent definition used for defining the agents in the problem solving agent layer, intelligent hybrid agent layer, intelligent agent layer and software agent layer is shown in Figure 4.

```
Name:
Parent Agent:
Goals:
Tasks:
Task Constraints:
Precondition:
Postcondition:
Communicates With:
Communication Constructs:
Linguistic/non-linguistic Features:
Psychological Scale:
Representing Dimensions:
Actions:
External     Tools:
Internal     Tools:
Internal     State:
```

Fig. 4. Generic agent definition

The generic definition of the agent includes communication constructs employed by the transformation agent. These communication constructs are based on human communicative acts like request, command, inform, broadcast, explain, warn and others. The linguistic and non-linguistic features represent the sensed data from the external environment as well as computed data by the agent. The parent agent construct identifies the generic agents in the four agent layers, whose constructs and services have been inherited by a particular application or domain based transformation agent. The precondition construct identifies the assumptions made by the agent for accomplishing its goals and tasks. The postcondition construct on the other hand, defines the competence level of the agent. The communication with construct in Figure 4 identifies all the agents and objects that a transformation agent communicates with in the five layers. The external tools construct in Figure 4 refers to those computer-based or other tools that are external to the definition of an agent. On the other hand, internal tools are defined by a transformation agent. The internal state construct refers to the beliefs of a transformation agent at a particular instant in time. Finally, the actions construct is used to define the sequence of actions for accomplishing various tasks.

4 Hardware Adapter Electronic Commerce Application

In this Section we describe the application of the human-centered intelligent distributed multi-agent framework for buying hardware adapters on the Internet. We particularly focus on the application of the problem solving agent layer of the distributed multi-agent framework. In order to do so, we firstly outline the need for a human-centered view of the electronic market. We follow it with the outline of the electronic brokerage architecture used for the hardware adapter domain. We then describe the application of problem solving agent layer and the five problem solving adapters of the human-centered intelligent distributed multi-agent framework how HCVM layered architecture allows the broker design to proceed seamlessly from a human-centered representation of (a portion of) the electronic market, based on a nominal scale, to the ordinal and interval-based representations that are more suitable for intelligent search agents. This will allow identification of the decision classes to be submitted to the user as the possible target for an electronic commerce transaction. As a by-product, we shall show how HCVM approach ensures generality and applicability of the brokerage system to a wide range of EC application domains.

4.1 A Human-Centered View of the Electronic Market

The electronic commerce research community has since long recognised the need to provide a systematic and complete view of the EC market. The `CommerceNet` consortium, including nearly 250 member companies providing solutions to EC technology issues, has been sponsoring some industry pilot projects in order to develop domain representation based on evolvable taxonomies [4]. An evolvable taxonomy functions much like a database schema and provides metainformation for agent searches. Those taxonomies are however `supply-side oriented`, being based on a classification of goods and services provided by a group of suppliers operating in a given application domain. Therefore, though they are useful in business-to-business transactions, in our opinion it is by no means guaranteed that they will present a view of the market that is satisfactory, or even comprehensible, for the casual user.

4.2 Electronic Brokerage Architecture

The reference model for electronic brokerage at the highest level of abstraction is shown in Table 2. The core concepts of this reference model are the roles of *customer*, *broker* and *supplier* and the actions of *search*, *order* and *deliver*.

Table 2. Roles and actions of the reference model

Roles	Customer/consumer/user	Broker	Supplier
Actions	Search	Order	Deliver

The broker acts as a supplier of information or services to the customers, and as a distribution mechanism for suppliers wishing to promote their products over the trading network. A basic assumption of this model is that brokers should acquire and maintain information about online services, in order to be able to locate the product required by the customers. This information is multimedia in nature and can be arbitrarily specialized, with special brokers for particular domains or geographical regions. The function of the broker is therefore to provide a path whereby the customer may find and obtain a product offering the required characteristics (and, of course, price) to the highest possible degree. Based on the reference model shown in Table 2 the brokerage architecture employed in the hardware adapter application is shown in Figure 5.

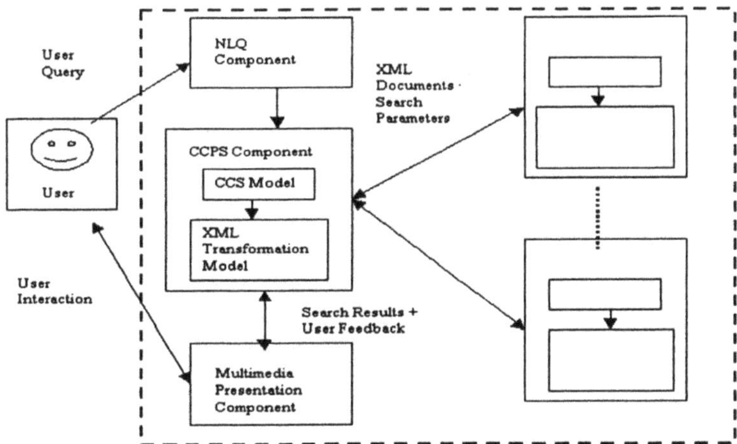

Fig. 5. The brokerage architecture

The brokerage architecture shown in Figure 5 consists of three components:

- Natural Language Query Component

- Consumer-Centered Product Search Component (CCPS)
- Multimedia Presentation and Communication Component

Natural Language Query (NLQ) Component The primary purpose of this component is to allow users to search products via a Web browser using natural language structures instead of supplier or technology based structures. Let's consider the following user query in natural language:

```
I want to buy PC hardware adapters under $ 200
```

This component eliminates any redundant or irrelevant words (e.g. `I want to buy`) from the natural language query and extract words (like product nouns, brand nouns, etc.) relevant for searching the products. The pre-processing agent of the problem solving agent layer in Figure 5 is used to transform the natural language query into a set of search strings to be used by the product search component. The pre-processing agent employs intelligent natural language processing techniques. The operation of this agent is not described in this paper.

Consumer(User)-Centered Product Search (CCPS) Component The consumer-centered product search component entails development of *Consumer-Centered Search* (CCS) model and *XML Transformation* model. The CCS model employs the decomposition, control and decision agents of the problem solving agent layer in Figure 4 for assisting users in developing mental models of the domain as well as systematizing and structuring their query. The CCS model uses the search strings from the natural language component to develop the user or buyer's mental model and structuring the query. The XML Transformation model is used to transform the CCS model into XML based representations in order to search and communicate with the *Supplier-Centered Product* (SSP) models on the Internet for a particular product (e.g., hardware adapters). In terms of the hardware adapter domain application we primarily focus on the workings of the CCS in this paper. The workings of the XML Transformation model can be found in [15].

Multimedia Presentation and Communication Component The purpose of the multimedia component is to present and communicate information content of various products that have different attributes/properties in a multimedia interface within a single application. The multimedia interface displays all the products' properties and features by integrating most if not all media, i.e. text, image, video and audio. The methodology employed for designing the multimedia component is described in [15] and is out of the scope of this paper.

4.3 Problem Solving Agents of the Hardware Adapter Domain

Figure 10 and Figureeps10 show the mapping of the generic decomposition, control and decision problem solving adapter agents of the human-centered intelligent distributed multi-agent framework to those in the CCS model of the hardware adapter domain. It shows the mapping of various constructs of the problem solving adapter agents to decomposition, control and decision agents of the CCS model. The decomposition agent of the CCS model relies on general features and structured features. General features are binary-valued and allow prompt identification of classes, since they can only belong to one class of the decomposition. For instance, in the Hardware Adapters domain, `AT_bus_interface` is a general feature that can be used to identify the class `Old_PC_Cards` (Figure 6). In passing, we note that this class, though very unlikely to be used in a supply-side oriented taxonomy of products, is indeed crucial in the users' perception of the market. Structured features, in turn, can have multiple discrete values (for instance a connector-type feature could have values DB-9, DB-25,...) and represent basic domain structure. The basic assumption we rely on is that the customer organises a mental model of the market via a limited number of general features, and an agent-based broker should be able to fully comprehend and utilise such a model.

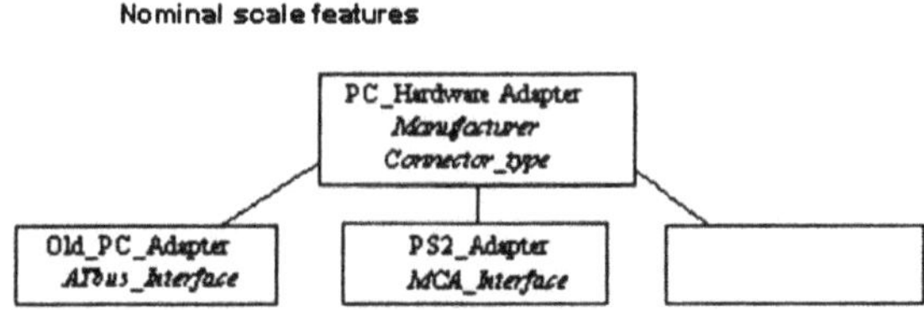

Fig. 6. A simplified decomposition of the PC hardware adapters sub domain

Hardware Old_PC Adapter Control Agent - Decision Level/Support Concepts The abstract classes identified by the decomposition agent present a model of the market that is familiar to the user. However, they are generally not related to the solution of any particular search problem. The Control Agent determines the decision support concepts within each abstract class identified by the decomposition agent. Decision support concepts are determined by this agent on the basis of finer-grain features whose values can be drawn on an ordinal or an interval-based scale. In our case, `price` or `price_band` is used as a fuzzy linguistic variable determining the decision support concepts or classes. It is also possible to use other user defined fuzzy linguistic variables for determining the decision support classes.

Agent / Construct	Decomposition	Control	Decision
Goal (Generic)	Restrict input context, reduce complexity, enhance reliability	Establish domain decision control constructs for orthogonal concepts based on desired outcomes from the system	Provide user/stakeholder defined outcomes from the system
Goal (PC H/W)	*Restrict input by connector-type of PC hardware adapter.*	*Define control knowledge for price-based adapter decision classes.*	*Provide a list of products to satisfy the requested properties (e.g. a multimedia adapter featuring 30 fps and 16KHz audio sampling rate*
Task (Generic)	Determine abstract orthogonal concepts	Determine decision level concepts	Determine decision instance
Task (PC H/W)	*Partition a global concept of hardware adapter into abstract classes Old_PC_Adapter, PS2_Adapter, New_PC_Adapter)*	*Determine price based decision classes that can be used with Old_PC_Adapter*	*Retrieve adapter specifications for the selected price based old PC adapter decision class*
Task Constraint (Generic)	Orthogonality, reliability, scalability	Imprecise and incomplete data, scalability, reliability, and other domain dependent	Imprecise, noisy data, generalization, adaptability, and other domain dependent
Task Constraint (PC H/W)	*Orthogonal types of adapter, scalable adapter classes*	Imprecise, fuzzy features	Imprecise, fuzzy features
Precondition (Generic)	Filtered/conditioned domain data	Orthogonal concept defined, concept related data available	Decision class case data, decision level concepts defined (optional)
Precondition (PCCC H/W)	*Domain of PC platform, filtered user query adapter data*	*Old_PC_Adapter class, fuzzy membership functions for various features*	*Price band,frame rate , data rate defined by user*
Postcondition (Generic)	Orthogonal abstract classes	Decision concepts/classes defined, control knowledge defined	Specific decision instance computed
Postcondition (PC H/W)	*Different types of adapters to select from*	*Price based decision classes defined and decision control knowledge for decision classes defined*	*Retrieved adapters based on user specifications and price, data scale, etc.*
Technology Artifacts (Generic)	Symbolic rule based, neuran networks, agent, multimedia	Agent neural networks, fuzzy logic,	Agent, fuzzy logic
Technology Artifacts (PC H/W)	*Perceptual (multimedia)*	*Fuzzy logic*	*Fuzzy logic/Division*
Domain Model (Generic)	Structural, functional, causal, geometric, heuristic, spatial, color, shape, etc.	Structural, functional, casual, geometric, heuristic, spatial, shape, color, etc.	Structural, functional, causal, geometric, heuristic, spatial, shape, color, etc.
Domain Model (PC H/W)	*Adapter Structure model.*	*Fuzzy price model*	*Functional specification model*

Fig. 7. Mapping of the generic decomposition, control and decision problem solving adapter agents (part I)

5 Hardware Adapter Decision Agent

The price based decision agents employ fuzzy linguistic variables exemplified by `frame_rate` and `audio_sampling_rate` (Figure 9) on the interval scale support concepts determined by the control agent are directly involved in the decision support process of the broker. It is interesting to observe that the model developed by the previous phase allows us to easily deal at this level with the user's implicit knowledge about the (sub)domain. For instance, the user's linguistic knowledge about a modem card may include the fact that it has a "fast" data rate. In this case, the meaning of "fast" depends on the

Agent / Construct	Decomposition	Control	Decision
Represented Features (Generic)	Qualitative/linguistic – binary, structured Non-linguistic – continuous features	Qualitative/linguistic – binary, structured, fuzzy data Non-linguistic – continuous data related to an orthogonal concept	Qualitative/linguistic – binary, fine grain fuzzy decision concept data Non-linguistic – continuous decision concept data
Represented Features (PC H/W)	*Binary-valued(e.g. AT_bus_interface)* *Structure (e.g. connector type DB-9, DB-25)*	*Fuzzy (price band), weight*	*Fuzzy (user selected frame rate, data rate. See Table 4 and 5), fuzzy division data*
Psychological Scales (Generic)	Nominal; Formal property; category	Nominal, ordinal, interval, ratio	Nominal, ordinal, interval, ratio, or none
Psychological Scales (PC H/W)	*Nominal (e.g. different manufacturer card products)*	*Interval (e.g. price)*	*Interval (user selected selected frame rate, data rate*
Representing Dimensions (Generic)	Shape, location, size, position, etc. on the nominal scale	Shape, size, length, distance, density, location, position, orientation, color, texture	Shape, size, length, distance, density, location, position, orientation, color, texture
Representing Dimensions (PC H/W)	*Shape, color*	*Orientation* *Price band* *50 75 25 100*	*Shape, length, color of retrieved adapter. Functional specification sheets*

Fig. 8. Mapping of the generic decomposition, control and decision problem solving adapter agents (part II)

modem card being compared with other cards of the same kind and not, say, with a digital communication adapter. In our model, being a decision class feature, the fuzzy linguistic variable **data_rate** may well have different definition intervals for different classes of adapters, thus dealing with the implicit different meanings of fast. Figure 9 shows the membership functions of fuzzy linguistic variable **frame_rate** in the hardware adapter domain. The user-

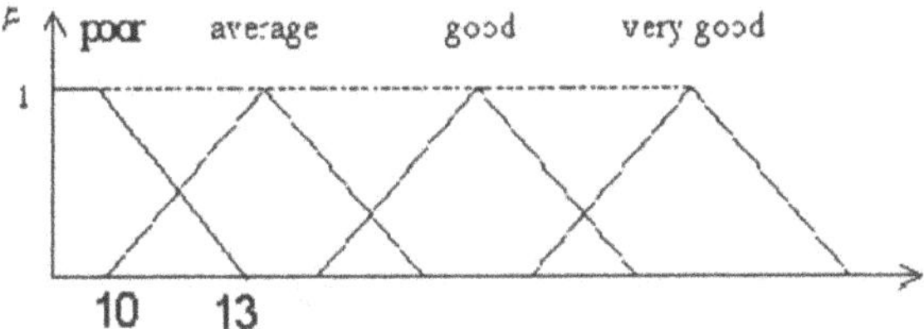

Fig. 9. A sample fuzzy feature for a video adapter

centered design of our architecture requires the broker to compute and retain information about the available products in the format of a class hierarchy. Classes at the higher levels exhibit general and structured features based on a nominal scale, while lower level classes present ordinal and interval-based features. To decompose the chosen subdomain on the basis of the nominal scale, the decomposition agent of the decomposition phase exploits the available body of domain knowledge. At the decision agent level, however, intervals and ordinal values must be computed on the basis of data published by supplier sites, which is multimedia in nature and whose format is likely to change across different vendors. In this Section, we shall outline how such a computation can be carried out through an example, exploiting a repository storing descriptors of the products available on the network. This repository can be carried out by a control agent, much in the same way as the service selection technique described in [2]. In our case, however, the repository is a structured collection of simplified descriptions of products properties [5] We consider such a repository to be associated with an application subdomain of EC or to a specific theme, such as, for instance, `Houseware`, `PC_Hardware Adapters`, `Fashion and Clothing`. In the repository, the O-O control level classes are stored as a set of fuzzy relations, which are defined by applying an imprecise criterion through a fuzzy predicate on a crisp relation. For such a fuzzy relation, built on a set of domains $\{D_i\}$, every t-uple is supplied with a membership degree μ_R, from 0 to 1, interpreting how this t-uple satisfies a fuzzy predicate P applied to the relation R. In the simplest case, the repository is a single fuzzy relation whose attributes are: `OID, feature, fuzzy element, weight`. Each feature corresponds to a linguistic variable having several fuzzy elements. To each fuzzy element of each feature a weight is associated, describing to which extent the corresponding property is offered by the object. From a purely syntactic point of view, features are expressed by nouns whereas adjectives describe fuzzy elements. Table 3 shows a fuzzy relation describing the properties of two audio/video adapters. This table was computed by the broker's control agent from crisp values supplied by vendor sites, by applying the definition of the `frame_rate` linguistic variable shown in Figure 9. The linguistic variables' definitions are a part of the domain knowledge stored by the broker. It is important to observe that this computation can take place both when the suppliers' servers sign up, i.e. communicate to the broker the availability of their products and services, and as they are periodically polled allowing the broker to take into account new prices or delivery conditions.

The broker's role is to help the client to choose among the available products. The decision agent of our broker uses a simple fuzzy technique to deal with values supplied by the user as reference values or as thresholds, rather than as absolute according to predicates definition, the input filter transforms crisp values provided by the user into weights. Here, we assume the availability of a Thesaurus allowing both functional and non-functional information about products to be uniformed through a naming discipline, in order to deal with a standard context-dependent vocabulary [5]. This allows both brokers and clients to use a domain-specific language to express features, without any explicit reference to the fuzzy model. Fuzzy elements and membership values, i.e. the internal knowledge representation, are only computed and dealt with

Table 3. An example of fuzzy descriptor relation

OID	Feature	Fuzzy Element	Weight
1	frame rate	good	0.8
1	frame rate	average	0.1
1	audio sampling rate	good	0.4
2	frame rate	good	1
2	audio sampling rate	average	0.5

inside the broker. A user, for example, could request to the broker a multimedia adapter having the following features: a frame rate of 30 frames per second and a audio sampling rate of 16 KHz. User input filtering computes a list of properties, each one associated with a certain fuzzy predicate and weighted by a value between 0 and 1. These values are obtained by transformation of crisp values according to the linguistic variable definition. The processed input defines a fuzzy request to the broker, which is nothing but another fuzzy relation shown in Table 4.

Table 4. A fuzzy query relation

Feature	Fuzzy Element	Weight
frame rate	good	1
audio sampling rate	average	0.5

In order to get the list of products satisfying the requested properties, the decision agent of the decision phase can simply compute the fuzzy relational division by the query table [5]. As we shall see in the next Section, various fuzzy operators are available to compute this division, among which the broker can perform a choice in order to obtain the semantics desired by the user.

5.1 The Division Operation

Let us consider two relations $R(X, A)$ and $S(Y, A)$ where A, X, and Y point out sets of attributes. The division of R by S, denoted $R[A/A]S$ is a relation on X, which can be defined as follows:

$$x \in R[A/A]S \ if \ \exists a \in S[A], (x, a) \in R. \tag{1}$$

Following [6], [7], we now examine the extension of the division to fuzzy relations. The operation of division of a relation R by another relation S can be considered as a set inclusion:

$$x \in R[A/A]S \Longleftrightarrow S[A] \in \Gamma^{-1}(x),\ with\ \Gamma^{-1}(x) = \{a, (x,a) \in R\} \quad (2)$$

This inclusion, in the case of the extension of the division to fuzzy relations, can be interpreted either using the concept of cardinality of a fuzzy set or using a *fuzzy implication*, as follows:

$$Inc(S \subseteq R) = min_S(\mu_S(a) \rightarrow \mu_R(x,a)). \quad (3)$$

The second type of division operation based on fuzzy implications is more appropriate in our case since it retains the logical aspect we are interested in. Among the main families of fuzzy implication connectives, only three are appropriate for our Decision Agent:

- *R-implications*, denoted $a \rightarrow b = \sup\ \{c \in [0,1], a * c \leq b\}$.
  - Goguen implication: $a \rightarrow b = 1$ if $a \leq b, b/a$ otherwise, if we associate T with the multiplication operation.
  - Goedel implication: $a \rightarrow b = 1$ if $a \leq b$, b otherwise, if we associate T with the minimum.
- *S-implications*, namely $a \rightarrow b = n(T(a, n(b)))$, where n is an involutive order reversing negation operation, and T a conjunction operation modeled by a triangular norm. This norm has to respect several properties such as associativity, commutativity, monotonicity and 1 as neutral element. We get:
  - Dienes implication: $a \rightarrow b = max(1 - a, b)$, if we associate T with minimum.
  - Goedel reciprocal $n(b) \rightarrow n(a) = 1$ if $a \rightarrow b, 1 - a = n(a)$ otherwise.
- *R&S-implications* such as the Lukasiewicz one, defined by: $a \rightarrow b = 1$ if $a \leq b$, $1 - a + b$ otherwise, obtained with Lukasiewicz norm $T(a,b) = max(a + b - 1, 0)$.

5.2 User-dependent Decision Semantics

By selecting an implication, the user assigns the intended meaning of μ_S degrees in the fuzzy division $R[A/A]S$, i.e. the semantics of the query submitted to the broker. If $\mu_S(a)$ values are considered as weights (i.e., we are interested in their importance), any element x will completely satisfy the query if, for each element a of S different from 0, we have a maximum membership degree for the corresponding t-uple (x, a) of R.

$$\mu_{R[A/A]S}(x) = 1 \Longleftrightarrow (\exists a, \mu_S(a) > 0 \Longrightarrow \mu_R(x,a) = 1). \quad (4)$$

In the same way, an element x will not satisfy at all a condition if there exists any element a of S which is completely important, or the t-uple (x, a) has membership degree equal to 0.

$$\mu_{R[A/A]S}(x) = 0 \Longleftrightarrow (\exists a, \mu_S(a) = 1 \wedge \mu_R(x, a) = 0). \tag{5}$$

This desired behavior leads to define the quotient operation by using Dienes implication. Then, we have:

$$\mu_{R[A/A]S}(x) = min_S\{\mu_S(a) \rightarrow \mu_R(x, a)\} = min_S\{max(1 - \mu_S(a), \mu_R(x, a))\}. \tag{6}$$

where S is a fuzzy normalised operation (i.e. $\exists a \in S, \mu_S(a) = 1$) in order to have a complete scale of importance levels.

5.3 An Algorithm for the Decision Agent

Whatever implication is chosen to perform the division, we can give the following naive algorithm for the Decision Agent in our example. The algorithm in Figure 10 sequentially seeks for each element x of the divided relation R, the t-uple (x, a) for each element a of the relation S.

```
for each x of R do
 μ(x) := 1.0;
 for each a of S do
  seek sequentially (x,a) in R;
  if found then
  μ(x) := μS(a) → μR(x,a);
  else
  μ(x) := μS(a) → 0;
  fi;
  μ(x) := min (μR/S(x), μcurrent(x));
 done;
done;
```

Fig. 10. The Decision Agent's algorithm

This simple algorithm is very costly in terms of memory accesses (when the t-uple (x, a) does not exist the algorithm examines the whole relation R). Improvements, based on heuristics and indexes, are necessary. For example, supposing the existence of a threshold λ that the products final weights must reach in order to be selected, the following heuristics can be used:

- A *heuristic of failure*, valid for any implication: element x will not be retrieved if $\exists a \in S, \mu_S(a) \rightarrow \mu_R(x,a) < \lambda$, since the division compute a minimum value.
- The second heuristic concerns the implications of Dienes and Lukasiewicz, as well as the reciprocal of Goedel implication. If we assume that S is sorted on decreasing μ_S membership degrees, one can stop the computation as soon as the current degree$\mu_{R/S}(x)$ is lower than $1-\mu_S(a)$. Indeed, in this case, if the values $1-\mu_S(a)$ are increasing then the degree of satisfaction for the considered element x can not decrease anymore. The element x will only be included in the division if $\mu_{current}(x) \geq \mu_S(a)$.

Finally, dealing with Goedel and Goguen implications, for a given element x, if there exists an element $a \in S$ such that the t-uple (x, a) does not exist in R, then we have $\mu_R(x,a) = 0$, and $\mu_S(a) \rightarrow \mu_R(x,a) = 0$. This heuristic can be used whenever the number of t-uples of any partition of the relation R is inferior to the number of t-uples of the relation S.

6 Conclusions and Future Work

In this paper we have outlined the need for a task-centered or problem driven approach for harnessing the modeling strengths of various intelligent technologies and their hybrid configurations. Based on this need, we have described a human-centered intelligent distributed multi-agent framework for Internet applications. We have also described the application of this framework in a hardware adapter e-commerce domain. We are currently exploring a number of other Internet applications of this approach. The development of a set of related software tools is also underway.

References

1. J. Hands, A. Patel, M. Bessonov and R. Smith, (1998), An Inclusive and Extensible Architecture for Electronic Brokerage, Proc. of the Hawaii Intl. Conf. on System Sciences, Minitrack on Electronic Commerce, 24–37.
2. P. Bosc, E. Damiani, (2000) Fuzzy Service Selection in Active Networks, Proc. of the IEEE Intl. Conf. On Fuzzy Systems, San Antonio, TX, 332–341.
3. R. Khosla, (1998) Human-Centered Virtual Machine of Problem Solving Agents, Intelligent Agents, Software Agents and Objects, Proc. Of the 3rd IEEE Symposium on High Assurance in Intelligent Systems, Washington,DC, 131–141.
4. J . Zhang, D. A. Norman, (1994), Distributed Cognitive Tasks. Cognitive Science, 84–120.
5. S. Hamilton, (1997), Electronic Commerce for the 21st Century. IEEE Computer, (30):5, 23–29.
6. E. Damiani, M.G. Fugini, (1997), Fuzzy Identification Of Distributed Components. In B. Reusch, Ed., Proc. of the 5th Fuzzy Days Intl. Conf., Dortmund, LNCS 1226,550–553.

7. P. Bosc, O. Pivert, (1995), SQLf: A Relational Database Language For Fuzzy Querying. IEEE Transactions on Fuzzy Systems, 3:(1), 138–145
8. P. Bosc, D. Dubois, O. Pivert and H. Prade, (1997), Flexible Queries In Relational Databases - The Example of The Division Operator. Theoretical Computer Science, (171):3, 147–163.
9. R. Khosla, (1997a), Tutorial Notes on Software Engineering Methodology for Intelligent Hybrid Multi-Agent Systems, Int. Conf. on Connectionist Information Processing and Information Systems, Dunedin, New Zealand.
10. R. Khosla and T. Dillon, (1997b), Engineering Intelligent Hybrid Multi-Agent Systems. Boston, USA, Kluwer Academic Publishers.
11. R. Khosla and T. Dillon, (1997c), Neuro-Expert System Applications in Power Systems. In: K. Warwick, A. Ekwue and R.K. Aggarwal, Eds., Artificial Intelligent Techniques in Power Systems. IEE Press, UK 238–258.
12. R. Khosla and T. Dillon, (1997d), Task Structure Level Symbolic-Connectionist Architecture. In: Connectionist-Symbolic Integration: From Unified to Hybrid Approaches, R. Sun and F.Alexandre, Eds., Lawrence Erlbaum Associates, 37–56.
13. R. Khosla and T. Dillon, (1997e), Fusion of Knowledge-Based Systems and Neural Networks and Applications. Keynote paper. 1st Int. Conf. on Conventional and Knowledge-Based Intelligent Electronic Systems, Adelaide, Australia, 27–44.
14. R. Khosla and T. Dillon, (1997f), Learning Knowledge and Strategy of a Generic Neuro-Expert System Arch. in Alarm Processing, in IEEE Trans. on Power Systems, (12):12, 1610–18.
15. R. Khosla, I. Sethi and E. Damiani, (2000), Intelligent Multimedia Multi-Agent Systems - a Human-Centered Approach, Kluwer Academic Publishers.
16. J.C. Bezdek, (1994), What is Computational Intelligence? In: Computational Intelligence: Imitating Life, Eds. Robert Marks et al. Eds., IEEE Press, New York.
17. L. Fu , L. C. Fu, (1990), Mapping Rule based Systems into Neural Architecture.Knowledge-Based Systems. 3(1): 48-56.
18. T. Fukuda, Y. Hasegawa and K. Shimojima, (1995), Structure Organization of Hierarchical Fuzzy Model using Genetic Algorithm. IEEE International Conference on Fuzzy Systems, 1(2): 295–299.
19. S. Gallant, (1988), Connectionist Expert Systems. Communications of the ACM, (2):3, 152–169.
20. G.E. Hinton, (1990), Mapping Part-Whole Hierarchies into Connectionist Networks. Artificial Intelligence, 46(1-2): 47-76.
21. H. Ishibuchi, H. Tanaka and H. Okada, (1994), Interpolation of Fuzzy If-Then Rules by Neural Networks. International Journal of Approximate Reasoning, 10(1): 3–27.
22. I. K. Sethi, (1990), Entropy Nets: from Decision Trees to Neural Networks. Proc. of IEEE, 78(10): 1605–1613
23. R. Sun (1994), CONSYDERR: A Two Level Hybrid Architecture for Structuring Knowledge for Commonsense Reasoning,. Proc. of the 1st Int. Symp. on Integrating Knowledge and Neural Heuristics. Florida, US, 32–39.
24. D. Srinivasan, A.C. Liew, and C.S. Chang, (1994), Forecasting Daily Load Curves using a Hybrid Fuzzy-neural Approach. IEE Proceedings on Generation, Transmission and Distribution. 141(6): 561–567.

25. M. Chiaberge, G.D. Bene, S.D. Pascoli, B. Lazzerini and A. Maggiore, (1995), Mixing Fuzzy, Neural and Genetic Algorithms in Integrated Design Environment for Intelligent Controllers, IEEE Int. Conf. on SMC, Vol. 4, pp. 2988–2993.
26. K. Hamada, T. Baba, K. Sato and M. Yufu, (1995), Hybridizing a Genetic Algorithm with Rule-based Reasoning for Production Planning. IEEE Expert (3) 4: 60–67.
27. G. Edelman, (1992), Bright Air, Brilliant Fire: On the Matter of the Mind. New York, USA, Raven Press.
28. J. Main, T. Dillon and R. Khosla, (1995), Use of Neural Networks for Case-retrieval in a System for Fashion Shoe Design. 8th Int. Conf. on Industrial and Engineering Applications of AI and Expert Systems. Melbourne, Australia, 151–158.
29. S.K.Tang, T. Dillon and R. Khosla, (1995), Fuzzy Logic and Knowledge Representation in a Symbolic-subsymbolic Architecture. IEEE International Conference on Neural Networks, Perth, Australia, 349–353.
30. S.K. Tang, T. Dillon and R. Khosla, (1996), Application of an Integrated Fuzzy, Knowledge-based, Connectionist Arch. for Fault Diagnosis in Power Systems. Int. Conf. on Intelligent Systems Applications to Power Systems 188–193.
31. T. M. Maybury, (1994) Planning Multimedia Explanation Using Communicative Acts. In: Intelligent Multimedia Interfaces, T. M. Maybury, Ed., AAAI Press, 60–74

A Soft Computing Framework for Adaptive Agents

Vincenzo Loia[1] and Salvatore Sessa[2]

[1] Dipartimento di Matematica e Informatica, Universitá di Salerno, 84081 Baronissi, Italy
[2] Dipartimento di Costruzioni e Metodi Matematici in Architettura, Universitá di Napoli "Federico II", Via Monteoliveto 3, 80134 Napoli, Italy

Abstract. We extend the actor-based model of concurrent and distributed programming toward a framework in which the agents can learn emerging behaviours through a fuzzy evolutionary structure. The framework is based on the notion of *FuzzyEvoAgent*, i.e. an entity that exploiting the basic issues of actors (asynchronous message passing, concurrent computation) is submitted to evolutionary laws that reinforce the most suitable behaviours respecting the environment. The behavior evolution is accomplished without the intervent of external stimulus, so that the actor (an entity that reacts only if it receives a command) may be considered as an adaptive agent. We propose a formal definition as well as an implementation model of FuzzyEvoAgents that has been verified via a simple simulation of Artificial Life.

Keywords: Fuzzy Evolutionary Systems, Agent-Based Systems, Actor Paradigm, Genetic Computation, Java Programming, Object-Oriented Technology.

1 Introduction

Agent technology characterizes the current state of software design in the area of distributed systems and applications [2]. Even though there is no universal definition accepted for the term "agent", the scientific community considers an agent as a software component running in specific environment. This component is equipped by a set of characteristics such as: autonomy, persistence, social ability, reactivity, pro-activeness. These features are important, especially, to handle real-world problems that are characterized by a large size of solution space. In this case, the difficulty (or often, the impossibility) to provide a complete, precise model of the problem is faced thanks to the agents' ability to tolerate and process (correctly) the approximation or vagueness of the problem.

As starting point of our work we point out a well-known design paradigm useful to describe medium-grained distributed and parallel system, the actor model [1]. This model is based on an essential entity, named actor, a computation object whose states are shown in Figure 1.

Briefly, the actor model can be presented as:

- the universe contains computational agents, called *actors*;

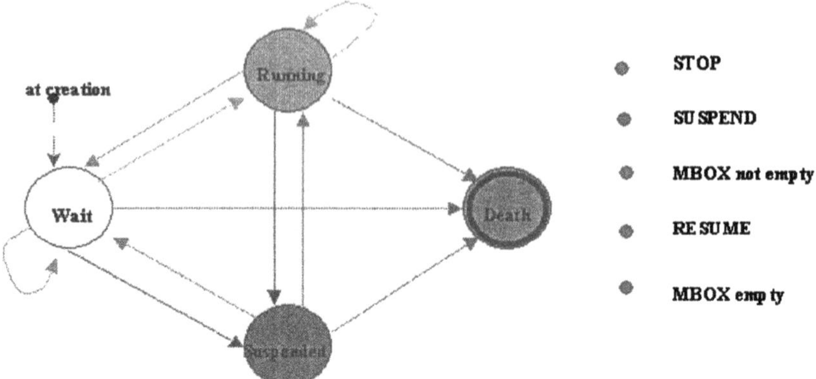

Fig. 1. Computational states of an actor

- actors perform computation through asynchronous, point-to-point message passing;
- each actor is defined by its state, a mail queue to store external messages and internal behaviour;
- an actor's state is defined by its internal data, not sharable by other actors. These local variables are named *acquaintances*;
- an actor reacts to the external environment by executing its procedural skills, called *scripts.*

The actor model is at the basis of the so-called object-oriented concurrent programming which constitute one of the most important paradigms employed to realize DAI (Distributed Artificial Intelligence) level architectures [3] [4]. Modelling software as collections of distributed, cooperative actors is a natural evolution of object-level languages. Object-oriented programming is based on a philosophy of software development through progressive refinements, strengthening the abstraction level as a result of the use of abstract data types and information hiding. The Actors combine object-oriented and functional programming in order to make the management of concurrency easier for the user.

Despite the considerable effort spent on the agent theory, a consistent definition has not been fully acknowledged. In general, agents own local duties which increase their ability in reasoning, in refusing orders, in negotiating commitments. We refer to the paper of S. Franklin in this issue for a more detailed discussion on the notion and role of the agents.

Our effort was concentrated in representing Agents as active objects (i.e. Actors) that are autonomous and learn (evolve) during their life cycle. The autonomy of Agents with respect to the Actor's behavior is ensured by a dynamic scheduling mechanism that selects (or generates) the next message by evaluating a procedure at running time overall the available knowledge.

In this paper we address the problem to provide a robust approach to treat the difference between the information available and the information necessary to the agent to make the best decision. Our approach is twofold: firstly, to manage these two kinds of information through a flexible interpretation of knowledge, namely fuzzy behaviors; secondly, to give to the agent the possibility to evolve, improving the ability to reason about the environment where it acts. For this reason, our main goal was to extend the notion of actor towards that one of agent, i.e. to inject in the actor the competence to adapt its behaviour according to the fulfilment of its local (sub)goals. Our result was the definition and implementation of the *FuzzyEvoAgent*.

We point out the basic issues of our model:

- The model is based on the notion of "FuzzyEvoAgents".
- FuzzyEvoAgents perform their computation in an asynchronous and independent way, exploiting concurrency and point-to-point and multicasting message passing.
- FuzzyEvoAgents are defined by their internal states, by a list of messages to process, and by their behaviour.
- FuzzyEvoAgents reacts to external stimulus, coming from other EvoAgents or from the environment.
- The scripts of a FuzzyEvoAgent are executed through an internal fuzzy control sub-system that takes into account a knowledge-base handled by an approximate reasoning engine.
- The rules represent the genotype of each FuzzyEvoAgent.
- FuzzyEvoAgent are adaptive entities, submitted to an evolutionary law.

2 Formal Definitions

As previosly stated, FuzzyEvoAgents are an extension of the basic notion of actor. Differently from the actors, the FuzzyEvoAgents are capable to ameliorate their behaviors during the life of the system.

Figure 2 shows the basic components of a FuzzyEvoAgent.

- A data section, containing the acquaintances.
- A script section, containing the tasks that the agent may perform.
- A Rule Base, formed by control fuzzy rules (FCRs).
- A Fuzzy Logic Control (FLC) that enables the execution of a task according to its knowledge base.
- A genetic engine (MEET) that allows the creation of new FuzzyEvoAgents by processing the genetic information contained in the knowledge-base of the agent.

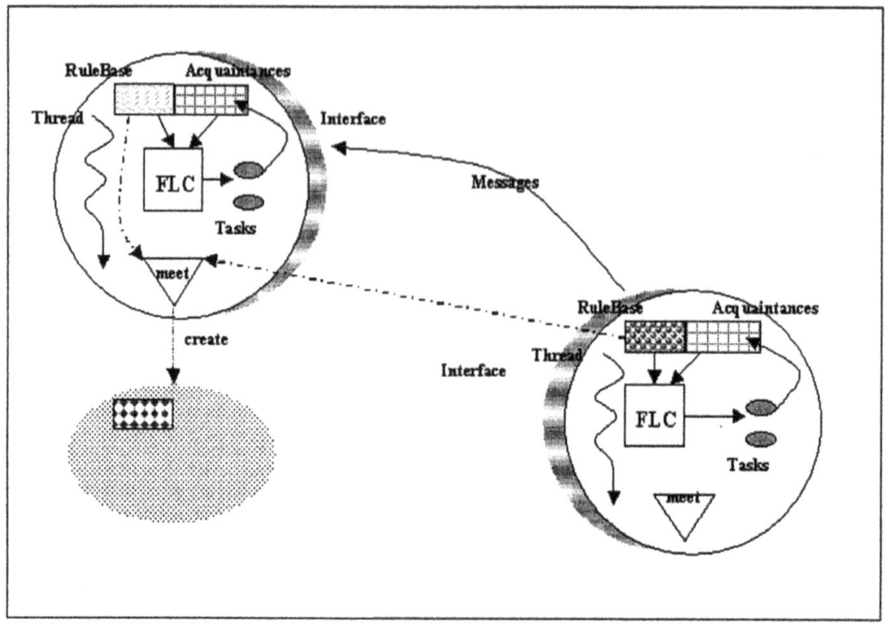

Fig. 2. FuzzyEvoAgent: they own a thread of control, an internal state, a rule base and a fuzzy control system.

Following [10] we use (1) to define our rule base as :

(1) $R = \bigcup_{i=1}^{m} R_i = \bigcup_{i=1}^{m} (X_i \rightarrow Y_i)$

In our model, a *fuzzy control rule* (FCR) R_i takes the form (2):

(2) "***if*** *acq_1 is α_{i1}, acq_2 is α_{i2},..., acq_n is α_{in}* ***then*** *$task_1$ is β_{i1}, $task_2$ is β_{i2},..., $task_m$ is β_{im}*"
where α_{i1}, α_{i2}, ..., α_{in} are fuzzy numbers representing the evaluation of the data set variables acq_i , and β_{i1}, β_{i2}, ..., β_{im} are fuzzy numbers representing the causality values of tasks with respect to the given data set (acq_1 ... acq_n, $task_1$ ... $task_t$) , having represented:

$$X_i = IF\ \{\text{acq}_1 \text{ is } \alpha_{i1} \text{ and} \ldots \text{and acq}_n \text{ is } \alpha_{in}\}, THEN\ Y_i = \{\text{task}_k \text{ is } \beta_{ik} \text{and} \ldots \text{and task}_t \text{ is } \beta_{it}\}$$

In the definition of a FuzzyEvoAgent, many fuzzy control rules may appear. The task activated is determined following a selection mechanism similar to a notion of a fuzzy control system [10] [11].

Strictly speaking, if {acq_1, acq_2, ..., acq_n} is the status , the ith rule says that the jth task, j=1...t, can be activated with possibility equal to:

$$\gamma_{ij} = \alpha_{i1}(acq_1) \cap \alpha_{i2}(acq_2) \cap \ldots \alpha_{in}(acq_n) \cap \beta_{ij}.$$

By setting

$$\pi_j = \bigcup_{i=1}^{m} \gamma_{ij}$$

we have the overall possibility value for the jth task to be executed, with respect to the set of fuzzy rules. The task actually activated is the one for which π_j achieves the maximum value.

Fuzzy rule (2) can be encoded as a string like the following:

$$R_i = c_s^{\gamma_s} \dots c_1^{\gamma_1} \tag{2'}$$

where $\{\gamma_1 \dots \gamma_s\}$ are fuzzy numbers defined below and every c_i is a subset of the data set whose elements have evaluation γ_i .

We remark that the string (2') is a compact, ordered version of the rule (2), where each evaluation appears exactly once only.

In this new form two fuzzy rules can be aggregated by using the following procedure [5] [6]:

given R_1 and R_2 as

$$R_1 = a_n^{\alpha_n} a_{n-1}^{\alpha_{n-1}} \dots a_1^{\alpha_1}$$

$$R_2 = b_m^{\beta_m} b_{m-1}^{\beta_{m-1}} \dots b_1^{\beta_1}$$

then

$$R_1 \Delta\, R_2 = (a_n^{\alpha_n} a_{n-1}^{\alpha_{n-1}} \dots a_1^{\alpha_1}) \Delta (b_m^{\beta_m}\, b_{m-1}^{\beta_{m-1}} \dots b_1^{\beta_1}) = c_{m+n-1}^{\gamma_m+n-1} \dots c_1^{\gamma_1}.$$

Here, without loss of generality, we can assume $n \geq m$:

$$c_i = \begin{cases} \bigcup_{j=1}^{i} (a_{i-j+1} \cap b_j) & 1 \leq i < m \\ \bigcup_{j=1}^{m} (a_{i-j+1} \cap b_j) & m \leq i < n \\ \bigcup_{j=i-n+1}^{i} (a_{i-j+1} \cap b_j) & n \leq i < m+m \end{cases}$$

$$\gamma_i = \begin{cases} \frac{1}{i} \sum_{j=1}^{i} 1/2\,(\alpha_{i+j-1} + \beta_j) & 1 \leq i \leq m-1 \\ \frac{1}{m} \sum_{j=1}^{m} 1/2\,(\alpha_{i+j-1} + \beta_j) & m \leq i \leq n-1 \\ \frac{1}{n+m-i} \sum_{j=i-n+1}^{m} 1/2\,(\alpha_{i+j-1} + \beta_j) & n \leq i \leq m+n-1 \end{cases}$$

where the $\cap$ and $\cup$ are the set-operations of join and meet.

From the rules:

$$R_1 = if\ acq_1\ is\ \alpha,\ acq_2\ is\ \beta\ then\ task_1\ is\ \gamma,\ task_2\ is\ \alpha$$

$$R_2 = if\ acq_1\ is\ \beta,\ acq_2\ is\ \alpha\ then\ task_1\ is\ \beta,\ task_2\ is\ \gamma$$

we get the representation (supposing $\gamma < \beta < \alpha$):

$$R_1 = [\text{acq}_1, \text{task}_2]^\alpha [\text{acq}_2]^\beta [\text{task}_1]^\gamma$$

$$R_2 = [\text{acq}_2]^\alpha [\text{acq}_1, \text{task}_1]^\beta [\text{task}_2]^\gamma$$

and aggregating R_1 and R_2 using operation Δ, we obtain the following string:

$$R_3 = [\text{acq}_2, \text{acq}_1]^{\delta_1} [\text{task}_2]^{\delta_2} [\text{task}_1]^{\delta_3}$$

which represents the rule:

$$R_3 = \text{“}\ if\ acq_1\ is\ \delta_1,\ acq_2\ is\ \delta_1\ then\ task_1\ is\ \delta_3,\ task_2\ is\ \delta_2\text{”}$$

where δ_1, δ_2 and δ_3, are fuzzy numbers yielded by the fuzzy aggregation operators defined above.

This aggregation is the basis for the evolution of the actors' knowledge base. We refer to R_3 as the *offspring* of the *mating* rules R_1 and R_2. Given a population of FuzzyEvoAgents Agt_1, Agt_2, ..., Agt_p, each agent keeps on with its fuzzy rules for a certain amount of time. During this period it would gain credit as the value of the function it has to maximize (agent's target or fitting function). Agent with large credit can continue their life. Agent with small credit finish to die and will be replaced by new agents, whose fuzzy rules are obtained by mating the knowledge base of the well performing agents. Moreover the resulting new population of agents undergoes a mutation operator. Mutation means that agents fuzzy rules can be modified (with small probability) by changing the fuzzy numbers attached to the tasks and acquaintances. We prefer to limit to the above description the fundamental concepts of our agents model. Further details are discussed in the next section, where the case study (a simple simulation of digital life) better help us in giving formal as well as pragmatic explanation through the software system description.

3 Ecosystem Framework

The term "artificial life" represents a complex discipline that covers different areas, such as biology, chemistry, economics, philosophy; its main goal is the study and the design of computational framework able to make sufficiently abstract the principles of biological phenomena, managing them in such a way to reproduce the dynamic behavior of evolutionary creatures, reducing the cost and complexity of alternative (biological) approaches [9].

In order to test the functionality of our model and its ability in representing ecomodels, i.e. models where the evolution changes the environment and vice versa, we sketched, with a rough approximation of the biological model, a naive representation of a simple natural scenario constituted by flies and frogs, that play the role of pray and predator. We focus our attention on the "action selection", that is the selection of the more appropriate behaviour in the range of the possible actions, taking into account the external (the environment) as well as internal (the knowledge) information available for the agents. The applicability of our testbed is measured in terms of simulating the evolution of the system, in particular the ability to propagate to the future generations of unpredictable emerging behaviours that lead to the survival of the species [7] [8].
The framework is essentially composed of two basic modules, as shown in Figure 3.

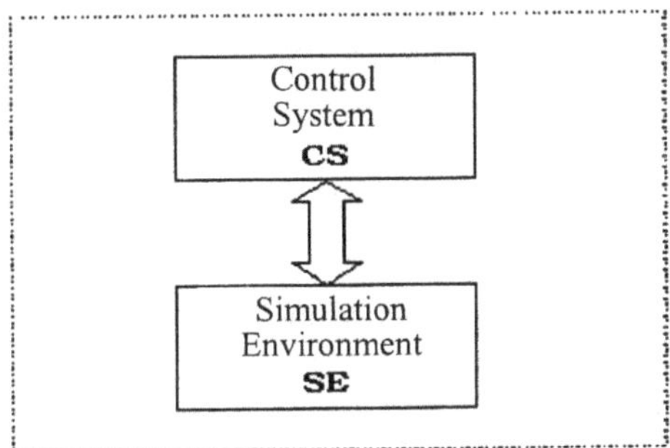

Fig. 3. CS (Control System) provides the primitives for the control flow management, whereas *SE (Simulated Environment)* provides the simulation environment.

The simulation environment is shown in Figure 4 according with an object-oriented modeling notation [12].

The entities *FuzzyEvoAgent* and *Actor* constitute the abstract or meta agents; this means that they are not strictly dependent from the specific application but they realize the basic primitives (concurrent and distributed evofuzzy reasoning) of the model.

The Control System module, given in Figure 5, is composed of two layers, the *GEC (Generational Evolutionary Controller)*, and the *PEC* (*Population Evolutionary Controller)*,i.e. the synchronizer of the overall simulation that manages the evolutionary phase of a certain population (in our case, fly and frog).

The GEC communicates the corresponding PEC to trigger the simulation for a given duration time T. Let us focus on the operational link between the CS and SE module. The control activities consist of four steps:

1. Setting of CS and SE.

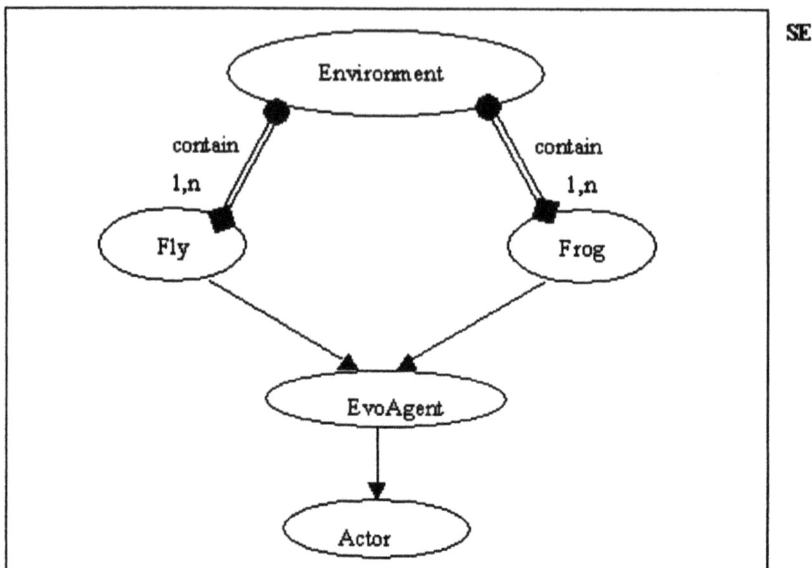

Fig. 4. An Entity-Relationship representation of the simulation environment

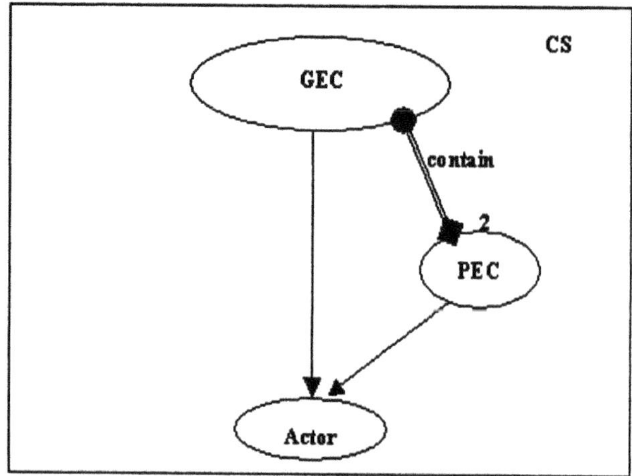

Fig. 5. The Control System in detail

2. *Trigger and simulate SE for a time T*
3. *Suspend the SE activity*
4. *Apply evolution*

We visualize these steps using circles to represent FuzzyEvoAgents, rectangles with single line to represent a set of FuzzyEvoAgents, rectangles with double line to characterize objects (non-agent elements). A dotted arrow means the agent's creation, continuous arrows represent messages. Labels indicate the kind of message and show a time ordering. A thin arrow pointing at a box represents a message sent to all the elements inside the box (multicasting). A thick arrow is used to characterize a set of identical messages sent from a set of entities to a single entity. Figure 6 depicts step1. As soon as the two PECs are generated, they trigger in parallel the creation of the FuzzyEvoAgents representing flies and frogs dutied with casual and approximate knowledge (rule base).

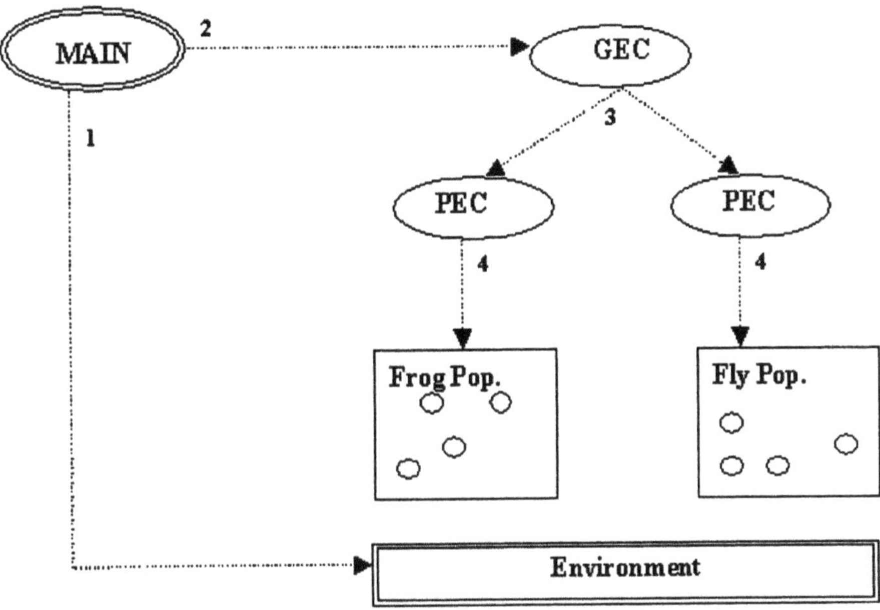

Fig. 6. First Step. The main program creates first the environment and then the GEC, that, in turn, generates the two PECs, skilled for the frogs and flies.

As shown in Figure 7, the simulation consists in an ecosystem running for a given time T: the PECs await that all the FuzzyEvoAgents react for a given observation time. The third step is characterised by the "suspension" (done by the PECs) of the FuzzyEvoAgents (see Figure 8).

This operation is important in order to avoid that the involved agents continue to interact with the environment (hence producing uncorrect side-effects). In the last step, given in Figure 9, the PEC, stimulated from the GEC, performs concurrently the evaluation of the FuzzyEvoAgents, choosing the agents to reproduce according to the fitness law.

To better understand the evolution phase, we deepen the behavior of the PEC after the reception of the message "evolute behaviour" and before the sending of the "reproduction" and "death".

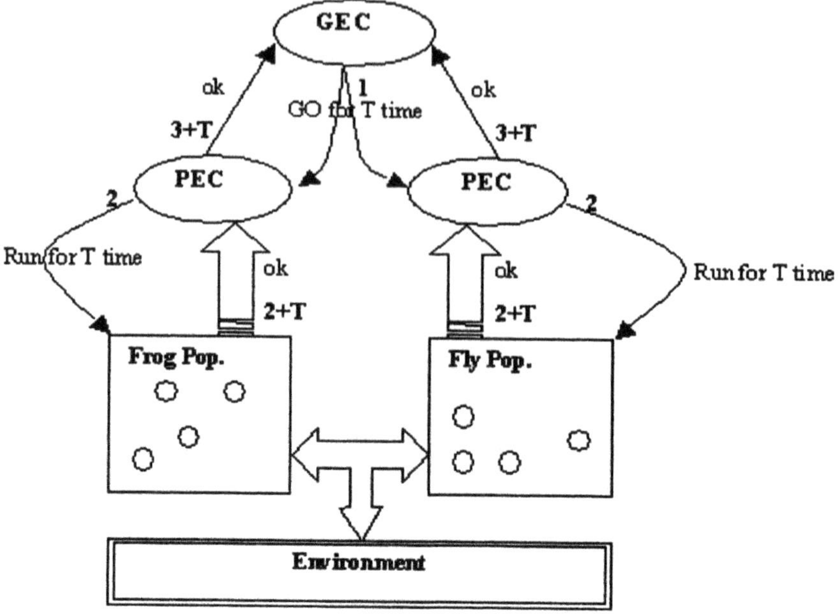

Fig. 7. Simulation of an ecosystem

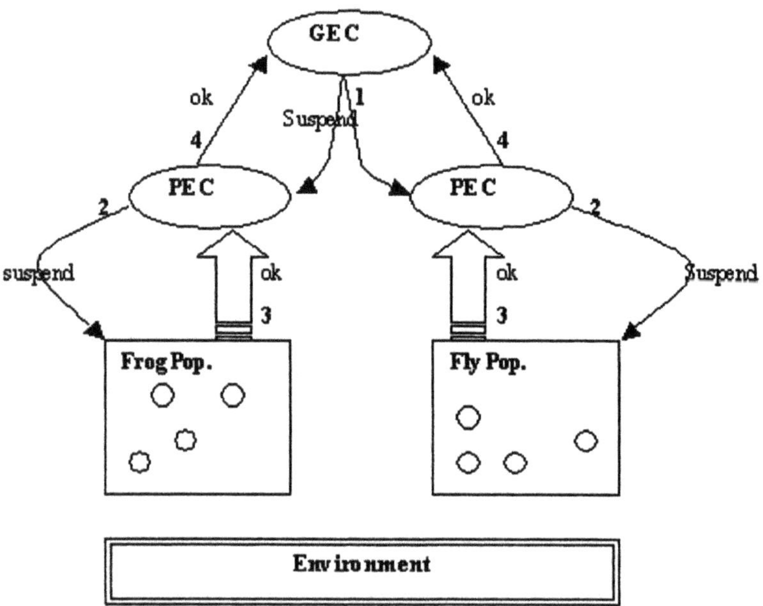

Fig. 8. The GEC communicates to the PECs to suspend the FuzzyEvoAgent activities.

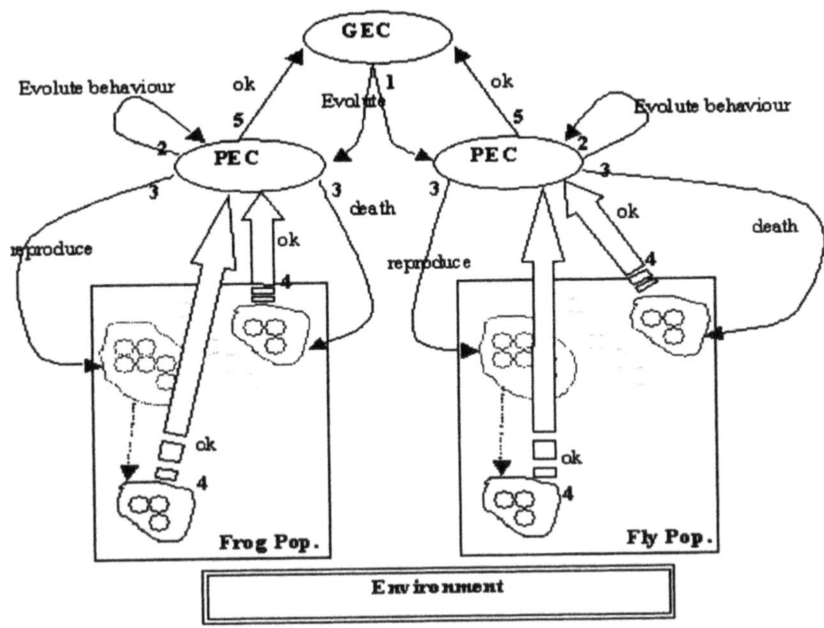

Fig. 9. The evolution step. The PEC, stimulated by the GEC, concurrently evaluate the corresponding agent populations, choosing the elements to destinate to the generation and eliminating the worst ones. At the end of this step, new FuzzyEvoAgents are created.

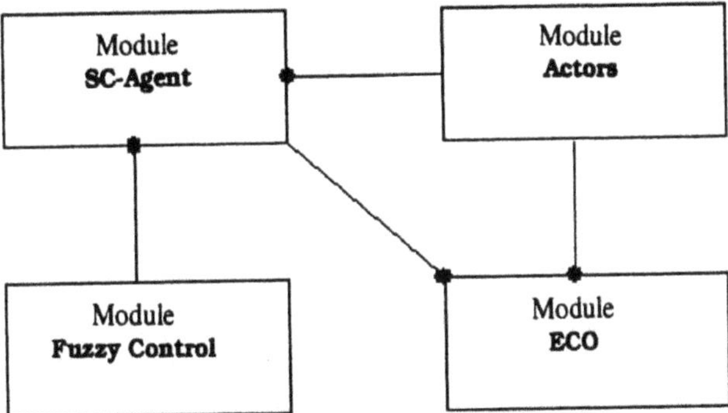

Fig. 10. The general architecture expressed in terms of basic modules and their aggregation.

At the reception of the message "Evolute behaviour", the PEC executes an internal script that individuates the best agent, the worst agents and an intermediate class, that will be maintained still for another generation.
These classes are determined exploiting the concurrency of the platform. More in detail, considering a set G=$\{(f_1,m_1),..,(f_{n/4}, m_{n/4})\}$ with f_i and m_i, respectively, the father and mother selected from the PEC over the n/2 "best" agents, then the PEC sends in parallel n/4 messagges "riproduce with m_i", to each f_i in G. This leads to the generation of n/4 new agents, (the blue group) that substitute the dead agents, characterized by the red group. This mechanism maintains constant the numbers of agents.

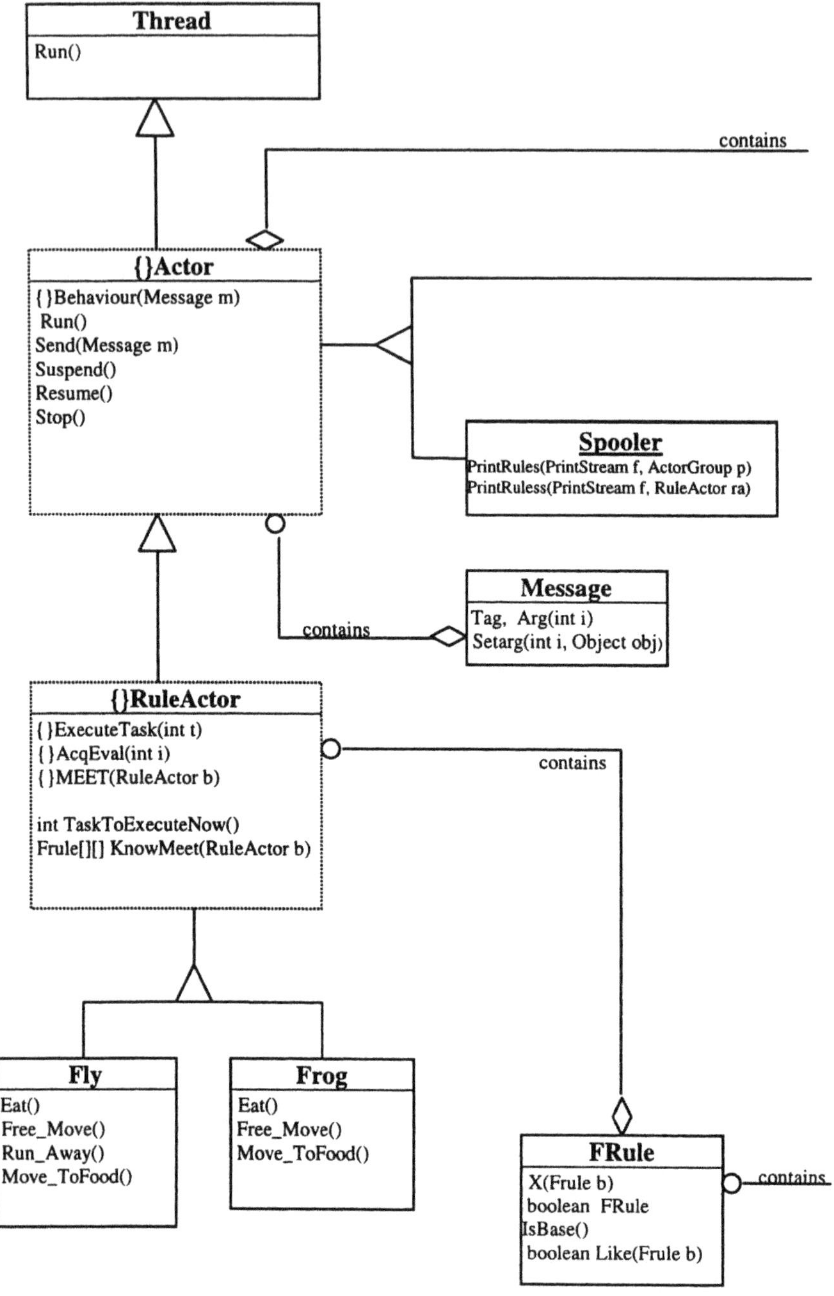
Thread
Run()
contains
{}Actor
{}Behaviour(Message m)
Run()
Send(Message m)
Suspend()
Resume()
Stop()
Spooler
PrintRules(PrintStream f, ActorGroup p)
PrintRuless(PrintStream f, RuleActor ra)
Message
Tag, Arg(int i)
Setarg(int i, Object obj)
contains
{}RuleActor
{}ExecuteTask(int t)
{}AcqEval(int i)
{}MEET(RuleActor b)
int TaskToExecuteNow()
Frule[][] KnowMeet(RuleActor b)
contains
Fly
Eat()
Free_Move()
Run_Away()
Move_ToFood()
Frog
Eat()
Free_Move()
Move_ToFood()
FRule
X(Frule b)
boolean FRule
IsBase()
boolean Like(Frule b)
contains

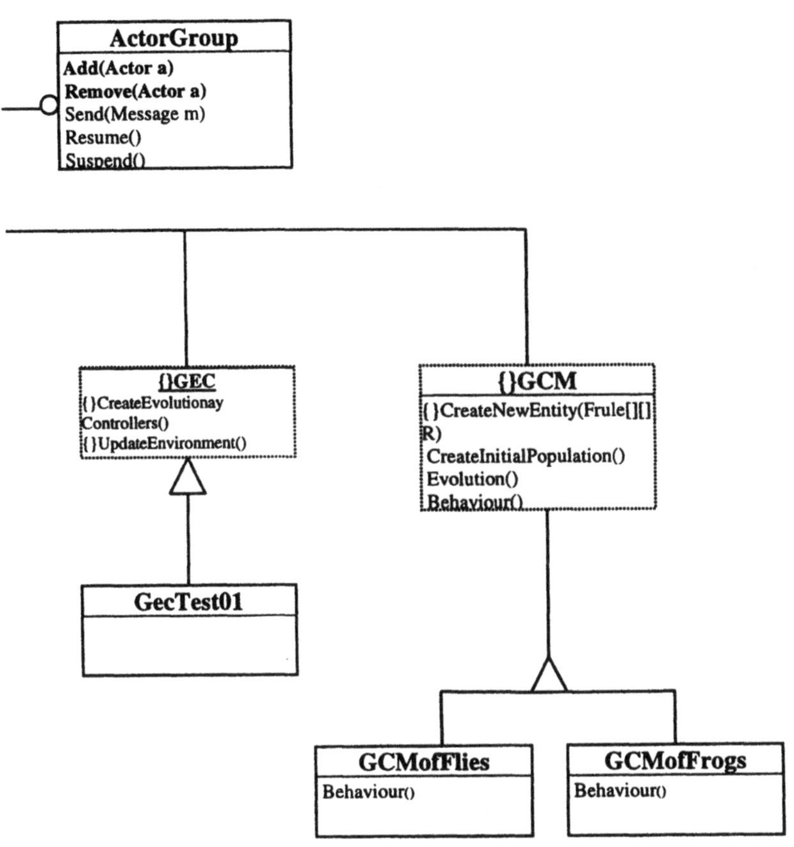

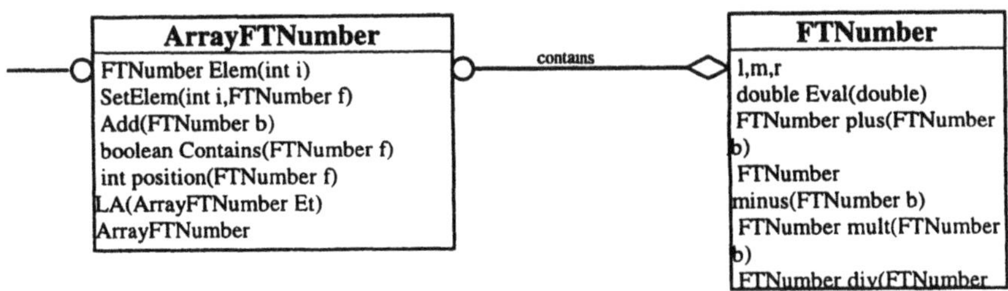

Fig. 11. An OMT representation of all the classes

4 Implementation

In this section we face implementation problems, in detailing the choices undertaken for the design a computation framework satisfable in terms of stability, extendibility and efficiency.

All the software is implemented in Java.
The overall framework is synthesized in Figure 10, while Figure 11 offers a more complete representation by showing all the classes. Figure 10 distinguishes four key modules:

- SC-Agent, identifying the basic notion of FuzzyEvoAgent.
- Actors, embodying the essence of the actor computational model.
- Fuzzy Control, realizing the control management of the behaviors of the agents (selection of the "best" task to trigger).
- ECO, representing the instance of the general framework obtained in the application of the eco-system.

In the following we evidenciate, for each of the four key modules in Figure 10, the most important features of each class.

4.1 Module Actor

As displayed in Figure 11, this module is composed of three classes: **Message, ActorGroup** and **Actor**. The first one implements the asynchronous communication among actors, the second one is designed to handle the interactions between a single actor and actor groups, the last class is devoted to the creation of actor entities. The scheletons of the three classes are given below.

In a "pure" OOP (*Object Oriented Programming)* framework, the objects communicate via synchronous message passing (i.e. the invoking object is blocked till the method is not completely accomplished). In the actor model it is necessary to overcome the "tiranny of the procedure call" thanks to asynchronous message passing protocol. This schema allows the actor to send the message and continuing its activities. Any message is received by the destination actor and stored in a local, private mailbox. The scheduling policy of the actor establishes the order in which the message shall be read and executed. This task is performed by the class **Message**.

Class Message
Description: the message in the actor model. *Attributes:* **String tag;** message identifier **Object[] parameter;** input/output parameters **len;** argument number *Constructors:* **Message(string name);** message instance

Message(string name, int n); message instance
Message(string name, Oject arg); message instance.

Operators:
Object arg(int i); argument selection
void Setarg(int i, Object obj); argument setting

Actors with common features may be grouped together. This is very important because a multicast message can be addressed concurrently to any actor in the group. The necessity to enrich the usual *point-to-point* communication *multicasting* is the goal of the class **ActorGroup**.

Class ActorGroup
Description: the management of an actor group logically identifiable

Attributes:
protected
String name; name of the group
Vector ActorList; the actors in the group

Constructors:
ActorGroup(string name); an empty group is created

Operators:
Int Len(); return the number of actors currently in the group
String getname(); return the name of the group
Synch. Void Add(Actor act); add an actor in the group
Synch. Void Remove(Actor act); delete an actor in the group
Actor[] Array(); the structure to implement the group
Void send(Message m); the multicast message to the group
Void sendFirst(Message m); a multicast message stored as first to read
Void resume(); resume the group
Void suspend(); suspend the group
Void stop(); stop the group eliminating its actors
Boolean AreAllSuspended(); true if the group is suspended
Boolean AreAllResumed(); true is the group is resumed
Void flush(); reset the mailboxes of the actors in the group

Let us recall that the actors as independent computation entities, able to work in a concurrent and distributed way. In order to implement this important issue, we used the Java Threads, as described in the class **Actor**.

Abstract Class Actor extends Thread
Description: the actor as an extension of the Java class Thread *Attributes:* *protected* **static ActorGroup MainActorGroup;** the default actor group **ActorGroup parentActorGroup;** the actual actor group **Vector mbox;** the message list to process **Actor self;** actor self-reference (this in java) **Boolean StopRequested;** state variable **Boolean isSuspended;** state variable **Boolean isWaiting;** state variable *Constructors:* **Actor();** init a default actor **Actor(String name);** init a designed actor **Actor(ActorGroup p, String name);** init an actor for a specific group *Operators:* **Void send(Message m);** send the message **Void sendFirst(Message m);** send a message with highest priority **Void Suspend();** suspend the actor **Void Resume();** resume the actor **Void Stop();** stop the actor removing it from the system **Boolean isSuspended();** test if the actor is suspended **Void flush();** clean the mailbox **Void setWaitON();** the actor is awaiting **Void SetWaitOFF();** the actor is not awaiting **Abstract synch void Behaviour(Message m);** abstract behaviors

4.2 Module FuzzyControl

This module is designed to perform our fuzzy control mechanism on the behavioral rules of the FuzzyEvoAgents. Let us recall the forms (2) and (2') of these rules:

$$\mathrm{R}_i = \text{“}\,\textbf{\textit{if}}\ acq_1\ is\ \alpha_{i1},\ acq_2\ is\ \alpha_{i2},\ \ldots,\ acq_n\ is\ \alpha_{in}\ \textbf{\textit{then}}\ task_1\ is\ \beta_{i1},\ task_2\ is\ \beta_{i2},\ \ldots\ task_m\ is\ \beta_{im}\text{”}$$

where α_i and β_i are fuzzy numbers, and the compact form of a FuzzyEvoAgent:

$$\mathrm{R}_i = \mathrm{c}_s^{\gamma_s} \ldots \mathrm{c}_1^{\gamma_1}$$

where $\{\gamma_1,\ldots,\gamma_s\}$ are fuzzy numbers defined in Section 2 and every c_i is a subset of the data set whose elements have evaluation γ_i.

In order to achieve best performance in applying the aggregation operation between FuzzyEvoAgents (see Section 2), it is better to consider a new form of fuzzy rules:

$$R_i = B^E$$

where $B=(c_s,..,c_1)$ is the basis of the rule and $E=(\gamma_s,..,\gamma_1)$ is the exponent.

It is important to note that the basis contains subsets of the data set where each acq_i and $task_j$ may appear once only (an agent does not modify the number of its local data and the number of its rules). Furthermore the evolution law must be applied to an agent belonging to the same typology (behaviors of a frog cannot be manipulated with those of a fly). This implies the use of two distinct arrays, one (A) dedicated to store the data/acquaintances of the agent, and the other one (T) for its behaviors/tasks:

$$A=(i_1,..w..,i_n) \text{ and } T=(j_1,..u..,j_m) \text{ with } i_k \text{ , } j_h \in \{1,..s\} \text{ where } 1 \leq k \leq n \text{ and } 1 \leq h \leq m$$

$$A[k]=w \Longleftrightarrow acq_k^{\gamma_w} \text{ with } 1 \leq k \leq n$$
$$T[h]=u \Longleftrightarrow task_h^{\gamma_u} \text{ with } 1 \leq h \leq m$$

and $w,u \in \{1,..,s\}$.

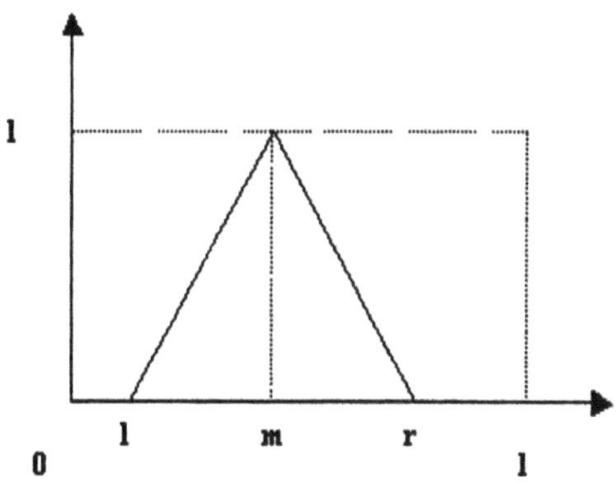

Fig. 12. Triangular fuzzy number

Afterwards it is necessary to find an appropriate representation for the fuzzy numbers. In our model, we refer to triangular fuzzy numbers defined in real unit interval [0,1] named **FTNumber**. Figure 12 represents graphically a FTNumber characterized by the three values [l,m,r].

The following class is designed for FTNumber management.

Class FTNumber

Description: define the triangular fuzzy numbers in [0,1]

Attributes:
Double left; the value l in figure 12
Double mid; the value m in figure 12
Double right; the value r in figure 12
String label; the label of the fuzzy number

Constructors:
FTNumber(); the number [0,0,0]
FTNumber(double l ,double m, double r); the number [l,m,r]
FTNumber(double l, double m, double r, string name); named num.

Operators:
Double Eval(double a); evaluation of fuzzy number on the axis Y
Boolean IsEqualTo(FTNumber b); true if a and b are equal
Void LA(ArrayFTNumber Et); linguistic approximation
FTNumber Plus(FTNumber b); add two fuzzy numbers
FTNumber Minus(FTNumber b); subtract two fuzzy numbers
FTNumber Mult(FTNumber b); multiply two fuzzy numbers
FTNumber Sprod(double c); multiplication for a constant
FTNumber Average(FTNumber b); give the average
Boolean GreaterThan(FTNumber b); greater number
...

To better manipulate the fuzzy number, the class ArrayFTNumber embodies the abstract concepts and basic operation to apply on the class itself. The fundamental structure is a vector of fuzzy numbers $\mathbf{A}=\mathbf{F}_n\mathbf{F}_{n-1}\ldots\mathbf{F}_1$, where F_i is a FTNumber.

Class ArrayFTNumber

Description: define an array of FTNumber

Attributes:
Private
Vector A; vector $A=F_n\ldots F_1$
Constructors:
ArrayFTNumber(); an empty vector of FTNumber
ArrayFTNumber(int n); n FTNumber [0,0,0]

ArrayFTNumber(Object[] obj); a vector A=F_n..F_1

Operators:
Int len; the length of the vector A
Void AddFirst(FTNumber B); the vector A= B F_n...F_1
Void removeElementAt(int i); delete F_i from A
FTNumber elem(int i); return the fuzzy number F_i
Boolean contains(FTNumber B); true if $B \in \{F_n \ldots F_1\}$
ArrayFTNumber clone(); duplicate the vector
Void sort(); order the vector such that $F_n \geq F_{n-1} \geq ... \geq F_1$
ArrayFTNumber Compose(ArrayFTNumber B); apply aggregation
ArrayFTNumber Product(ArrayFTNumber B); apply multiplication
ArrayFTNumber Average(ArrayFTNumber B); apply average
...

We can now give the basic information of the class that handle the fuzzy behaviors of the agents.

Class Frule

Description: implementation of the fuzzy control on the behavior rules of an agent with n acquaintances and m tasks

Attributes:
Private
Int[] T; array for tasks
Int[] A; array for acquaintances

Public
ArrayFTNumber Exp; the exponent of a rule FCR: E=(γ_s,..,γ_1)
Int taskLen; cardinality of task
Int acqLen; cardinality of acquaintances

Constructors:
Frule(Object[] obj); build the rule

Operators:
Frule clone(); duplicate the rule
Int Task(int i); return the index k | "$task_i$is γ_k"
Int Acq(int i); return the index k | "acq_i is γ_k"
Void setTask(int i, int k); set "$task_i$ is γ_k"
Void setAcq(int i, int k); set "acq_i is γ_k"
FTNumber expTask(int i); return γ_k | "$task_i$ is γ_k"
FTNumber expAcq(int i); return γ_k | "acq_i is γ_k"
Frule X(Frule B); apply aggregation operation.
...

4.3 Module SC-Agent

This module provides the basic functionality of the FuzzyEvoAgent, formally defined in Section 2. The classes inside the module define the data structures necessary to represent the agent as well as the algorithm that rules the agent evolution.

The knowledge base of the agent is a collection of rules , $R = \bigcup_{i=1}^{m} R_i = \bigcup_{i=1}^{m} (X_i \rightarrow Y_i)$ where each R_i accomplishes a sub-task, namely a sub-task fuzzy control rule SFCR. Formally, let r_{ik} be a SFCR:

$$r_{ik} = \text{"IF } acq_1 \text{ is } \alpha_{i1} ,\ldots, acq_n \text{ is } \alpha_{in} \text{ THEN } task_k \text{ is } \beta_{ik}\text{"}$$

then the complete set of rules is $R=R_1 \cup \ldots \cup R_m$, where $R_i = \bigcup_{k=1}^{w} r_{ik}$, R_i being composed from w sub-tasks r_{ik}. The task that the agent performs can be sketched as follows.

Let $I=\{acq_1,..,acq_n\}$ be the state vector containing the values of the acquaintances of the agent, and let r be a SFCR.

We define:

$$\mathbf{Elhs(r|I)}=\alpha_1\mathbf{(acq_1)}\cap \ldots \cap \alpha_n\mathbf{(acq_n)}$$

as the evaluation of the left hand size of a SFCR given the state vector I, and β(r) as the fuzzy number related to the SFCR. Then the task that is performed by the FuzzyEvoAgent is :

1) $\forall$i=1,...,m compute $\mu_i = \bigcup_{k=1}^{m} \; (Elhs(r_{ik}|I)) \wedge \beta(r_{ik})$

2) compute an index h such that $\mu_h = \bigcup_{i=1}^{m} \mu_i$

3) $task_h$ is the task to execute.

In order to enable any agent to perform at least one task (in the evaluation of Elhs(r) may happen that $\alpha_i(acq_i)=0$ and due to the $\cap$, Elhs(r)=0), we set the following conditions:

- Each α_i in a SFCR is represented by a FTNumber [0,m,1]. Such FTNumber is named **Basic Fuzzy Number.**
- Each agent possesses a rule base of (at least) 2^n SFCR rules, such that each $\alpha_i \in$\{ONE, ZERO\} , with ONE=[0,1,1] and ZERO=[0,0,1] as FTNumbers. Such rules are named **Basic Rules.**

Now let us concentrate on the evolution of FuzzyEvoAgents. We consider their behavioral rules (FCR) as their genetic features (genotype) that must be submitted to the evolutionary law.

Genetic Framework Genetic algorithm is a search method that uses some principles of evolution and selection in nature to find an optimum solution for a problem. It is generally used in situations where the search space is relatively large and cannot be traversed efficiently by classical search methods. This is mostly the case with problems whose solution requires evaluation and equilibration of many apparently unrelated variables.

As an initialization step, genetic algorithm generates randomly a set of solutions to a problem (a population of genomes). Then it enters a cycle where fitness values for all solutions in a current population are calculated, individuals for mating pool are selected (using the operator of reproduction), and after performing crossover and mutation on genomes in the mating pool, offspring are inserted into a population and some old solutions are discarded. Thus a new generation is obtained and the process begins again.

Genetic algorithm stops after the stopping criteria are met, i.e. the number of generations has reached its maximum value.

There are several issues of importance that have to be considered when designing a genetic algorithm for a problem:

- representation of genomes, it defines a search space and describe a complete solution of a problem in the form of a data structure. This solution is referred to genome or individual.
- definition of the fitness function, whose task is to determine which solutions are better than others;
- definition of the crossover operator, used to produce a new offspring by combining genetic material from two parents, each of them characterized with a high fitness function;
- definition of the mutation operator, used to introduce some randomness in the population ad thus slow down the convergence and cover more of the search space;

Let A and B be two FuzzyEvoAgents to mate. Let K and Z be their corresponding rule bases. The genetic algorithms works by differentiating the knowledge recombination and the knowledge mutation as follows.

Knowledge Recombination

We compute the rule base R=KΔZ. R is the recombination of two sets of rule bases (with obvious meaning of the symbols) K=$K_1 \cup \ldots \cup K_p$ and Z=$Z_1 \cup \ldots \cup Z_q$.

In particular:

R= $R_1 \cup \ldots \cup R_s$, where every $R_j = K_h \Delta Z_u$, 1≤h≤p, and 1≤u≤q, K_h and $Z_u$being randomly selected in their set **K** and **Z**, respectively.

Knowledge Mutation

To the Rule Base R, previously computed, is applied a mutation function (*mutate*), obtaining R'=mutate(R), which represents the actual rule base of the new FuzzyEvoAgent.

Strictly speaking, we have three types of mutation:

- *mutation of an* α_{ik} *of a FCR*
- *mutation of a* β_{jk} *related to the task given by the FCR*
- *shift position between two rules belonging to two different rule bases* R_1 *and* R_2

The following schema gives the internal definition of the class EvoAgent, realizing the notion of FuzzyEvoagent.

Abstract Class EvoAgent extends Actor
Description: FuzzyEvoAgents as an extended actor *Attributes:* *Public* **Int m;** number of available task **Int n;** number of acquaintances **Frule[][] R;** the Rule Base **Double fitness;** the fitness **String parents;** the parents *Costructors:* —- same of actor — *Operators:* **Abstract double AcqEval(int i);** value of acq_i **Abstract void ExecuteTask(int i);** perform $task_i$ **Abstract void MEET(EvoAgent B);** mating with the agent B **Protected int taskToExecuteNow();** what task to perform **Frule[][] KnowMeet(EvoAgent A, EvoAgent B);** the new rule base ...

4.4 Module ECO

This module realizes the simulation of the ecosystems. In particular we deepen the implementation details of the classes inside the simulation environment

SE (**Environment, Fly, Frog**) and the classes related to the control system CS (**GEC, PEC**). The classes **Printer, Scheduler** are not herein described because they are used just for testing and evalutation purpose.

The (spatial) environment where the agents (frogs and flies) live is implemented as a statical object *Space*. In particular:

- Space[i][j][0] contains the quantit of food available for fogs and flies in position (i,j);
- Space[i][j][1] contains the list of frogs present in that instant in (i,j);
- Space[i][j][2] contains the list of flies present in that instant in (i,j);

Class Environment
Description: manage the space where the FuzzyEvoAgents live *Attributi Private* **Int SpaceDim;** size of the environment **Int food;** the totality of food available **Object[][][] Space;** data structure of the environment *Costruttori:* **Environment(int N);** create the space NxN *Operatori:* **Int getDim();** returns the size of the environment **Synch. Void distributeFood(int qt);** randomly spread the food **Int getFoodFrom(int i,int j);** the food in the position (i,j) **Synch. Boolean removeFoodFrom(int i, int j, int qt);** remove the food **Synch void AddFrogIn(Frog f, int i, int j);** add a frog in position (i,j) **Synch void AddFlyIn(Fly f, int i, int j);** add a fly in position (i,j) **Synch void removeFlyFrom(Fly f, int i, int j);** remove a frog **Synch void removeFrogFrom(Frog f, int i, int j);** remove a fly **Synch Frog getaFrogFrom(int i, int j);** select randomly a frog **Synch Frog getaFlyFrom(int i, int j);** select randomly a fly ...

The FuzzyEvoAgent Frog is a predator entity with the following acquaintainces:

- acq_1 = time occured from the last meal;
- acq_2 = distance from a possibile pray (fly)

and the following tasks:

- Task_1 = eat a fly. This happens when the fly is close to the frog.
- Task_2 = bring near a fly. The frog is dutied of a visibility degree v that allows it to see within a distance equal to $\sqrt{2}v$. If a flies is detected then the frog tries to catch it moving on a not diagonal path (see Figure 13).
- Task_3 = move in the environment. The movement mimics a not linear path.

Here follows the schema of the class Frog.

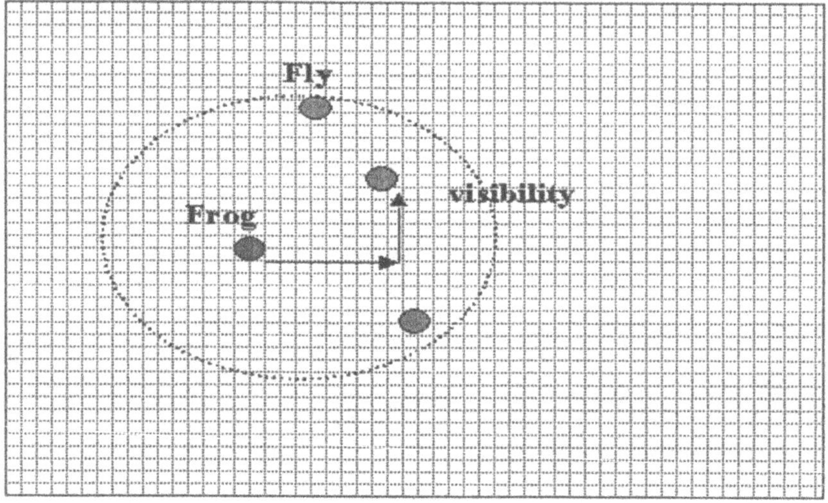

Fig. 13. An OMT representation of all the classes

Class Frog extends EvoAgent
Description: a frog and its behavior *Attributes:* **Static int totalFrogs;** number of frogs in the ecosystem **Static int eyeDistance;** visibility scope of a frog **Environment myEnv;** where the frog lives **Point myPos;** where the frog is located **Double deltaTime_eat;** acq_1 **Double foodDistance;** acq_2

PEC handle; the management of a frog population

Constructors:
Frog(PEC sup, Printer p, Scheduler[] synch, ActorGroup g, Environment env, FRUle[][] R); create a frog

Operators:
Double AcqEval(int i); return the acquaintance acq_i of a frog
Synch void ExecuteTask(int i); execute $task_i$
Synch void MEET(EvoAgent B); the generation of a new frog
Synch void Behaviour(Message m); the behavior of the frog
Synch protected void Eat(); action $task_1$
Synch protected void MoveTo(); action $task_2$
Synch protected void FreeMove(); action $task_3$

The FuzzyEvoAgent Fly is a prey entity with the following acquantainces:

- acq_1 = time spent from the last eating;
- acq_2 = distance from a nearest food
- acq_3 = distance from a nearest predator (frog)

and with the following tasks:

- $task_1$ = eat
- $task_2$ = reach a food
- $task_3$ = move in the environment
- $task_4$ = escape from a predator (frog).

As noted, the class Fly is very similar to Frog.

Class Fly extends EvoAgent
Description: a fly and its behavior *Attributes:* **Static int totalFlies;** number of flies in the ecosystem. **Static int eyeDistance;** visibility scope of a fly **Environment myEnv;** where the fly lives **Point myPos;** where the fly is located **Double deltaTime_eat;** acq_1 **Double foodDistance;** acq_2 **Double predatorDistance;** acq_3 **PEC handle;** the management of a fly population *Constructors:* **Fly(PEC sup, Printer p, Scheduler[] synch, ActorGroup g, Environment env, FRUle[][] R);** create a fly *Operators:* **Double AcqEval(int i);** return the acquaintance acq_i of a fly **Synch void ExecuteTask(int i);** execute $task_i$ **Synch void MEET(EvoAgent B);** the generation of a new fly **Synch void Behaviour(Message m);** the behavior of the fly **Synch protected void Eat();** $task_1$ **Synch protected void MoveTo();** $task_2$ **Synch protected void FreeMove();** $task_3$ **Synch protected void RunAway();** $task_4$ ...

The classes GEC (Generational Evolutionary Controller) and PEC (Population Evolutionary Controller) have been described in Section 3. We avoid to discuss further details about their functioning.

5 Evaluation

In order to evaluate our framework it is necessary to establish the evolution law, i.e. the fitness function. This function appears as $fitness_t = fitness_{t-1} + V_t$, where V_t is a *feedback* value related to the time t. This value is deduced from the environment as effect of an execution of task. V_t may be a positive value if the corresponding action has ameliorated the status of the agent or negative in the case of a impoverishment of its state (for example, considering a frog, choose a "wrong" direction , i.e. a path without prey). More in detail, the testing has been performed by considering the following data:

1. N: size of the environment
2. T: time of the generation time
3. G: number of generations to observe
4. Test: kind of test (without evolution, with evolution, with evolution + learning).

Being T a constant, and fixed the size of the population, the total number of actions perfomed in each generation is $\mathbf{N}_g$=**T*(P**$_{frog}$**+P**$_{fly}$**)**, where T is the observation time dedicated to the generation, P_{frog} is the number of frogs, and $P_{fly}$the number of flies. Let a_i and b_j be, respectively, the number of "good" action performed by the ith frog and by the jth fly. Then the global evaluation parameter (GEP) associated to a generation G is the following:

$$GEP_G = \frac{\sum_{i=1}^{P_{frog}} a_i + \sum_{i=1}^{P_{fly}} b_j}{N_G}$$

The testing has been performed on a population if 12 frogs and 26 flies, in an environment of size 20x20. The generation time is composed of 20 units (20 actions executed by each agent for each generation). The total number of generation executed was fixed equal to 50. The results given in Figure 14 have been computed by averaging the data obtained in any single simulation.

As further parameter considered in our experimentation, we estimated the impact in next generation. In essence, when an agent performs a coherent rule, this rule will receive a major consideration in the next agent generation. This means that, if K is a Rule Base, after the application of the fuzzy rules, the rule base is changed in K'. Letting $r_i(t)$ by the ith SFCR rule of K that implies the task t , and being δ the "good" application of the rule and γ its total number of applications then:

- Change the task t associated to the rule $r_i(t)$ where $0 \leq \delta(r_i(t))/\gamma(r_i(t)) \leq \iota$ with $\iota < 0.5$.
- Change the possibility value β to trigger the task t of a rule $r_i(t)$, such that:
  $\beta=\beta^*c$, where $c>1$, if $\delta(r_i(t))=\gamma(r_i(t))$
  $\beta=\beta^*c$, where $c<1$, if $\delta(r_i(t))/\gamma(r_i(t))=0.5$

6 Conclusions

Soft-Computing technologies offer new tools to achieve higher functionality control even in the design of complex agent-based architecture. Recently we noticed a growing interest in combining DAI approaches with soft-computing, with an immediate benefit in sketching more efficient and manageable models of interaction, cooperation and learning. The results are reported in different areas, with frequent intersections. Among these we underline the following:

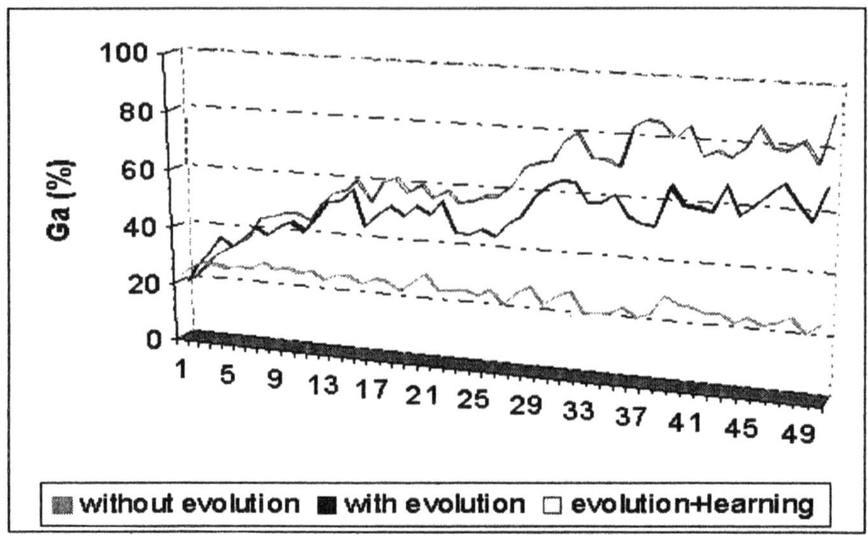

Fig. 14. Performances of ECO

- Using Fuzzy Logic as an inference engine for complex distributed, rule-based applications [13] [14] [15]. Here fuzziness is usually used to represent and reason about vague knowledge with fuzzy production rules. The distributed approach is applied as an optimization boost to the construction and maintenance of fuzzy knowledge bases, an activity that is quite time consuming. Often, the deductive model inherits its properties from a variant of control in fuzzy logic.
- Using genetic computation as a powerful exploratory method to acquire knowledge, with reduced efforts in human design, in highly evolutionary environments [16]. This approach is nowadays one of the most popular ones: the simple biological metaphor at the base of genetic processing has been widely acknowledged as an efficient engine to design reactive, adaptive, and evolving agents. The assumption that genetic algorithms are a promising approach to be used for modeling adaptive systems has been successfully verified in many experiments and in different areas such as, for instance, information retrieval/filtering [17], engineering design [18] and robot construction [19], where the genetic algorithm is chosen to engineer the action selection functionality.
- Using artificial neural networks (ANNs) to optimize Agent behavior. The impact of multi-agent strategies, often associated to evolutionary behaviors, shows to be beneficial for the transfer of knowledge across multiple functions [20] and for a successful multifunctional learning of the systems [21].

Our main goal is to extend the notion of an Actor towards that one of Agent, i.e. to inject in the Actor the ability to adapt its behaviour according to the fulfillment of its local (sub) goals. Our result is the definition and implementation of the FuzzyEvoAgent. The adaptive functionality of our Actors may be well integrated with other Agent architecture that, however, lack learning and adaptability.

References

1. Agha, G., *Actors. A Model of Concurrent Computation in Distributed Systems*, MIT Press, (USA), 1986.
2. Genesereth, M.R., and Ketchpel, S.P., Software agents, *Communications of the ACM,* 37(7) (1994), pp.48-53.
3. Cerri, S.A., Gisolfi, A., and Loia, V., Towards the Abstraction and Generalization of Actor-based Architectures in Diagnostic Reasoning, in *Collaboration between Human and Artificial Societies, Coordination and Agent-Based Distributed Computing,* (J. A. Padget, Ed.) vol. 1624, Lecture Notes in Artificial Intelligence, Springer-Verlag, (1999), pp. 115-131.
4. Guessoum, Z., and Briot, J-P., From active objects to autonomous agents, *IEEE Concurrency,* 7(3): (1999) pp. 68-76.
5. Gisolfi, A., and Loia, V., A Complete Flexible Fuzzy-Based Approach to the Classification Problem, *Internat. J. Appr. Reasoning* , 13(1995), pp.156-183.
6. Cicalese, F., and Loia, V., A Fuzzy Evolutionary Approach to the Classification Problem, *Int. Journal of Intelligent and Fuzzy System*,6(1) (1998), pp. 117-129.
7. Holland J.H., *Adaptation in Natural and Artificial Systems*, The University of Michigan Press, Ann Arbor, (USA), 1975.
8. Goldberg D., *Genetic Algorithms in Search, Optimization and Machine Learning,* Addison-Wesley, 1989.
9. Langton, C.G., Preface, in *Artificial Life II,* (C.G. Langton, C. Taylor, J.D. Farmer and S. Rasmussen, Eds.) pg. xiii-xviii, (1992), Addison-Wesley.
10. Mandami, E.H., and Assilian, S., An experiment in linguistic synthesis with a fuzzy logic controller, *Int. J. Man Machine Studies*, 7(1), (1975), pp. 1-13.
11. Zadeh, L.A., A theory of approximate reasoning, in *Machine Intelligence* (P. Hayes, D. Nuchie, and L.I. Mikulich Eds.), Halstead Press (USA), 1979, pg. 149-194.
12. White, I., *Using the Booch Method: a Rational Approach*, Benjamin/Cummings Pub., Redwood (USA), 1994.
13. Song, H., Franklin, S., and Negatu, A., SUMPY: A Fuzzy Software Agent, *Proceedings of the ISCA Conference on Intelligent Systems*, Reno (USA), 1996.
14. Nebot, A., Cellier, F.E., and Linkens, D.A., Synthesis of an Anaesthetic Agent Administration System Using Fuzzy Inductive Reasoning, *Artificial Intelligence in Medicine*, 8(3) (1996), pp.147-166
15. Sanz, R., Matia, F., de Antonio, A., and Segarra, M. J., Fuzzy Agents for ICa, *Proceedings of FUZZ-IEEE 1998*, IEEE Press (1998), pp.545-550.
16. Ackley, D., Littman, M., *Interactions between Learning and Evolution*, in Artificial Life II, (C. Langton, C. Taylor, J. Farmer and S. Rasmussen, Eds.), Addison Wesley, 1991.
17. Moukas, A.G., Amalthaea: Information Discovery and Filtering using a Multiagent Evolving Ecosystem, *Proceedings of the Conference on Practical Application of Intelligent Agents and Multi-Agent Technology*, London, 1996.

18. Hoffmann, F., Incremental tuning of fuzzy controllers by means of evolution strategy, *Proceedings of GP-98 Conference*, Madison (USA), 1998, pp. 550-556.
19. Pollack, J. B., Lipson, H., Funes, P.O, Ficici, S. G., and Hornby, G., Coevolutionary Robotics, *Proceedings of the first NASA/DoD Workshop on Evolvable Hardware* (John R. Koza, Adrian Stoica, Didier Keymeulen, and Jason Lohn, Eds.), IEEE Press, 1999.
20. Wermter, S., Panchev, C., and Arevian, G., Hybrid Neural Plausibility Networks for News Agents, *Proceedings of the Sixteenth National Conference on Artificial Intelligence*, Orlando (USA),1999.
21. Wang, F., and Mckenzie, E., Multifunctional Learning of a Multiagent based Evolutionary Artificial Neural Network with Lifetime Learning, *Proceedings of IEEE International Symposium on Computational Intelligence in Robotics and Automation*, Monterey (USA), 1999, pp.332-337.